UNDERSTANDING DEVIANCE AND CONTROL

UNDERSTANDING DEVIANCE AND CONTROL:

THEORY, RESEARCH AND SOCIAL POLICY

CRAIG B. LITTLE
State University of New York, Cortland

F.E. PEACOCK PUBLISHERS, INC.
ITASCA, ILLINOIS 60143

Copyright ©1983
F.E. Peacock Publishers, Inc.
All rights reserved
Library of Congress
Catalog Card No. 82-061588
ISBN 0-87581-289-9
Printed in the U.S.A.
Third Printing, 1988

To my parents, Dorothy and John

CONTENTS

Chapter 1: EXPLANATIONS OF DEVIANCE 2
    DEVIANCE AND DEVIANTS 4
    DEFINITIONS OF DEVIANCE AND THE FIELD OF INQUIRY ... 4
        Objective Rule-Breaking and Perceptions by Others 5
    TYPES OF DEVIANCE 6
    THEORY, RESEARCH, AND SOCIAL POLICY 9
    LEVELS OF EXPLANATION 11
        Biogenetic 12
        Psychological 14
        Social Psychological 14
        Sociological 15
    SUMMARY 19

Chapter 2: SEXUAL DEVIANCE 26
    TYPES OF SEXUAL DEVIANCE 28
        Normal Deviance 28
        Pathological Deviance 28
        Social-Structure Generating Deviance 29
    PROSTITUTION 29
        Definition 29
        Historical and Cultural Perspectives 30
        Prostitution in the United States Today 32
            Types 32
            Extent of Prostitution 35
        Explanations of Prostitution 35
            Functions 35
            Social Psychological Development 36
            Career Movement and Labeling 38
        The Political Economy of Prostitution 39
            Prostitution and the Law 39
            Commercialized Vice and the American Way 40
    PORNOGRAPHY 42
        What Is It? 42
        Cultural and Historical Context 43
        Types and Extent of Erotica 45
        Effects of Sexual Materials 45
            Psychosexual Stimulation 45
            Satiation 46
            Effects Upon Sexual Behavior 46
            Attitudinal Responses 47
            Emotional and Judgmental Responses 47
            Criminal and Delinquent Behavior 48
        Explanations of Pornography 49
            Functionalism 49
            Guilt, Sexism, and Violence 50
            Status Politics 52

viii UNDERSTANDING DEVIANCE AND CONTROL

    HOMOSEXUALITY 54
        Historical and Cultural Attitudes 54
        Defining Homosexuality 56
        Masters and Johnson: Homosexual Physiology 57
        Bell and Weinberg: Homosexual Diversity 58
            Close-Coupleds 59
            Open-Coupleds 59
            Functionals 60
            Dysfunctionals 60
            Asexuals 60
        Subcultural Patterns 61
            Coming Out 61
            Meeting Places: Bars, Baths, and Tearooms 63
            One-Sex Environments: Prisons and the Military 67
        Explanations of Homosexuality 70
            Heredity and Hormones 70
            Psychoanalytic Perspectives 71
            Learning 72
            Societal Reaction 73
            The Politics of Definition 73
    SWINGING 74
        Meeting, Motives, and Manipulation 75
        The Sociological Significance of Swinging 76
    SUMMARY 77

Chapter 3: MENTAL DISORDERS 84
    IMAGES OF MADNESS 85
        Mental Disorder in Western History 85
        Cross-Cultural Perspectives 86
    DEFINITION OF MENTAL DISORDERS 88
    TYPES OF MENTAL DISORDERS 89
    THE DISTRIBUTION OF MENTAL DISORDERS 92
        Counting Cases 92
    SOCIOCULTURAL FACTORS AND MENTAL DISORDERS 94
        Age 94
        Sex 94
        Race 95
        Rural-Urban Settings 95
        Social Class 96
    EXPLANATIONS OF MENTAL DISORDERS 98
        Nature Versus Nurture: The Genetics-Environment Issue 98
        Social Disorganization: The Ecological Approach 99
        Social Structural Strain 102
            Condition of the Economy 102
            Anomie 103
        Family Dynamics 104
        Labeling 106
    REACTIONS TO MENTAL DISORDER 111
        Public Attitudes 111
    MENTAL HOSPITALS 112
    PUBLIC POLICY 114

Deinstitutionalization and Community Mental Health 114
MENTAL DISORDER AND THE LAW 117
    Involuntary Commitment 117
    Incompetency to Stand Trial 118
    The Insanity Defense 119
    Policy Suggestions 121
SUMMARY 121

Chapter 4: SUICIDE 128

HISTORICAL AND CULTURAL ATTITUDES 129
VARIATIONS IN THE SUICIDE RATE 131
    International Rates 131
    Suicide in the United States 133
    Evaluating Official Statistics 133
SOCIAL CORRELATES OF SUICIDE 137
    Sex, Age, and Race 137
    Occupation, Marital Status, and Religion 138
    Adolescent and Young Adult Suicide 140
EXPLANATIONS OF SUICIDE 141
    Social Integration and Regulation 141
        Durkheim 141
    Status Integration 144
        Gibbs and Martin 144
    Social Disorganization 144
        Cavan 144
    Frustration and Aggression 146
        Henry and Short 146
    Suggestibility, Societal Reaction, and Social Meaning 148
        Suggestion 148
        Societal Reaction 149
        Social Meaning 149
    Suicide Notes 150
    A Basic Suicide Syndrome 152
SUICIDE PREVENTION AND SOCIAL POLICY 153
SUMMARY 154

Chapter 5: ALCOHOL AND OTHER DRUGS 160

AN OVERVIEW OF DRUG USE 161
    What is a Drug? 161
    Alcohol as a Drug 163
    Drug Use as Deviance: Laws and Perceptions 164
MAJOR DRUGS AND THEIR EFFECTS 165
    Central Nervous System Stimulants 166
    Central Nervous System Depressants 168
        Analgesics 168
        Sedative-Hypnotics 169
    Hallucinogens 170
    Marijuana 170
    Trends and Prevalence of Drug Use 171
EXPLANATIONS OF DRUG ABUSE 172

Alcoholism 172
　　　The Disease Model 174
　　　　Heredity 174
　　　　The Jellinek Classification and Alcoholics Anonymous 175
　　　Sociocultural Models 176
　　　　Norms, Ambivalence, and Integration 176
　　　　The Social Functions of Drinking 180
　　　　The Politics of Definition 181
　　　　Public Attitudes and Public Policy 182
　　　Marijuana Use 184
　　　　Social Learning 184
　　　　"Turning Off" 186
　　　　Medicine and Morals: Marijuana as a Public Issue 187
　　　The Political Economy of Drugs 189
　　　　The Control of Drugs: The Case of Opiates 189
　　　　Drugs as Control: The Legal Drug Epidemic 193
　　SUMMARY 196

Chapter 6: ELITE DEVIANCE 204
　　THE AMERICAN CLASS STRUCTURE 205
　　　Who are the Elites? 205
　　　　Individuals 205
　　　　Corporations 206
　　　Elites and the Exercise of Power 208
　　THE WHITE-COLLAR CRIME TRADITION 211
　　　Problems of Definition 213
　　ELITE OCCUPATIONAL DEVIANCE 214
　　　Illegal and Unethical Behavior in the Professions 214
　　　　Physicians 214
　　　　Lawyers 216
　　　　Professors 217
　　　Official Deviance 219
　　　　Theories of Official Deviance 221
　　CORPORATE DEVIANCE 222
　　　What Is a Corporation? 222
　　　Why Study Corporate Crime? 224
　　　The Costs of Corporate Crime 225
　　　　Economic Costs 225
　　　　Physical Costs 226
　　　　Social and Moral Costs 227
　　　Types of Corporate Deviance 228
　　　　Customers as Victims 228
　　　　Employees as Victims 230
　　　　The Public-at-Large as Victims 232
　　　　Owners as Victims 233
　　　How Much Corporate Deviance Is There? 234
　　　Explanations of Corporate Deviance 236
　　　　Social-Psychological Factors 236
　　　　Culture of the Corporation 238
　　　　Structure of the Corporation 239
　　　　Structure of the Economy 240

    Societal Reaction and Social Control 242
    Control of Corporate Deviance 244
        Legal and Penal Reform 244
        Consumer, Employee, and Public Action 247
        Changes in Corporate Attitudes and Structure 248
  SUMMARY 250

Chapter 7: DEVIANCE, CONTROL, AND SOCIAL POLICY 258
  IMAGES OF DEVIANCE IN WESTERN HISTORY 259
    Sin, Crime, and Sickness 259
    The Medicalization of Deviance 262
  THE POLITICS OF DEVIANCE 264
    The Social Construction of Deviance 264
    The Emergence of Social Policy 264
    The Responsibility of the Human Sciences 267
  THE PRACTICE OF CONTROL 269
    Overreach and Underreach of the Criminal Law 269
    Deviance as Control 271

List of Tables and Figures

Chapter 1 Figure 1.1 Levels of Explanation, p. 13
Chapter 2 Figure 2.1 The Kinsey Heterosexual-Homosexual Continuum, p. 57
            Table 2.1 A Typology of Sexual Experience, p. 59
            Table 2.2 Social Contexts in Which Respondents "Came Out," p. 62
Chapter 3 Figure 3.1 The Major Categories of Mental Disorders According to the DSM, 3 Classification, p. 90
            Table 3.1 Number and Percent Distribution of Resident Patients by Diagnosis, State and County Mental Hospitals, United States, 1978, p. 91
            Figure 3.2 Class Position and Types of Mental Illness, p. 96
            Table 3.2 Total Admissions to State and County Mental Hospital Inpatient Services and Total Admissions to Private Mental Hospital Inpatient Services by Primary Diagnosis, United States, 1975, p. 97
            Figure 3.3 Sub-Communities Based on Census Tracts of Chicago, p. 100
            Figure 3.4 Flow Chart — Stabilization of Deviance in a Social System, p. 108
            Table 3.3 Psychiatric Hospital Use Rates, 1960-1979, p. 114
Chapter 4 Table 4.1 Suicide Rates of Selected Countries (Rate per 100,000 population), p. 132
            Figure 4.1 U.S. Homicide and Suicide Rates, 1960-1978, p. 134
            Table 4.2 U.S. Suicides, 1978, By Sex and Method, p. 137
            Figure 4.2 U.S. Suicide Rates by Sex, Race and Age Group, 1978, p. 139
            Figure 4.3 Predictions of Durkheim's Theory of Suicide, p. 143
            Figure 4.4 Predicted Relationship between Social Disorganization and Suicide, p. 145
            Figure 4.5 Henry and Short's Predicted Relationships Between Type of Restraint and Suicide, p. 147
Chapter 5 Figure 5.1 The Legal Status and Perceptions of Drug Use, p. 165
            Figure 5.2 A Typology of Drugs and Their Effects, p. 167
            Table 5.1 Percent of People Reporting Having Ever Used Drugs: Youth, Young Adults, Older Adults, and College Students, p. 173
            Table 5.2 Economic Costs of Alcohol Misuse and Alcoholism in the United States, 1975, p. 174
            Figure 5.3 Two Models of Alcohol Dependence, p. 177

List of Tables and Figures CONTINUED

Chapter 6 Table 6.1 The American Class Structure, p. 207
          Figure 6.1 The Growth and Development of the Corporation, p. 209
          Table 6.2 Occupations of Members of the House of Representatives, p. 210
          Figure 6.2 Capitalist Elite — Ruling Elite Linkages, p. 212
          Figure 6.3 Gains to Perpetrators and Losses to Victims of Selected Types of Illegal Corporate Actions, p. 229
          Table 6.3 Large Nonsubsidiary Corporations Involved in 1961 and 1976 Price-Fixing Cases, p. 246

Chapter 7 Figure 7.1 Broad Historical Trends in Western Images of Deviance and the Practice of Social Control, p. 261
          Figure 7.2 The Process of Defining Deviance and Creating Social Policy, p. 266

PREFACE

As its subtitle suggests, this book relates theories and research on deviant behavior to the social policies aimed at controlling it. First, Chapter 1 establishes a framework for helping students think clearly about theories of deviance. The approach is comprehensive in the following sense: a given activity, say marijuana smoking, can be best understood with reference to several different theories. The appropriate theory, of course, depends upon the way a question about a phenomenon is asked. Different theories might apply depending upon whether one is interested in the differing *rates* of marijuana use among various age groups or whether one wishes to explain the *process* that generally leads people to smoke grass regularly. Approaching marijuana smoking from still another perspective, a theory could be proposed about how, when, and why the activity became an object of public and legal concern. Because we can ask a number of distinct questions about human activities, a variety of theoretical perspectives can enhance our understanding of those behaviors that have been labeled deviant.

The next five chapters describe the research and explanations most widely represented in the literature on several types of deviance including prostitution, pornography, homosexuality, mental disorders, suicide, alcohol and drug use, and elite deviance. In each case, explanations of the behavior are clearly reviewed with the intention of helping students learn how to recognize and evaluate them. Discussions of social control and social policy occur at appropriate points in each chapter and these issues receive special attention in the concluding Chapter 7.

The approach of the book has been developed primarily from that which I have found most successful in my own teaching. Usually this includes supplementing the core text in a course with a reader plus monographs, paperback narratives, or articles. By design, then, this book is intended to integrate flexibly with supplemental materials and should be useful in deviant behavior, criminology, and social problems courses.

All of one's debts in an enterprise of this sort cannot be pinpointed. Certainly I deeply appreciate the guidance, encouragement, and critical reactions offered by scores of teachers, colleagues, and students over the years. More specific thanks go to Harold Firestone, Fred Halley, Arnold Linsky, Elaine Little, Earl Rubington, Richard Stephens, Stuart Traub and Lynn Zimmer, who each read part or all of the manuscript, contributing valuable suggestions for revisions. Nancy Galambos was a very helpful research assistant, as was Joe Montuori who became indispensible in a number of ways, big and small, during the last stages of the project. I am grateful to the SUNY Cortland Library staff for their always cheerful, able assistance. Yvonne Becker and Mary Anne Mead carefully typed and retyped several drafts of the manuscript. Ted Peacock, Joyce Usher, and the fine staff at F. E. Peacock Publishers never waivered in their excellent editorial advice and steady attention to details.

Finally, my thanks to Elaine and Heather for their support and understanding as late nights at my office accumulated. They helped in so many ways to make it all worthwhile.

Cortland, N.Y. Craig B. Little
January 1983

Chapter 1
EXPLANATIONS OF DEVIANCE

DEVIANCE AND DEVIANTS
DEFINITIONS OF DEVIANCE AND THE FIELD OF INQUIRY
  Objective Rule-Breaking and Perceptions by Others
TYPES OF DEVIANCE
THEORY, RESEARCH, AND SOCIAL POLICY
LEVELS OF EXPLANATION
  Biogenetic
  Psychological
  Social Psychological
  Sociological
SUMMARY

Why people behave as they do has long been a question asked by parents and teachers, police and politicians, psychologists and sociologists. And more to the point, they often want to know why some people are not well behaved and others are. This question implicitly suggests that people who have a reputation for misbehavior are importantly different from the rest. The underlying assumption is that deviants are different. From this point of view, the task of those seeking to explain deviance is to discover (1) what characteristics distinguish deviants from nondeviants, and (2) to develop a logical explanation (a theory) consistent with the differences observed. A great many social scientists have devoted time and effort to understanding deviant behavior using this strategy and some of what their research tells us about deviance will be discussed in this book.

Of course, deciding what constitutes proper behavior versus misbehavior is frequently a matter of opinion not easily resolved. For example, as almost anyone who has attended elementary school knows, some teachers are very permissive while others are very strict. Students are quick to pick up these distinctions and most of them easily learn that the same behavior, such as talking softly in class, may be grounds for punishment by the strict teacher but lead to no sanction by the permissive teacher. In other words, there is nothing inherently "deviant" about talking in class. Rather, the deviant quality of the behavior is conferred upon it by the teacher who backs up her definition of classroom–talking with the power to punish.

Looking at deviant behavior from this perspective suggests that it is important to ask what factors lead certain activities to be defined as deviant in a particular time and place. For example, the history of laws regarding drinking in the U.S. illustrates that the same behavior, selling alcoholic beverages, may be legal, as it was prior to 1919 and after 1933, or illegal as it was during the period of the Prohibition Amendment. In response to this observation, students of deviance might seek to explain why the sale of alcoholic beverages was outlawed in 1919 and why that decision was later reversed. Increasingly, social scientists are directing their attention to questions of this kind.

DEVIANCE AND DEVIANTS

Let us further elaborate on the two broad perspectives on the study of deviance suggested by what has been said so far. One of the more obvious but important points to recognize is that understanding deviance involves studying both those who break rules and those who make rules. Studying the rule breaker begins with such questions as: "Why does a person become a homosexual?" Research in response to this question has yielded some fascinating theories and evidence that suggest genetic transmission (Kallmann, 1952), family dynamics (Cory, 1951), and failure of proper sex identification (Freud, 1930b) among many possible "causes." On the other hand, studying the rule makers stimulates questions like: "Why is homosexuality considered to be deviant, rule-breaking behavior at all? Has it always been so in human societies? How did rules against homosexuality come about, and how are they changing? Are rules against homosexuality applied equally to everyone in the society?" Here the issue is, essentially, how the rules that establish an activity as deviant come to be made and how they are enforced.

The two types of questions asked above point to an important distinction when trying to evaluate explanations of deviance. The first question, "Why does a person become a homosexual?" is aimed at understanding a deviant person. We might call it a *type-of-person* question which leads us to explore the etiology (causes) of the deviant's activity. The second question, "Why is homosexuality deviant at all?" is directed at understanding how the behavior is classified. It is a *type-of-behavior* question which leads us to analyze the development of rules and laws. Both concerns are legitimate aspects of the field of deviant behavior. However, being aware that some theories are attempts to explain deviants' behaviors while others deal with the labeling of behaviors as deviance should enable one to see how very different theoretical perspectives are sometimes applied to the same kind of deviant behavior—because fundamentally different questions can be asked about it. Some theories clearly focus on the causes of deviants' behaviors while others emphasize why and how certain behaviors come to be labeled deviance.

DEFINITIONS OF DEVIANCE AND THE FIELD OF INQUIRY

Defining deviant behavior is not an easy task. However, in struggling with some of the difficulties, insight may be gained. Howard S. Becker (1963) has identified two broad American traditions in the sociological study of deviance which differ in their approaches to defining deviant behavior. The first simply emphasizes whether a particular activity objectively breaks the rules or not. If a person's behavior violates the rules, which are usually written laws in literate societies or widely shared understandings of what constitutes rule-breaking behavior in nonliterate ones, then that behavior is defined as deviant. In this straightforward legalistic view, if an activity breaks the rules, it is deviant. Otherwise, it is not.

The second approach emphasizes how others perceive and react to an activity, regardless of whether there is an explicit rule against it or not. For example, there is no rule or law against stuttering when one speaks. However, as stutterers know to their discomfort, other people often react to them by breaking off conversations, avoidance, or other negative responses. In other words, people often treat stutterers as though they are deviant. Thus, from this point of view, deviance is not defined in relation to rules or laws. Rather, an activity is considered deviant simply if it arouses negative reactions in others.

Objective Rule-Breaking and Perceptions by Others

Now, consider the implications of defining deviance either in terms of objective rule-breaking or the perceptions of others. The *objective rule-breaking* orientation assumes that the rule in question is very clear and agreed upon by most people in the society. This approach to defining deviance seems to work best when dealing with especially serious problems such as murder, assault, or theft. There is consensus in American society that these things are not to be tolerated, and there are clear laws against them which are more or less strictly enforced. We say that this approach "works best" with regard to serious violations because almost everybody agrees that murder, for example, is something that ought to be prevented, and when it occurs something ought to be done about it. A behavior is easily defined as deviant when there is a clear rule (law) against it and there is consensus that the rule should be enforced.

However, the objective rule-breaking approach does not seem to work as well if we realize that many times when the law is broken (objective rule-breaking occurs) the rule-breaking is treated as though it were not deviant at all. For example, in many jurisdictions there are blue laws which prohibit stores from opening on Sunday. However, these blue laws are seldom obeyed or enforced. Indeed, in some localities, in the eyes of other store managers and many customers, the store operator who kept his or her retail business closed on Sunday would be the deviant, regardless of the law. In this case, it can be argued that keeping one's store open is deviant from an objective rule-breaking point of view, but not deviant according to the perceptions of most others.[1]

We might also consider cases in which people do not actually break the law but are treated by others as though they had. For example, there may not be a law in a particular community stating that one must occasionally mow the lawn. However, failure to cut the grass may, after a while, earn a person the hard glances, scandalized whispers, and ostracism of the neighbors. Similarly, hippies, Jesus people, commune dwellers, stutterers, the handicapped, and numerous others sometimes find themselves treated as though they were rule breakers despite not having broken the law.

An understanding of deviance clearly requires attention to objective rule-breaking. But as the examples above suggest, defining deviance only in terms of the objective rules may lead us to overlook some very significant kinds of behavior which produce negative reactions from others. Moreover, in our consideration of deviance we should be sensitive to cases in which, despite the law being broken, there is not much negative reaction to the infraction.

TYPES OF DEVIANCE

Conforming behavior neither objectively breaks any rules, nor is it perceived by most others as deviant. It is important to remember that even most individuals who become labeled deviants whether they are hippies, whores, murderers, or thieves actually engage in conforming behavior *most* of the time. Conforming behavior is the norm in most social groups, and even most deviant individuals abide by both the formal and informal rules the vast majority of the time. Students of deviance are, of course, less interested in conforming behavior than various types of deviance except to the degree that conformity is the standard against which deviance is measured.

In contrast to conformity, much of what we commonly call crime is both objectively rule-breaking and perceived by others as deviant. In American society ordinary crime is well represented by the FBI's eight Index crimes that make up the annual crime rates widely cited from the *Uniform Crime Reports* (UCR). They are: murder, aggravated assault, rape, robbery, burglary, larceny, auto theft, and arson. Numerous other behaviors such as counterfeiting or kidnapping would fit into the criminal category. If most Americans were asked to give examples of criminal behavior, it is probably safe to assume that activities such as the eight Index crimes would head the list.

There is no question that criminal behavior is deviant, and an entire specialized discipline, criminology, is devoted to its study. This book is intended specifically to reflect the interest of specialists in deviance who frequently leave to criminologists the study of ordinary crime. Therefore, traditional criminal behavior of the sort on the UCR Index will not be extensively treated in this book. As the field of deviant behavior has emerged, it has tended to concern itself mostly with types of behavior that are especially controversial in respect to their causes, the extent of their harm, and what should be done about them. Examples of the deviant behaviors to be discussed in subsequent chapters include prostitution, homosexuality, mental disorders, suicide, drug use, and illegal activities by corporations. In contrast both to conforming or ordinary criminal behavior, these types often do not generate strong public consensus on whether or how to control them. However, as we shall see, it is the very ambiguous or marginal nature of these deviant activities—often behind the everyday social scene, at the center of political conflict or at the vanguard of social change—that makes them highly interesting.

Sometimes an activity is definitely against the rules, but it is either so well hidden that nobody sees it or, if it is seen, nobody seems to do anything about it. Becker (1963) called such behaviors secret deviance. For example, numerous sexual activities such as swinging (extramarital sexual relations), fetishism, sodomy, and the like are quite illegal and probably occur quite frequently but usually in private without the attention of nonparticipants. In these cases it is not so much that the behavior in question is not perceived as deviant by others as that others do not see the behavior at all.

Closely related to secret deviance in some respects is "victimless" crime. Edwin Schur (1965) coined this term referring "essentially to the willing exchange, among adults, of strongly demanded but legally proscribed goods or services" (p. 169). He describes abortion, homosexuality, and drug addiction as examples. To these we might add prostitution, illegal gambling, and numerous other forms of vice. Their outstanding characteristic is a transaction between two parties who both desire to enter into the exchange relationship.[2] As a result, these crimes violate laws which are relatively unenforceable because neither party in the interaction desires to make a complaint. Thus, without the active searching out of the behavior by the law enforcement authorities, usually vice squads, most activities of this sort simply go on with neither person involved claiming harm nor reporting the behavior as deviant.

Keeping deviant behavior secret is often related to the ability of the person engaging in the activity to cover up the transgression. Therefore, secret deviance is often the deviance committed or controlled by the powerful.[3] Power usually implies the ability to affect the social control machinery—to "fix the ticket"—to avoid prosecution and public humiliation. And power, embodied in very high social status, also permits one to transcend the potentially debilitating stigma of a deviant label. For example, leaders of organized crime, whose interests are usually embedded both in the world of vice and legitimate business, are often revered and treated with great respect both within their own ethnic communities and beyond. Or in another case, Schwartz and Skolnick (1964) found that physicians with malpractice convictions suffered relatively little professional, economic, or social damage compared to less powerful law breakers. Likewise, judges have been characteristically unwilling to apply sentences to business executives convicted of corporate crimes, responding to their lawyers' pleas that their clients, although law breakers, are not "real" criminals.

Finally, there are instances when there has been no objective rule-breaking, but the behavior is perceived as deviant by others. Probably the most common examples of this situation are what we sometimes call alternative life-styles. Hippies, commune dwellers, religious zealots, hobos, and tramps all sometimes find themselves persecuted by others as though they had broken the law when they have not objectively done so. Becker calls these law abiders who nonetheless become pinned with a deviant label the "falsely accused." A broad category of behavior that Scheff (1966) calls residual rule-breaking also fits into this type. In Scheff's discussion of mental disorder, residual rule-breaking is behavior "for which our society provides no explicit label, and which, therefore, sometimes lead(s) to labeling of the violator as mentally ill . . ." (p. 34). In other words, residual rule-breaking is not strictly illegal in a way that allows us to categorize the violator as a murderer, thief, arsonist, etc., but others do find the behavior so annoying or disconcerting that they seek removal from their midst of the person who engaged in it. For example, refusing to reply when spoken to, or uncontrolled laughing at inappropriate moments are incidents of residual rule-breaking. Excessive residual rule-breaking—the persistent violation of everyday informal rules of interaction—can, under certain circumstances, according to Scheff, become officially labeled as mental illness.

False accusation, or deviant labeling without illegal conduct, is more likely to be the lot of the relatively defenseless. These types of deviance are, therefore, often the deviance of the powerless. The behavior receives the reprehension of others, not because it is strictly illegal—for it is not—but because it is different and those who engage in it lack the power to resist a stigmatizing deviant label.

There has simultaneously been a contraction and broadening of the field of deviance. The definition of the field has been contracting in the sense that deviance specialists have generally been moving toward the study of behaviors on the margin of the strictly illegal and left the study of what is usually considered ordinary crime to the criminologist. Substantively, this orientation of the field translates into the study of mental disorder, sexual deviance, suicide, hidden deviance among social elites, unconventional life-styles, and other marginal activities. At the same time, there has been an effort to broaden the definition of deviance to include behavior by elites that *is* definitely illegal, but has been largely ignored due to lack of awareness or accessibility to researchers and the public. Indeed, the serious indictment of the field for failure to encompass and examine elite deviance is reflected by the call for less attention to relatively powerless "Nuts, Sluts and 'Preverts' " (Liazos, 1972) and more attention to "covert institutionalized violence" (e.g., unsafe working conditions, environmental damage, consumer fraud) committed by the powerful (Thio, 1973). Thus, many contemporary theorists in the field of deviance have developed a special concern for the relative status and power of rule makers and rule breakers. The types of deviance discussed in subsequent chapters of this book reflect the more restricted concern for marginal behavior by largely excluding the broad category of deviance that is popularly known as criminal. At the same time, the expanding concern for elite deviance and questions about the relative power of rule makers and rule breakers are also taken into account.

THEORY, RESEARCH, AND SOCIAL POLICY

The words "theory" and "research" sometimes have a forbidding connotation that implies highly complex statements and equally esoteric procedures of scientific investigation. At root, however, there need not be anything mysterious about either. In fact, even while hardly knowing it, at a fairly basic level, each of us theorizes about human behavior and conducts research on it every day. We theorize when we try to explain something. A theory, in its broadest sense, is simply an explanation for some event or phenomenon. Thus, in response to the observation that little Billy is an active child who is always getting into everything, a grandmother may reply, "He comes by it naturally; he's just like his father was at that age." The grandmother has stated a theory of Billy's behavior—specifically, a genetic theory implying that hereditary characteristics explain the behavior. To be sure, the theory is not precisely formulated, as it would be by a social scientist. Still, by recognizing that a theory has just been proposed and then trying to understand the mechanism (heredity) that it implies, we can learn to think clearly about different kinds of explanations.

Research can take many forms ranging from simple observation to elegant, controlled experiments. However, regardless of the strategy or technique, observation is the basic component of all research. In this sense, as we experience the world around us—often unconsciously making comparisons, searching for regularities, identifying differences—we engage in research. The major differences between our everyday observations and those of the social scientist are that the social scientist's are apt to be more systematic—often guided by the test of a theory—and more precise—sometimes aided by sampling techniques to assure representativeness or careful training to minimize biased data gathering.

The findings from research observations may be used in at least two ways. First, the results of observations can become the basis for generating a theory. For example, by carefully recording many people's accounts of how they initially came to smoke marijuana, one researcher (Becker, 1963) constructed a theory of how marijuana smoking is usually an activity learned from others. The second way to use research findings is to test a theory. For example, to test the theory that poor economic conditions lead to higher rates of mental disorders (a "stress" theory of mental disorder), we might examine the relationship between economic indicators (e.g., levels of employment) and mental hospital admission rates over a long period of time. One researcher (Brenner, 1973) has found evidence for this relationship. In either case, *generating* theory or *testing* theory, research is a way of linking our ideas about explaining an event or phenomenon with actual occurrences in the world around us.

So far, we can see that research is important to constructing and testing theories. But we might reasonably ask: Why are theories so important? Why is it important to be able to understand and evaluate them? The answer that is most central to the goals of this book has to do with the role of theory in the formulation of social policy. Put simply, the accepted theory about what causes a particular pattern of behavior sometimes guides our attempts to control or change it. For example, if we theorize that certain strange behavior on the part of some people is due to demonic possession, we might devise a social policy that emphasizes religious exorcism, ritual, or punishment to drive away the evil spirits. (This happened in 17th century colonial America during the witchcraft hysteria.) Throughout most of the last century, theories of bizarre behavior have conceptualized it as an indication of illness or disease and, therefore, hospitalization and treatment according to a medical model have dominated social policy toward mental disorders. On the other hand, if we theorize that publicly labeling and stigmatizing a person who exhibits odd behavior as mentally ill actually *increases* his tendencies to act strangely (Scheff, 1966), we might initiate a social policy designed to minimize the humiliation and isolation of mental hospitalization by releasing mental patients to local community care facilities. Such a "deinstitutionalization" policy, largely consistent with labeling theory, has been accelerating over the past decade.

While we usually think in terms of theory being a guide to some particular social action, this is not always the case. Sometimes, social policymakers (society's elite class, politicians or government officials) may decide on a particular course of action and then promote a theory to rationalize it. For example, the real reasons for releasing mental patients back to their communities might be to lower the cost and responsibility for psychiatric care for the state (Scull, 1977). However, a labeling theory like Scheff's that suggests deinstitutionalization as a way of avoiding the damaging stigma of hospitalization might be used by policy makers to rationalize and mask the real reasons for increased reliance on community-based outpatient facilities.

Theories, then, are important because they serve both to guide and to rationalize social action or inaction. In a democracy, where citizens are presumably able to influence social policy decisions by pressuring legislators and voting, the capacity to understand and evaluate theories is essential. Deciding the best course for social policy depends upon an ability to make an informed, reasoned judgment about the theories implied by various social policy choices. To avoid being hoodwinked, we must understand theories sufficiently to decide when they are being used as smoke screens by social policy makers to hide the true intentions of the laws they pass and would have us accept. From this viewpoint, full, meaningful participation in a democratic society demands learning how to think clearly about theories of behavior, including deviance, in order to exercise true freedom of choice as a citizen.

Chapters 2 through 6 of this book each have a section devoted to explanations (theories) of various types of deviance and the evidence (research findings) that relates to those explanations. As a framework for helping to organize theories into sensible categories, we next turn to an overview of several different levels of explanation.

LEVELS OF EXPLANATION

Explanations of deviant behavior range from those attributing its cause to the basic constitution of the individual (the person's nature) through how one is socialized (the person's nurture) to larger environmental variables such as the opportunities available to advance one's social status (opportunity structure) and the transmission of cultural values (subculture). Broadly speaking, it is sometimes useful to think of explanations in terms of their levels of analysis such as those outlined in Figure 1.1: (1) Biogenetic, (2) Psychological, (3) Social Psychological, and (4) Sociological. In the next few pages we will briefly discuss each of the four levels of analysis indicating examples of theories from the deviance literature.[4]

Biogenetic

The biogenetic level has most to do with innate physiological characteristics of the individual. In the late 1700s and early 1800s phrenologists theorized that irregularities in the shape of a person's brain, as manifested by bumps one could feel on the head, were a significant cause of criminal behavior. Likewise, Lombroso's (1911) famed theory of atavism claimed that some criminals were physically and mentally degenerate throwbacks to prehuman apelike forms. Others, more recently, have tried to establish a causal relationship between body type and deviance, especially delinquent behavior (Sheldon, 1949; Glueck & Glueck, 1956). Although there probably is a tendency for delinquents more frequently to be mesomorphs (muscular body types) rather than ectomorphs (lean, delicate body types) or endomorphs (round, fat body types), it is doubtful that such a relationship is causal (Sutherland & Cressey, 1970; Mannheim, 1965). Indeed, each of the foregoing examples of a biogenetic explanation of deviance has been largely discredited.

Currently the most controversial biogenetic theory postulates a relationship between chromosome composition and antisocial behavior, especially violence (Jacobs *et al*, 1965). This theory states that a propensity to violence in some males is due to the presence of an extra Y (male) chromosome in their bodies' cells. The extra Y chromosome is thought to add an aggressive tendency to these men's psychophysiological constitutions. At this point the weight of evidence has not swung clearly for or against the chromosomes and violence hypothesis (Fox, 1971; Hook, 1973) and the debate on this theory is far from conclusive (Witken *et al*, 1976).

Finally, a number of other theories of deviance either explicitly state or imply that the behavior is at least partly due to a genetically inherited physiological predisposition and there is some evidence to support them (Ellis, 1982). For example, the results of one study on rates of alcoholism in families showing that 52% of alcoholics had at least one alcoholic parent suggest the possibility that genetic inheritance may be a factor (Catanzaro, 1967, p. 34). Of course, to establish clearly the role of genetic transmission, the role of nongenetic factors such as family structure or parental attitudes toward drinking would have to be isolated.

Level	Kinds of causal variables	Examples
Biogenetic	Head shape or other physical anomaly	Phrenologists
	atavism	Lombroso (1911)
	somatotype	Sheldon (1949)
		Glueck and Glueck (1956)
	Genetic transmission	
	Chromosome composition (XYY theory)	Jacobs (1965)
Psychological	Instinctual drives	Ardrey (1961)
	(and/or their suppression)	Freud (1930)
	Mental pathology	Glueck and Glueck (1959)
	Maternal deprivation	McCord and McCord (1956)
Social Psychological	Socialization	
	superego development	Henry and Short (1954)
	Social learning	Akers et.al. (1979)
	imitation	Bandura et. al. (1961)
	Influences of significant others	
	differential association	Sutherland (1970)
	Labeling	Scheff (1966)
Sociological	Social structure	
	"Needs" of the society	
	functionalism	Durkheim (1938)
		Erikson (1966)
	Social change	
	social disorganization	Faris and Dunham (1939)
	anomie	Durkheim (1951)
	Opportunity structure	Cloward and Ohlin (1960)
	anomie	Merton (1968)
	Culture	
	transmission of values and attitudes	Shaw and McKay (1942)
	delinquent subculture	Cohen (1955)
	subculture of violence	Wolfgang and Ferracuti (1967)
	Control	
	social bond	Hirschi (1969)
	deterrence	Braithwaite and Geis (1982)
	Political economy	
	class structure	Quinney (1970)
		Chambliss (1975)
	class conflict	Taylor et.al. (1973)

FIGURE 1.1. LEVELS OF EXPLANATION

Psychological

Psychological level theories also emphasize variables that have to do with the individual's personal traits, especially those like instincts or IQ that might be important to behavioral predispositions. For example, in *Civilization and Its Discontents,* Freud (1930a) postulates that numerous types of deviance including intoxication, religious fanaticism, withdrawal, and madness can be attributed to sublimation of humans' basic sexual, aggressive instincts. Ardrey (1961, 1966) argues that much of the violence in human societies is rooted in man's inherited aggressive instincts which derive from his need to gain and defend territory.[5] In addition to instinctual drives, psychological level explanations of deviance have involved variables such as mental pathology (Glueck & Glueck, 1959), maternal deprivation (McCord & McCord, 1956), hormonal imbalance, and epilepsy (Shah & Roth, 1974).

Social Psychological

Psychological explanations depend upon factors that become part of a person's personality at birth, or very shortly thereafter. Social psychological theories emphasize variables that emerge as a result of the person's interactions with others. For example, some theorists suggest that deviance is a product of a person's failure to develop sufficient internal controls during the socialization process. Punitive child-rearing practices, most common in the lower class, seem to retard superego development. In Freudian terms, this weak superego means that a person does not possess the internal restraints or sense of guilt to prevent them from engaging in antisocial, illegal, or especially violent behavior (Coser, 1967). On the other hand, it has been hypothesized that middle-class, love-oriented child-rearing techniques run the risk of a too strong superego which inhibits outwardly directed hostility in the face of frustrations and can lead to inwardly directed responses such as depression or even suicide (Henry & Short, 1954).

Another social psychological approach emphasizes imitation and role modeling. For example, Bandura and his colleagues (Bandura, 1962; Bandura *et al.,* 1961, 1963; Bandura & Walters, 1959) have developed a social learning theory which suggests that exposure to adult deviant role models, even through the media (e.g., television violence), leads to the learning and imitation of such behavior by young children. Similarly, Sutherland's (Sutherland & Cressey, 1970) famous theory of differential association states that a person will come to violate rules through his or her learning by association with rule breakers. Importantly, the learning includes both the development of skillful techniques (how to pick a lock, juggle the account books, or pick up a "john") and psychological defenses (rationalization, projection, etc.) to reduce or eliminate guilt. The latter are often referred to as neutralizations (Sykes & Matza, 1957) or rationalizations for having broken a particular rule.

Still another example of the social psychological level of analysis is labeling theory. This approach states that the single most important event leading to a person being locked into a deviant role is official labeling. When a person is officially identified as a drunk, a thief, a prostitute, crazy, or any other disvalued status, the label: (1) helps to convince the person so identified that he or she is indeed different, possibly bad, even dirty; and (2) sometimes closes off legitimate opportunities for the person to go straight. Thus, for example, prostitutes often become caught in a sequence of revolving door justice where they are picked up on the street for hustling "tricks," go to court to be fined or placed on bail for prostitution, and soon find themselves stigmatized and back on the street with no better opportunities to make a living than before. To earn money for bails, fines, and simply to live they have few alternatives other than continued prostitution.

Sociological

Theories at the sociological level of analysis tend to emphasize how different social structures or social environments exert pressures on people to engage in deviant activity. One of the earliest sociological theories of deviance is Durkheim's (1938) functional analysis of crime.[6] He argues that since deviance is present in all societies, it must serve some positive function or else it would not persist. Put another way, because it is present in all known societies, deviance must fulfill some needs of a society for its survival. Durkheim goes on to suggest that the deviant does serve a positive role in the social organization by helping to define and publicize the rules for others, by creating increased social cohesion as an outsider for people collectively to react against, and by sometimes acting as a forebearer of social change. Durkheim concludes that because deviance is positively functional in every society, every society has its "normal" rate of deviant behavior.

Another group of American sociologists working in the first half of the 20th century thought that conditions such as suicide, mental disorders, and delinquency seemed to be concentrated in certain areas of cities (Cavan, 1923; Faris & Dunham, 1939; Shaw & McKay, 1942). They hypothesized that the reason for higher rates of deviance in these locations was the social disorganization to be found in them. These theorists argued that the rapid social changes in American cities, epitomized by massive immigration, industrialization, and urbanization, led to a weakening of social norms. The weakened social norms, or social disorganization, was proposed to be the underlying cause of deviance. The social disorganization theorists sought evidence in support of their theory by relating indices of social disorganization in an area of a city such as the proportion of foreign born, property values, and types of dwellings to rates of deviance found there. They did find that areas with the greatest social disorganization by their account had higher rates of deviance.

Durkheim, the French sociologist who made the first detailed argument for a functionalist theory of deviance, also introduced the concept *anomie* (normlessness) to explain differing rates of suicide among nationalities and other social groupings. Durkheim's (1951) anomie theory is based on the idea that people must have their desires for ever increasing social status checked or restrained by normatively proscribed limits or they will be doomed to perpetual unhappiness. In a sense, Durkheim was saying that norms tell people what reasonably to expect in their social positions and, in effect, to "know their place" in the society. However, when the norms in a society are seriously disturbed because of economic upheaval—economic boom or bust—the resulting condition called anomie leads to increased rates of suicide. Note that both the American social disorganization theorists (writing in the first part of the 20th century) and Durkheim (writing in the latter part of the 19th century) ultimately turn to the rapid social changes in society as a variable central to their explanations of rates of deviance.

In addition to anomie, or normlessness, Durkheim also offered social integration or social cohesion as a key variable to understanding rates of deviance. Specifically regarding suicide, he suggested that people who lacked cohesive ties with others in the social structure would have higher rates of suicide. As evidence of this he noted that the married have lower suicide rates than the widowed or divorced, the young lower than the old, and Jews (highly cohesive group) lower than Protestants (less cohesive). Suicide resulting from lack of social integration Durkheim called *egoistic*. At the other extreme, he noted suicides that were an expression of an individual's intense integration into the group—to the point where he or she makes the ultimate sacrifice for it. For example, hara kari or kamikaze suicides in Japanese society reflect cohesive bonds so intense that the individual willingly dies for the supposed good of the group. Durkheim called these *altruistic* suicides. Thus, egoistic suicide is due to a lack of social integration at one extreme and altruistic suicide represents highly intense social integration at the other.

Another American sociologist, Robert K. Merton, further developed Durkheim's anomie theory. The key variable in Merton's theory is what others (Cloward & Ohlin, 1960) have called *opportunity structure*. Merton (1968) states that in some societies there may be an imbalance between cultural goals (things that people generally think are valuable and worth striving for) and institutionalized means (the legitimate, legal ways to attain the valued goals). In American society there tends to be great emphasis on attaining material wealth like cars, good clothes, a home, appliances, etc. These are culturally valued symbols of success in the United States. Everyone is expected to strive for these goals and each of us is constantly urged, through advertising, to pursue them. However, the means to reach these goals are not universally available. Not everyone has the same educational or occupational opportunity. This overemphasis on the goals without adequate availability of means to all for reaching the goals puts intense pressure on some individuals to use illegitimate, illegal means to reach the goals. Merton suggests that higher rates of deviance (especially crime) are apt to be found at points in the society where the disjunction between cultural goals and legitimate opportunities is greatest. Put another way, an imbalance of emphasis in the social structure creates the conditions for a breakdown of norms, or anomie.

Some theorists at the sociological level of analysis postulate the cultural transmission of values and attitudes which actually support rule-breaking. Much of the theory and research in the area of juvenile delinquency has centered on the question of the values to which delinquents adhere. While there are certainly those who argue against it (see Sykes & Matza, 1957), cultural transmission theorists describe a delinquent subculture which, in distinct contrast to the culture of the society at large, actually values negativistic, nonutilitarian, malicious behavior (Cohen, 1955). Similarly, Wolfgang and Ferracuti (1967) ascribe higher rates of homicide in areas such as the American South or "among a relatively homogeneous subcultural group in any large urban community" (p. 52) to a value system that constitutes a subculture of violence. In other words, the deviance is theorized to result from a unique set of norms and values shared by members of a particular group through their culture.

Control theory assumes that people will commit deviant acts unless they are restrained in some way. Thus, while most of the theories previously described respond to the question: "Why does the deviant do it?" control theory responds to the question: "What prevents the nondeviant from committing deviant acts?" This perspective assumes that deviance is not problematic. All of us, given free rein, would commit deviant acts out of greed, selfishness, contempt, or simple meanness unless we were restrained. However, people do limit their behavior according to the constraints of disappointing others, guilt, fear of getting caught, spoiling of reputation, and other mechanisms of social control. Thus, rather than focusing upon the conditions such as genetic predisposition, psychological trauma, family upbringing, or social pressures that might impel a person into deviance, control theory concentrates on the social mechanisms that deter people from deviant activity.

Hirschi's (1969) formulation of control theory states that an individual's bond to the society is what restrains him from committing deviant acts. When people have a sense of attachment, commitment, and involvement with law-abiding others in the society and have learned to believe in the morality of the law, it is unlikely they will be deviant. They will conform because they have a "stake in conformity" (Toby, 1957). In this sense, control theory looks at the other side of the deviancy coin and might be considered more a theory of conformity rather than one of deviance.

Another variation of control theory concentrates on conventional techniques of punishment and deterrence. For example, Braithwaite and Geis (1982) argue that although sanctions such as fines or imprisonment have not been particularly effective deterrents against ordinary street criminals, such measures have a high probability of success in reducing high-status corporate crime. They reason that since corporate crimes such as price fixing or health and safety violations are often based on the rational determination of possible gain, making the risks clearly outweigh the benefits would make law-abiding behavior the normal, rational decision. Moreover, high-status individuals who have the most to lose from traditional criminal penalties like fines and the public humiliation of imprisonment would be most deterred by those measures.

Finally, some contemporary sociological theorists emphasize class structure as central to the development and application of criminal law in capitalist societies (Quinney, 1970; Spitzer, 1975). Beginning with the premise that society is dominated by a ruling elite, these sociologists show how rules (laws) are formulated in the interest of the elite and then applied to protect the powerful, to threaten the powerless, and to maintain the inequitable status quo. Deviance from this perspective is best understood in relation to class conflict. The powerful are presumed to manipulate the legislation and execution of laws in their interests through control of the criminal justice system and the powerless are seen as more vulnerable to a disproportionate application of criminal sanctions (Chambliss, 1975). Thus, the appearance of greater amounts of deviance in the lower classes is attributed mainly to class discrimination in the making and enforcement of the laws.

Explanations of deviance operate at different levels of explanation ranging from biogenetic to sociological. Each of the levels of explanation just described is represented several times in subsequent chapters. However, each type of explanation has not been applied to every type of deviance we will examine. Any particular form of deviance may seem to be more amenable to certain explanations than others. For example, although prostitution has not been explained by biogenetic theories, social psychological (learning theories) and sociological (functionalist) explanations have been widely accepted. On the other hand, heredity and hormones (biogenetic explanations) have been given significant consideration in the theory and research on homosexuality. The sections on explanations of the types of deviance discussed are intended to represent the types of theories, and the levels of explanation, most predominantly applied in each case. You might find it helpful occasionally to return to Figure 1.1 as you read.

SUMMARY

In this chapter you have been introduced to the study of deviant behavior as a field of inquiry. We began by distinguishing between explanations aimed at understanding the behavior of deviant individuals (*deviants*) and explanations dealing with how a particular sort of behavior becomes labeled deviant (*deviance*). Another way to put this distinction is to note the difference between type–of–person theories directed to the question, "Why does the person act that way?" and type–of–behavior theories responding to the question, "Why are certain activities treated as deviant while others are not?" The discussion of types of deviant behavior emphasized that the field of deviance is primarily concerned with marginal activities. Unlike conforming or ordinary predatory criminal behavior such as murder or rape, marginal deviant activities often do not generate a strong public consensus on what should be done about them. This suggests that interest-group conflict, politics, and power are frequently central to understanding deviance.

Next we turned to the importance of theories (explanations) and research (systematic observations) for the formation of social policies directed at changing or controlling deviance. Because theories frequently serve as guides or rationalizations for social action or inaction, it is important for effective citizens in a democratic society to understand and evaluate the theories surrounding various social policy choices. Research, in turn, is both a source for generating and a means for testing theories. Most of the rest of this book is devoted to explanations—theories—of various types of deviance and the evidence—research findings—that relate to those explanations.

Finally, there was a brief review of approaches to explaining deviance which can be organized according to levels of analysis: biogenetic, psychological, social psychological, and sociological. These levels move generally from locating the cause within the individual (nature) to locating the cause in the social environment (nurture). In subsequent chapters, the foregoing analysis of explanations should be useful in understanding the research and theories about each specific type of deviance. For example, when trying to grasp a particular explanation of deviance, it is usually helpful to ask oneself the following questions:

Does the explanation deal with how a *person* becomes deviant or how the *behavior* became deviance?

What is the *level of analysis* of the explanation? Does it emphasize the individual's "nature" or socioenvironmental "nurture"?

What is the main *causal variable* in the theory? Social integration? Anomie? Social learning? Social class?

NOTES

1. An interesting question can be raised when old, discarded laws like the blue laws become the objects of renewed attention and attempts at enforcement. For example, see Chambliss (1973). This issue is discussed later at various points in this book.

2. While Schur (1965) identifies the transactional nature of victimless crimes as their underlying commonality, there is heated debate revolving around his label for them. For an excellent exchange on the issue of whether "victimless" crimes really have no victims, see Schur and Bedeau (1974).

3. Of course, the most famous recent example of the failure on the part of the powerful to maintain the secrecy of their deviance is the collapse of the Nixon administration brought about by the Watergate episode.

4. Although we have noted that the field of deviant behavior can be distinguished from criminology by the types of behavior most frequently studied, theories developed specifically to explain criminal behavior have been important to the development of explanations of the marginal activities studied by deviant behavior specialists. Thus, some of the theories reviewed refer to crime as the type of deviance they were designed to explain. Nevertheless, the same principles used by earlier theorists to explain crime can often be used to explain more marginal deviance.

5. Ethology is the study of how animal behavior relates to that of humans. Ardrey (1961) finds ethological evidence for his theory in the study of territoriality among fish, birds, and subhuman primates. A similar argument is advanced by Lorenz (1966).

6. While Durkheim applies his functional analysis specifically to crime, the logic of the argument holds equally well for the broader category, deviance. For example, see Erikson (1966).

REFERENCES

Akers, R., Krohn, M.D., Lanza-Kaduce, L., & Radosevich, M.
    1979 Social learning and deviant behavior: A specific test of a general theory. *American Sociological Review, 44*, 636–655.

Ardrey, R.
    1961 *African genesis.* New York: Atheneum.

Ardrey, R.
    1966 *The territorial imperative.* New York: Atheneum.

Bandura, A.
    1962 Social learning through imitation. *Nebraska Symposium on Motivation.* Lincoln: University of Nebraska Press.

Bandura, A., Ross, D., & Ross, S. A.
    1961 Transmission of aggression through imitation of aggression models. *Journal of Abnormal and Social Psychology, 63*, 575–582.

Bandura, A., Ross, D., & Ross, S. A.
    1963 Imitation of film-mediated aggressive models. *Journal of Abnormal and Social Psychology, 66*, 3–11.

Bandura, A., & Walters, R. H.
    1959 *Adolescent aggression.* New York: Ronald.

Becker, S.
    1963 *Outsiders.* New York: Free Press.

Braithwaite, J., & Geis, G.
    1982 On theory and action for corporate crime control. *Crime and Deliquency, 28*, 292–314.

Brenner, M. H.
    1973 *Mental illness and the economy.* Cambridge, Mass.: Harvard University Press.

Catanzaro, R. J.
    1967 Psychiatric aspects of alcoholism. In D. J. Pittman (Ed.), *Alcoholism.* New York: Harper and Row.

Cavan, R.
    1923 *Suicide.* Chicago: University of Chicago Press.

Chambliss, W. J.
    1973 The law of vagrancy. *Warner Modular Publication,* Mod. 4, 1–10.

Chambliss, W. J.
    1975 Toward a political economy of crime. *Theory and Society, 2*, 149–170.

Cloward, R., & Ohlin, L. E.
    1960 *Delinquency and opportunity: A theory of delinquent gangs.* New York: The Free Press.

Cohen, A. K.
    1955 *Delinquent boys.* Glencoe, Ill.: Free Press.

Cory, D. W.
    1951 The homosexual in America. New York: Greenberg.

Coser, L. A.
    1967 Violence and the social structure. In *Continuities in the Study of Social Conflict.* New York: Free Press.

Durkheim, E.
  1938 *The rules of sociological method.* S. A. Solovay & J. H. Mueller (Trans.), E. G. Catlin (Ed.). New York: Free Press.

Durkheim, E.
  1951 *Suicide: A study in sociology.* Translated by J. A. Spauldey & G. Simpson (Trans.). Glencoe, Ill.: Free Press.

Ellis, L.
  1982 Genetics and criminal behavior. *Criminology 20,* 43–66.

Erikson, K. T.
  1966 *Wayward puritans.* New York: John Wiley and Sons.

Faris, R., Dunham, E. L., & Dunham, H. W.
  1939 *Mental disorders in urban areas.* Chicago: The University of Chicago Press.

Fox, R. G.
  1971 The XYY offender: A modern myth? *The Journal of Criminal Law, Criminology and Police Science, 62,* 59–73.

Freud, S.
  1930a *Civilization and its discontents.* J. Riviera (Trans.). London: The Hogarth Press.

Freud, S.
  1930b *Three contributions to the theory of sex.* A. A. Brill (Trans.). New York: Nervous and Mental Disease Publishing Co.

Glueck, S., & Glueck, E.
  1959 Mental pathology and delinquency. In *The Problem of Delinquency.* Boston: Houghton Mifflin.

Glueck, S., & Glueck, E.
  1956 *Physique and delinquency.* New York: Harper and Row.

Henry, A. F., & Short, J. F., Jr.
  1954 *Suicide and homicide.* New York: Free Press.

Hirschi, T.
  1969 *The causes of delinquency.* Berkeley, Calif.: University of California Press.

Hook, E. B.
  1973 Behavioral implications of the human XYY genotype. *Science, 179,* 139–150.

Jacobs, P. A., Bunton, M., Melville, M. M., Brittain, R. P., & McClemont, W. F.
  1965 Aggressive behavior, mental subnormality, and the XYY male. *Nature, 208,* 1351.

Kallmann, F. G.
  1952 A comparative twin study on the genetic aspects of male homosexuality. *Journal of Nervous and Mental Disorder, 115,* 283–298.

Liazos, A.
  1972 The poverty of the sociology of deviance: Nuts, sluts, and 'preverts'. *Social Problems, 20,* 102–120.

Lombroso, C.
 1911 *Crime, its causes and remedies.* H. P. Horton (Trans.). Boston: Little, Brown.
Lorenz, K.
 1966 *On aggression.* M. K. Wilson (Trans.). New York: Harcourt, Brace and World.
McCord, W., & McCord, J.
 1956 *Psychopathology and delinquency.* New York: Grune and Stratton.
Mannheim, H.
 1965 *Comparative criminology.* Boston: Houghton Mifflin.
Merton, R. K.
 1968 Social structure and anomie. In *Social Theory and Social Structure.* New York: Macmillan.
Quinney, R.
 1970 *The social reality of crime.* Boston: Little, Brown.
Scheff, T. J.
 1966 *Being mentally ill: A sociological theory.* Chicago: Aldine.
Schur, E. M.
 1965 *Crimes without victims.* Englewood Cliffs, N.J.: Prentice-Hall.
Schur, E. M., & Bedeau, H. A.
 1974 *Victimless crimes: Two sides of a controversy.* Englewood Cliffs, N.J.: Prentice-Hall.
Schwartz, R. D., & Skolnick, J. H.
 1964 Two studies of legal stigma. In H. S. Becker (Ed.), *The other side.* New York: The Free Press.
Scull, A. T.
 1977 *Decarceration—Community treatment and the deviant: A radical view.* Englewood Cliffs, N.J.: Prentice-Hall.
Shah, S., & Roth, L. H.
 1974 Biological and psychophysiological factors in criminality. D. Glaser (Ed.), *Handbook of criminology.* Chicago: Rand McNally.
Shaw, C. R., & McKay, H. D.
 1942 *Juvenile delinquency and urban areas.* Chicago: University of Chicago Press.
Sheldon, W. H.
 1949 *Varieties of delinquent youth: An introduction to constitutional psychiatry.* New York: Harper and Row.
Spitzer, S.
 1975 Toward a Marxian theory of deviance. *Social Problems, 22,* 638–651.
Sutherland, E. H., & Cressey, D. R.
 1970 *Criminology,* 9th ed. Philadelphia: Lippincott.
Sykes, G. M., & Matza, D.
 1957 Techniques of neutralization: A theory of delinquency. *American Journal of Sociology, 22,* 664–670.
Taylor, J., Walton, P., & Young, J.
 1973 *The new criminology.* New York: Harper and Row.

Thio, A.
   1973   Class bias in the sociology of deviance. *The American Sociologist, 8,* 1–12.

Toby, J.
   1957   Social disorganization and stake in conformity. *Journal of Criminal Law, Criminology and Police Science, 48,* 12–17.

Witken, H. A., Mednick, S. A., Schulsinger, F., Bakkestrom, E., Christiansen, K. O., Goodenough, D. R., Hirschhorn, K., Lundsteen, C., Owen, D. R., Phillip, J., Rubin, D. B., & Stocking, M.
   1976   "Criminality in XYY and XXY men." *Science, 193,* 547–555.

Wolfgang, M. E., & Ferracuti, F.
   1967   *The subculture of violence.* New York: Tavistock.

Chapter 2
SEXUAL DEVIANCE

TYPES OF SEXUAL DEVIANCE
  Normal Deviance
  Pathological Deviance
  Social Structure Generating Deviance
PROSTITUTION
  Definition
  Historical and Cultural Perspectives
  Prostitution in the United States Today
  Explanations of Prostitution
  The Political Economy of Prostitution
PORNOGRAPHY
  What Is It?
  Cultural and Historical Context
  Types and Extent of Erotica
  Effects of Sexual Materials
  Explanations of Pornography
HOMOSEXUALITY
  Historical and Cultural Attitudes
  Defining Homosexuality
  Masters and Johnson: Homosexual Physiology
  Bell and Weinberg: Homosexual Diversity
  Subcultural Patterns
  Explanations of Homosexuality
SWINGING
  Meeting, Motives, and Manipulation
  The Sociological Significance of Swinging
SUMMARY

For survival as a species, humans must obviously engage in sexual relations, and most people feel the effects of a biologically based sexual drive for a significant portion of their lives. While a fundamental human sex drive undeniably exists, it is equally clear that human sexual behavior takes highly diverse forms. It is channeled, molded, restricted, repressed, or stimulated by a huge number of beliefs, customs, and sanctions in various cultures around the world. The extent of human cultural diversity is displayed most dramatically in the customs and taboos surrounding basic human functions like eating—an activity necessary for short-term survival of individuals, and sex—an activity necessary for long-term survival of the species. For example, one way in which people identify their group in contrast to another, is the set of taboos or customs dictating what is allowable, proper, or desirable to consume as food. Thus, taboos against mixing meat and dairy products or eating beef, or preferences for steak and kidney pie or spaghetti and meatballs immediately identify certain groups. Likewise, norms vary widely regarding sexual attractiveness (fat or thin, old or young, big breasts or small), availability of sexual partners (permissive or severely limited access), marital-sexual arrangements (varying from strict monogamy to polygamy), and acceptance of nonprocreative sexual practices (sexual foreplay, homosexuality, masturbation, etc.)—to name but a few.

Because contrasting standards of conduct have evolved in different cultures in regard to even the most basic human functions like eating or sex, simple, general definitions either of deviant consumption habits or sexual behaviors are impossible. Likewise, especially in regard to sex, standards of behavior are apt to change very rapidly in any given society. Within a generation in the United States, for example, there has been a dramatic increase in the availability of sexually explicit materials; more permissive attitudes toward premarital intercourse, mouth-to-genital sex, and masturbation with corresponding increases in these behaviors. There also has been a more open treatment of human sexuality, especially female sexuality, and a considerable shift away from the double standard (Hunt, 1974).

Recognizing the inevitable difficulties in defining and precisely classifying various sexual activities as either deviant or not, we next turn to the rationale for choosing the types of sexual behavior discussed in this chapter: prostitution, pornography, homosexuality, and swinging.

TYPES OF SEXUAL DEVIANCE[1]

Normal Deviance

A number of sexual activities are quite frequent even though they violate the law, offend the normative standards of most people in a community, or both. For example, a recent survey found that 86% of males and 60% of females between 18 and 34 had had premarital coitus. Mouth-to-genital techniques (fellatio and cunnilingus) were a part of the repertoire of sexual practices used by more than 50% of high-school educated married Americans (Hunt, 1974). This is despite the fact that nonmarital sex and mouth-to-genital contact technically violate the law in most states.

These types of behavior have been called normal deviance by Gagnon and Simon (1967) because they are so widespread and occur with such low social visibility that only a small number of people are ever sanctioned for doing them. Statistically speaking they are the norm rather than deviant and, even if technically illegal, they possess the characteristics of secret deviance discussed in Chapter 1: They are usually done behind closed doors and they are victimless because no one directly involved would seek a legal complaint.

Pathological Deviance

This is behavior which is against the law, is believed by most people to be harmful, and is engaged in by relatively few individuals. Examples include incest, sexual contact with children, exhibitionism, voyeurism, and aggressive offenses such as rape. Activities of this sort exist without supportive group structures to recruit participants, train them, gather people together to perform the act, or provide social support for the actor. Instead, pathological deviance involves an offender who is acting alone out of particular psychological needs. Causes for the behavior are most likely to be found at the psychological or social psychological level of explanation—in the early experiences and resulting personality structure of the individual as opposed to the more immediate social environment.

Social Structure Generating Deviance

In contrast to both normal and pathological deviance, this type includes behavior that generates specific social structures which may serve to recruit, train, gather participants together, or provide social support for the actor. Examples are nudism in nudist camps, pornography, prostitution, homosexuality, and swinging. Of course, any of these behaviors may be explained, in part, by reference to the psychological history of the participants. However, in each case, an elaborate set of ongoing relationships provides the participant with specialized knowledge to help manage interactions with partners or clients. Through such relationships the deviant can also learn the attitudes and rationalizations that allow him or her to place the behavior in the best possible light. The social structures generated by this type of deviance are implicit when one speaks of the "homosexual community" with its bars, steam baths, publications, organizations, and argot. Likewise, when a female prostitute enters "the life," she becomes part of an occupational culture with an elaborate set of social networks including pimps, other prostitutes, steerers, clients, and vice officers.

This chapter deals with social structure generating sexual deviance. It is the type for which the sociological perspective is most appropriate. In the analysis of female prostitution, one can see clearly how widely shared sexist and commodity-orientated values converge with the career contingencies of many women in our society to make prostitution both a viable option and even an apparently rational choice. The legislative and enforcement battles surrounding pornography provide a particularly vivid example of deviance at the center of political struggle. The discussion of male and female homosexuality continues the subcultural and political themes raised in respect to prostitution and pornography. And finally, swinging appears to be an example of a middle-class, sexually deviant social movement that never really caught on.

PROSTITUTION

Definition

If asked in our mind's eye to visualize a prostitute, most of us would probably imagine a lone "painted" woman, seductively clothed, walking the streets of a city. Such an image does, in fact, conform partly to reality—although we shall see that not all prostitutes are street walkers, ostentatious in their physical appearance, or even female. Indeed, rather than relying upon appearance, prostitution is better defined first by the unique properties of what a prostitute does. One expert defines prostitution as any sexual exchange where the reward for the prostitute is neither sexual nor affectional (James, 1977, p. 369). Thus, anyone—including young boys, wives, or girl friends—prostitutes him- or herself when they exchange access to their bodies for material gain (money, clothes, promotion, or entertainment). While this definition makes logical sense, as a practical and legal matter prostitution may be defined more precisely. First, although instances of gigolos (males who provide sexual services to women for pay) and male homosexual prostitution (Gandy & Deisher, 1970) unquestionably exist, they receive relatively little attention from the law. Historically, prostitution by any definition has overwhelmingly involved women as the sexual providers in the relationship. Thus, we will here be dealing only with female prostitution.

Second, sexually active women who receive gifts from lovers, can be distinguished from prostitutes by taking the woman's self-image into account. Thus, Heyl (1979) favors Polsky's (1967, p. 191) definition:

> Prostitution is the granting of nonmarital sex *as a vocation.* . . . Although women accepting gifts regularly from lovers may be engaged in a commercialized relationship, they usually do not view it that way. Prostitutes, on the other hand, see the sex-money exchange as the business transaction that constitutes their job. (Heyl, 1979, p. 2)

In this chapter, our discussion of prostitution will be confined to women who, as a business, exchange sex for money.

Historical and Cultural Perspectives

Although there are no firm grounds for the claim that prostitution is the world's oldest profession, it does appear that relationships approaching prostitution have existed for a very long time. We say "approaching" because arrangements that might appear to be prostitution by Western cultural standards are sometimes not viewed that way in other societies. For example, in Urga (outer Mongolia) merchants and lamas took women as companions on short journeys. After one group of women was paid and discharged, they simply sought others as replacements. However, from the buyers' point of view these were not prostitutes but temporary wives. Similar arrangements existed among some American Indian tribes where it was customary for a woman to accompany a man on an extended hunting trip to satisfy both his material and sexual needs in exchange for a share of the expedition's profits. The arrangement would be terminated at the end of a hunt.

Likewise, some writers have classified as prostitution the Eskimo hospitality tradition of a male host offering his wife to a visitor for which she received a small gift. By Western cultural standards this may appear to be a case of prostitution, but according to Eskimo culture it is not (Bullough & Bullough, 1978). In still other non-Western accounts, examples of prescribed promiscuity, religious ritual, serial marriage, or polygamy might be interpreted as prostitution depending on the viewpoint of the observer. The point is that since prostitution is so much a matter of definition according to the standards of a particular society, cross-cultural generalizations about its development in primitive societies, especially, are difficult.

In Western history, references to prostitution date back to ancient Greece where there was widespread prostitution of various types ranging from upper-class courtesans (*hetaira*) to lower-class streetwalkers who in poetic accounts sound similar to those encountered in urban areas today. During the earliest Greek period, prostitution, along with homosexual behavior and very sexually explicit art, was condoned. Later, in Plato's time, there was a growing hostility toward sex. This historical ambivalence of the Greeks toward prostitution with early tolerance—even encouragement—and later hostility, seems to have been paralleled in Roman attitudes. In Rome there were temple prostitutes, brothels, and streetwalkers, while upper-class courtesans were not romanticized as in early Greece. The prevailing popular attitude treated the prostitute as a low-status person and her occupation as a necessary evil.

During the early Christian period, stigmatizing attitudes toward prostitution, and indeed all sexual activity, hardened still further. At the same time, prostitution continued to flourish with the reluctant toleration of the Church.

> The fact that Christianity, with its open and avowed hostility toward sexual intercourse, tolerated prostitution as a necessary evil indicates how deeply the subordination of women and the double standard are set in Western culture. Though Christians attempted to ameliorate some of the conditions of the prostitute, they never challenged traditional attitudes enough to grant sexual equality or to regard women, except for the virginal unmarried woman, as other than part of the family unit. (Bullough and Bullough, 1978, p. 66)

During the latter Middle Ages, prostitution became widely accepted and most attempts to eliminate it were abandoned. Sexual inequality, the acceptance of women as sex objects and the impossibility of an unmarried woman supporting herself by other means all contributed to widespread prostitution and apparently resigned attitudes toward it.

From the 15th century to the present day, European public policy and attitudes toward prostitution have varied considerably. Toward the end of the 15th century, an epidemic of syphilis coupled with the reform ideology of the Protestant movement fostered attempts at repression. By the 17th century the syphilis epidemic declined and courtesans among the elite—such as Madame de Pompadour, mistress of Louis XV—were frequent additions to the royal courts. Likewise, prostitution among the more lowly increased, in brothels and in the streets. Through the late 18th and early 19th centuries, despite renewed epidemics of venereal disease, prostitution was practically tolerated with the emphasis on regulation rather than reform or elimination. Toward the mid-19th century Victorian era, a less flamboyant approach toward sexuality in general brought a return of reformist attitudes toward prostitution.

Present-day images of the prostitute and, indeed the historical attitudes that serve as a foundation for the continued existence of prostitution, are rooted in recurrent themes and conditions present from the outset of Western civilization. Women have historically been viewed as subordinate to men and, in contrast to men, women have been viewed as asexual in nature—two conditions that have served as the foundation for the sexual double standard. The double standard, encouraging widespread sexual activity on the part of men while demanding the withholding of sexual favors on the part of most "good" women, inevitably pushed a small population of enterprising women into the lucrative business of meeting the high demand.

Prostitution in the United States Today

Types. Prostitutes are available to fit almost any sexual demand across a wide range of prices for the service. The business styles include, but are not limited to, streetwalkers, bar girls, studio models and escorts, masseuses, hotel and convention prostitutes, house prostitutes, and call girls. Although between the extremes the relative status of the types is not clear, streetwalkers fall at the lower end of the professional hierarchy and call girls are at the top. A comparison of these two highlights the differential risks, independence, styles of client relationships, economic opportunities, and future prospects of women from the bottom to the top of the profession.

Streetwalkers are the most visible of prostitutes. In most large urban areas they may be found especially in red light areas on streetcorners or in doorways awaiting potential customers who walk or drive by. Usually, the streetwalkers will be approached by a man; the price and type of sexual service (fellatio, intercourse, etc.) negotiated; and agreement reached on where to meet for the exchange—usually a cheap hotel that provides rooms for prostitution, or even the client's car. The fee usually ranges from $20 to $100 a "trick" with an average of about half a dozen "johns" a night.

Street prostitutes are most frequently members of a racial or ethnic minority or young runaways from white homes. They have a high incidence of drug abuse and are often both the dispensers and victims of violence. Because for short periods of time they are apt to carry substantial amounts of cash, these women are targets of muggers. Increasingly, the street prostitutes themselves rob from their clients—sometimes in teams, one member of which steals from the john while he is engaged in sex with the other. The street hooker lives in a world of pimps, roach-infested hotels, vice officers, "pros wagons," night courts, bail bondsmen, prostitution lawyers, and day-to-day existence with a criminal record. The risk of arrest is great; the likelihood of long-term financial success is small; and the physical toll is enormous.

Sheehy (1973) puts it well:

> It sounds unbelievably glamorous. Come to the big city and make a minimum of $200 a night doing what comes naturally. Work six nights a week while you're young and pretty. It's the fastest way to make money in the shortest time. How else can a girl earn $70,000 a year?
>
> There are several critical facts the recruiter fails to mention. The average *net* income for a streetwalker is less than $100 a week. "To the pimp she's nothing but a piece of meat," says one police veteran of prostitution vans. And she ages very quickly. Prostitution is a physically punishing business. Right from the start a working girl begins to worry about her age. This is one profession in which seniority is not rewarded. (pp. 12-13)

Most urban street prostitutes are part of a stable of from two to a dozen women overseen by a pimp. The characteristic pattern is for the woman to turn over the money she earns to the pimp in exchange for his expertise in administering her professional and personal life—paying bail bondsmen or otherwise attending to the consequences of brushes with the law; allowing her to share the status he derives from his ostentatious lifestyle which usually includes fancy clothes, a customized car, and a general aura of a celebrity; and providing her with a secure sense of belonging. This latter factor seems to explain, in part, why street prostitutes so readily become attached to pimps, despite the overbearing, inequitable, sometimes violent aspects of the relationship. Women in America are generally socialized to feel that they need a man to care for them, and there is no reason to suspect prostitutes feel otherwise.

A pimp named Silky describing the pimp-prostitute relationship provides insights into how he operates with his women and why they stay.

> It's almost inevitable that a prostitute ends up with a player. It's hand and glove. Birds of a feather. The two just go together. Their heads are in the same place. We have the same thought patterns about life. We live the same life. Most girls look at everyone besides pimps as tricks. Some people think that pimps are whores because they take money, and that whores are tricks because they pay the pimps. It's true that without money a girl can't be mine, no way. A date can't have her unless he pays her. That is a similarity. But the relationship between a pimp and a whore is also a man–woman relationship. Our personal relationship is number one. Money is part of that relationship because money is a rule and a law of life.
>
> A girl who is a prostitute becomes good at manipulating men. Because I am aware, I don't allow her to manipulate me. With me, she has the one relationship that isn't a "use" relationship. She needs a pimp for her personal life. He's the only one who can understand, appreciate and handle her. (Hall, 1972, pp. 5–6)

The call girl, in contrast to the streetwalker, is at the pinnacle of the profession. She is usually white, attractive, socially sophisticated, discreet, and independent. Her business is arranged mostly by telephone over which she receives calls for "visits" or "dates" with customers. The call girl may begin building up a "book" of clients by taking the extra customers of another call girl to whom she pays a share of the fee. Current customers sometimes refer friends or business associates to her. While there usually is some contact with other call girls, this mode of prostitution is not enmeshed in a web of threatening or parasitic relationships like those that surround the streetwalker.

Sheey (1973) quotes from an interview with a "liberated" call girl:

> Take a woman of my age. Twenty-five. Divorced. After a woman has lived with a man and reaches a certain age, she needs sex. That's why being a working girl is so great. I take only champagne tricks, $100 an hour. My men are all very welldressed and successful with styled hair and young wives in Southhampton, that group. They're men I would date if I weren't in the business. It's a protection for me because I'm always afraid of getting involved. I don't want another unhappy marriage. So being a call girl is like taking out sexual insurance. I get paid for it. Plus when I want to enjoy it, I enjoy it ... (p. 205)

And another call girl is described:

> Today she is determined to build up a good book in New York. Her goal is to chin up the social ladder toward a rich husband. By now she has assembled a $6,000 wardrobe, paid off most of her furniture, and has almost "done her teeth." The apartment belongs to another working girl

who is living with a client in Italy. The address, the chandeliered lobby, the patina of hand-polished bronze elevators—all these things are critical if one is to maintain a champagne clientele. But she pays off no one. (Once a girl begins paying off, there is no end to the overhead.) In the interest of discretion, she allows no more than five of her most distinguished clients per week past the nosy doorman . . . Now that she has had a taste of independent high living on $600 to $1,000 a week, her sights have been raised. She wants to hit the top as a call girl. She keeps telling herself it is the true liberation. There is only one thing missing in her two years in New York; she has not seen or held a man for anything but business. (Sheehy, 1973, pp. 211–212)

Extent of Prostitution. There is obviously no way to count accurately the number of prostitutes in the United States even if a satisfactorily precise definition existed. One widely cited source estimates that as many as 500,000 women earn over one billion dollars per year in the occupation. Prostitution also exacts a major commitment from the criminal justice system. FBI statistics (1983) show that in 1980, over 64,000 women were arrested for "prostitution and commercialized vice." Moreover, a substantial portion of the additional 21,000 female arrests for "curfew and loitering law violations" or "vagrancy" probably involve at least suspicion of prostitution, and approximately 30% of female jail inmates are there on a prostitution charge (James, 1977).

Explanations of Prostitution

Functions. The earliest attempt to explain the prevalence of prostitution was made by Kingsley Davis (1937) who posed the question this way: "Why is it that a practice so thoroughly disapproved, so widely outlawed in Western civilization, can yet flourish so universally?" (p. 744). He begins by noting that human sexual behavior has social significance beyond mere reproduction. Because human females are sexually receptive year round, sex is a permanent part of human social life. Sex can be and is used for purposes other than the individual's own erotic gratification. Indeed, the employment of sex for nonsexual ends characterizes not only prostitution but all of our institutions involving sex, such as courtship and marriage. Looked at from this way, prostitution is not unique simply because in it sex is used for nonsexual reasons.

On the other hand, prostitution does differ from the legitimate sex-linked institutions, such as marriage, by not encouraging or demanding relative permanence or emotional feeling—qualities that are conducive to stable families in which to raise children. Thus, since prostitution does not exist for reproduction or child rearing, it is broadly condemned. "Commercial prostitution stands at the lowest extreme; it shares with other sexual institutions a basic feature, namely the employment of sex for an ulterior end in a system of differential advantages, but it differs from them in being mercenary, promiscuous and emotionally indifferent. From both these facts, however, it derives its remarkable vitality" (Davis, 1937, p. 749).

Davis goes on to argue that when rules restricting sexual activity to marriage are strong, opportunities for sex are greatly diminished. Prostitution is one way to fill the male sexual demand in a society with rules inhibiting the supply of available females. Moreover, it allows relatively few females to satisfy many men and does so without requiring any commitment beyond the man's ability to pay. The prostitute–client relationship is commercial, impersonal, and transitory. Prostitution is, then, an institution complementary to the traditional marriage and family because it provides an outlet for immediate sexual gratification without directly threatening the family. It follows that as sexual norms liberalize and women are less closely tied to the traditional family, prostitution should decline. However, while Davis foresees a simultaneous reduction in both family stability *and* prostitution, he does not predict the total elimination of either.

> ... even if present trends continue, there is no likelihood that sex freedom will ever displace prostitution. Not only will there always be a set of reproduction institutions which place a check upon sexual liberty, a system of social dominance which gives a motive for selling sexual favors, and a scale of attractiveness which creates the need for buying these favors, but prostitution is, in the last analysis, economical. Enabling a small number of women to take care of the needs of a large number of men, it is the most convenient sexual outlet for any army, and for the legions of strangers, perverts, and physically repulsive in our midst. It performs a function, apparently, which no other institution fully performs. (p. 755)

Social Psychological Development. A functionalist theory like Davis' is aimed at explaining why a practice like prostitution exists. One can, of course, seek an answer to a very different sort of question. Why do certain women become prostitutes? One approach in response to this question has been to assume that something must be fundamentally wrong—even sick—with a woman who sells sex. Various psychoanalytic or psychological studies of prostitutes have reported motivations such as being oversexed or frigid, latently homosexual, or having other difficulties in psychosexual development (see for example, Greenwald, 1970; or Winick & Kinsie, 1971). However, the evidence to support these assertions is weak and contradictory. For example, in a study specifically aimed at uncovering evidence concerning theories of psychological abnormalities, Gebhard (1969) found that among 127 prostitutes there was no unusually high incidence of frigidity, homosexuality, or hatred of men.

One researcher (Heyl, 1979) has ruefully observed that analyses of prostitutes based on Oedipal/Electra complexes, penis envy, or infantile regression would make more sense if applied to their male clients. After all, the prostitute's motivation is probably largely utilitarian—she does it to earn a living. However, the client's motivation, being less utilitarian, might be more appropriately explained by *his* psychosexual development. Nevertheless, the extant research at the psychological level focuses overwhelmingly on the prostitute rather than the client.

Aside from psychoanalytic motivations, the reasons for becoming a prostitute can be classified under three headings: predisposing factors, attracting factors, and precipitating factors. Predisposing factors typically include parental abuse and neglect (Davis, 1971; and Gray, 1973). Coincident with disruptive family backgrounds, women who become prostitutes typically leave home permanently and have their first sexual experiences at an earlier age than other women. These factors are especially characteristic of street prostitutes and to some extent, although to a lesser degree, for call girls. At a more general level, in regard to call girls, Rosenblum (1975) has argued that socialization into the female sex role is a predisposing factor—the attitudes that both call girls and nondeviant women learn toward sex and men are not qualitatively different.

> Desirability for both the call girl and the nondeviant woman is most basically measured by physical appearance and the ability to make a man feel "masculine." Neither the call girl nor the nondeviant woman have high expectations about receiving sexual gratification (though to differing degrees), and both expect some type of "pay off" for their desirability (though the prostitute's payment is more tangible). The difference between the utilization of and the expectations regarding sexuality is only one of degree. The decision to become a call girl simply requires an exaggeration of one aspect of the situation experienced as a nondeviant woman. (p. 180)

Factors attracting women to prostitution include comparative career advantages such as independence, adventure, money, and sexual gratification. In a review of 26 studies of prostitution, James (1977, pp. 390–391) found that "economics" was mentioned as an important conscious motivation in 14 and "adventure" was the next most frequent reason mentioned in 10 studies. There are few occupations widely available to women that promise the high economic payoff that prostitution does, especially for call girls, for whom the risks of arrest or physical harm are least.

> ... prostitution may be regarded as an entrepreneurial endeavor, at least on certain levels of its pursuit, replete with all of the advantages that self-employment offers (including the opportunity to easily avoid payment of income taxes). One has no bosses, and retains the right to choose whether one cares to work at given times. Perhaps, in an ironic way, prostitution can be seen as much as anything else as fulfilling the vocational wish, expressed today by so many altruistically inclined young persons, that they "like to work with people." (Geis, 1972, p. 177)

The precipitating factors that finally motivate a woman to take up prostitution vary greatly. Economic pressures, an unhappy love affair or marriage, having a marginal occupation like cocktail waitress in bars catering to men who are "cruising," or positive contact with a pimp or other prostitutes may all contribute to drifting into "the life." The general pattern reported repeatedly in studies of street prostitutes is estrangement from home while quite young (Davis, 1971) and a supportive relationship with a pimp or other prostitutes who provide for the insecure novice what appears to be a secure place in a well-defined (even if authoritarian) social world (Gray, 1973).

Career Movement and Labeling. How does a woman begin to see herself as a prostitute? This question goes beyond establishing the *factors* associated with becoming a prostitute to the description of the *process* through which a deviant identity is established. Davis (1971) has delineated three stages in the process of career movement and role commitment: (1) the process of drift from promiscuity to the first act of prostitution; (2) transitional deviance; and (3) professionalization.

In stage 1, promiscuity may be used as a status tool to gain attention—especially if the girl comes from an unstable home. She becomes identified by others, and comes to see herself, as different or a troublemaker. The drift from promiscuity to the first act of prostitution generally occurs in late adolescence. She becomes gradually aware that the already established pattern of promiscuous behavior can also be profitable.

> It was either jump in bed, and go with every Tom, Dick and Harry, and just give it away, so I decided to turn tricks instead.... The money was so easy to get. (Davis, 1971, p. 305)

Being institutionalized in a correctional facility appears to speed the process leading to self-conception as a prostitute. Being incarcerated with established prostitutes facilitates learning the techniques and attitudes required to take up the role herself.

In stage 2, transitional deviance, many girls show a zigzag pattern of behavior between conventionality and deviance. They may make verbal commitments to stop prostituting and return to home, school, or job. There is motivational ambivalence between the fears of acquiring the inevitable stigma as a prostitute and the desire to establish economic independence. A few at this stage may move permanently in the direction of conventional behavior due to negative experiences with a pimp, a client, or the police. For others, economic motives seem to provide the strongest reason to increase the frequency of prostitution. During this stage, for those who continue, their links with pimps and other prostitutes provide "in-service training" which includes:

> (1) Willingness to satisfy a broad range of client requests, requiring certain social and sexual skills; (2) elimination of fears regarding clients who are defined as "odd" (sadomasochists); (3) adaptation to police surveillance and entrapment procedures; (4) avoidance of drunken clients, or those unable or unwilling to pay; and (5) substitution of a "business" ethic for the earlier one of "gaming" or excitement concerns. (Davis, 1971, p. 315)

In stage 3 of deviant involvement, professionalization, there is the "unequivocal perception of a deviant self" (p. 315). Prostitution has become the daily routine in which sex is the vocation. The woman is now firmly implanted in a social network of johns, pimps, other prostitutes, and police with whom she must deal regularly and skillfully. For example, the actual social relations between prostitutes and police are far less hostile than their legal relationship would imply. The veteran prostitute will provide services for vice officers such as counselling or instructing troublesome hookers, acting as informants, and providing sex for the officers themselves or others such as judges or politicians. Thus, prostitutes are able to attain one of their primary goals by helping vice officers attain theirs. The successful prostitute avoids arrest by providing services for officers: information, friendship, emotional support and sex (Atkinson & Boles, 1977, p. 227).

The Political Economy of Prostitution

Prostitution and the Law. Legal sanctions, in the United States as well as most societies, are directed almost exclusively at the prostitute with little or no attention directed toward the client. This is not to say that men who purchase the service of prostitutes are acting legally. In most jurisdictions, being a client of a prostitute is strictly illegal; however, men clients are almost never arrested or prosecuted. For example, during a two-month period in New York City when a 1967 law took effect that called for arrest of *both* prostitutes and patrons, only 6% of the arrests were for patronizing. Of the 508 convicted cases, only 8% were for patronizing and there was a distinct lack of media publicity regarding the men who were arrested "obviously extending a courtesy to patrons which (the media) do not extend to prostitutes" (Roby, 1969, p. 99).

Strong forces clearly exist to support differential enforcement of the law in a way that protects patrons. The reason is to be found in the relative statuses of the prostitute and the client. Generally speaking, the prostitute is from a lower- or working-class background while the customer is middle class. Moreover, the client is more thoroughly attached to valued institutions in the society. As Flexner (1920) has accurately observed:

> The professional prostitute being a social outcast may be periodically punished without disturbing the usual course of society ... The man, however, is something more than a partner in an immoral act; he discharges important social and business relations, is a father or brother responsible for the maintenance of others, has commercial or industrial duties to meet. He cannot be imprisoned without damaging society. (p. 108)

In other words, those with influence due to their more valued status receive preferred treatment before the law.

Aside from the preferential treatment of clients over prostitutes, there is further discrimination legally. As we have already noted, the lower-status street prostitute is much more likely to be arrested than the higher-status call girl who serves an elite clientele. Clearly, having the resources to operate discreetly provides considerable protection from the law. And even the cast of characters who reap the greatest profits from their association with the street prostitute—including pimps, doormen, hotel operators, and commercialized-vice landlords—go relatively untouched by the law. The heaviest burden of the law, and the resulting stigma, falls on the women with the least political and economic resources to resist.

Commercialized Vice and the American Way. A careful examination of the prostitute and her occupation reveals a paradox. The prostitute herself is an outcast, an outsider—a true deviant with a spoiled identity who must manage as best she can to find compensation for her loss of social standing from her income and the relationships that make up her subculture. At the same time, prostitution as an occupation is consistently integrated with numerous fundamental American beliefs and institutions.

Prostitution is supported by widely shared discriminatory attitudes toward women. First is the sexual double standard that portrays men as having normal sexual needs to "sow their wild oats" or engage in extramarital sex while women are idealized as asexual, unpromiscuous, and faithful. To the degree that such a double standard exists, a relatively few women (the bad girls, the sluts, and the whores) will be required to service relatively many men thus creating obvious pressures for some women to take economic advantage of the supply-demand imbalance.

Second, learning the traditional female sex role that emphasizes sexual attractiveness and pleasing men for a "payoff" is consistent with sex as a vocation. Moreover, when women are subtly taught that they need to be attached to a man for economic security and emotional fulfillment, the stage is set for the domination exercised over many prostitutes by pimps.

Third, the inferior status of women to men and resultant job discrimination make prostitution an economically viable opportunity for many. Financial advantage is not the sole motivator, but the information presented in this chapter clearly establishes it as a potent force.

Finally, an array of people profit from prostitution indirectly, and it is in their interest to have the activity go on relatively undisturbed by serious attempts to eliminate it. Lemert's (1951) assessment is as good as any since:

> If (the prostitute) works on her own, the cab driver and the bellhop have to be paid. The disreputable medical examiner and the abortionist take a portion of the prostitute's income, as do the attorneys who obtain her release when she is arrested. Apart from the attorney's fees, money has to go to the "fixer" who sees to it that she escapes prosecution or conviction. The bail bondsman levies his toll, and often the policeman on the beat is not loath to practice crude extortion on the prostitute either in trade or money... Real-estate owners and managers are able to earn far more on their investments and properties by renting to prostitutes or vice-resort operators than to other tenants. Better class hotels, along with the cheaper ones, owe part of their revenue to the prostitute, as well as taxicab companies, laundries, amusement parks, vacation resorts, and contraceptive manufacturers and distributors. The sale of liquor has always been intimately connected with prostitution, brought out by the large number of contacts between prostitutes and customers made in taverns and bars.... In other words, prostitution has been, and remains, integrated into many functions or organizations which are sanctioned enterprises in the community and important in our economy. (p. 91)

Prostitution, despite the deviant status of the women who practice it, is not an activity separate from the ideology and the legal or the economic institutions of our society. Prostitution persists—even thrives in some places—because it provides relatively risk-free economic benefits to the powerful despite the high risks, punishing life-style, and rampant exploitation of the women who provide the service.

PORNOGRAPHY

What Is It?

The word is derived from the Greek *pornographas,* meaning literally "the writing of harlots," and today most people would probably agree that pornography is sexually oriented material intended to arouse vulgar, shameful, lewd, or disgusting thoughts. In the abstract, then, pornography is fairly easy to define. The difficulty arises when trying to determine whether any particular book, painting, film, videotape, or record is pornographic because any attempt to define pornography in terms of its effects (sexual arousal) requires an accounting of the audience and the setting in addition to the pornographic work itself. For example, to many adolescent, middle-class boys a generation ago, women's lingerie ads or photographs of bare-breasted women in *National Geographic* magazine were sexually arousing enough to stimulate masturbation. Would it then be correct to define these materials as pornographic? The point is that pornography is very much in the eye of its beholders and this fact is at the heart of the problem both social scientists and lawyers have encountered when trying to apply a definition. Indeed, the subjectivity and value judgment required for designating material as obscene or pornographic is well illustrated by Supreme Court Justice Potter Stewart's statement in a 1946 decision that although he probably could never succeed in defining intelligently the types of material he would call pornographic, . . . "I know it when I see it." Subsequent Supreme Court decisions have applied the analagous principle of "they'll know it when they see it" by ruling that local community standards of decency be the definitional guideline.

In 1967, a commission on obscenity and pornography was appointed by the President to assess the extent and effects of such materials and to make legislative recommendations. To study the effects of pornography, of course, requires that one define it precisely and the commission was no less perplexed than lawyers and judges. In the end, the commission decided to use the term "erotic materials" in place of pornography or obscenity, stating the following:

> In the absence of well-defined and generally acceptable definitions of both obscenity and pornography, the Commission conceptualized the

relevant stimuli as erotic materials, sexual materials, or sexually explicit stimuli over a range of media (photographs, snapshots, cartoons, films, and written materials in books, magazines and typewritten stories) which are capable of being described in terms of the sexual themes portrayed: e.g., "a man and a woman having sexual intercourse," or "mouth–sex organ contact between man and woman." (Report, 1970, p. 181)

Pornography and obscenity revolve around erotic or sexual themes. However, it does not follow that all erotica is pornographic or obscene, for beyond the explicit, objective content of the material pornography requires a subjective value judgment on the part of the viewer that it is vulgar, shameful or offensive.

Cultural and Historical Context

Erotica have existed from earliest recorded history. Sculptures of female fertility goddesses, phalluses, and copulating couples date back thousands of years. Elaborate visual erotica existed at least as long ago as the famed whorehouse murals found in Pompeii and the ancient Hindu temple erotic sculpture found in India. Likewise, written descriptions of sexual activities date at least from the Roman poet Ovid's *The Art of Love* at about the time of Christ and the Oriental *Kama-Sutra* of Vatsayama from Western India in the fourth century A.D. The existence of such materials, at those times, was certainly not regarded as a major social problem worthy of large scale efforts to control them. Rather, erotic art and writing were frequently integrated into the religious customs and beliefs of the society (Hyde, 1964).

Western prohibitions against sexually oriented materials are relatively recent partly because, until the invention of the printing press, relatively cheap methods of papermaking, and the subsequent increased rates of literacy, erotica were not readily available to the general population. Even after the invention of printing, the Roman Catholic church, the most powerful censor in history, bothered little about erotic books *per se*. It was only when "the bawdy was combined with heresy or a satire or attack upon the church, as in the *Decameron*, that the work was ecclesiastically proscribed or at least not permitted to be read by the faithful until it had been 'expurgated' " (Hyde, 1964, p. 164). The earliest English legal cases aimed at erotic writing were based on charges of sedition against the crown or blasphemy against the church rather than any "threat to public morals" posed by sexually oriented themes.

In mid-19th century Victorian England the first obscenity legislation passed was aimed specifically at the importation and dissemination of "lewd" works. Beyond advancing printing technology and increased literacy, Muedeking (1977) suggests several other factors that encouraged erotica and thus stimulated its legal control in England. These included:

> ... The rise of the state (Crown) and the decline of the Church as the supreme institution and the corresponding necessity for the state to replace custom with uniform laws for the control of behavior; the fear of satirical erotica undermining the authority of the state; and the development of a lucrative underground market in erotica (which, interestingly enough, arose out of the very existence of antipornography laws). (pp. 485–486)

In the United States, the relative lack of concern for erotica paralleled that in Britain until the mid-1800s. At that time a reformist zealot named Anthony Comstock took it upon himself to ensure enforcement of an 1868 New York obscenity statute. By rallying support of various groups including the Young Men's Christian Association (YMCA), Comstock mounted sufficient political pressure to get himself appointed by the President to the Post Office department as a censor. There he was authorized, under the 1865 Federal Mail act, to open any letter or package and judge whether its contents were obscene. From then until 1957 most states passed obscenity statutes to supplement the federal legislation concerning the mails.

Obscenity became a constitutional issue when the Supreme Court, in a 5 to 4 decision, ruled in the famous 1957 *Roth* v. *United States* case. It said:

> Obscene material is material which deals with sex in a manner appealing to prurient interests. I.e., material having a tendency to excite lustful thoughts ... (to) the average person, applying contemporary community standards, the dominant theme of the material taken as a whole appeals to prurient interest ... All ideas having even the slightest redeeming social importance—unorthodox ideas, even ideas hateful to the prevailing climate of opinion—have the full protection of the guarantees [of the First Amendment] ... But implicit in the history of the First Amendment is the rejection of obscenity as utterly without redeeming social importance.

This ruling, for a time, undermined existing obscenity statutes and led to greater openness and availability of sexually oriented materials. However, more recent Supreme Court decisions, especially *Miller* v. *California* in 1973, appear to be aimed at restraining the "permissive" trend. Briefly, the key sections of these rulings state that: (1) There can be no "national" definition of what is "offensive"—communities and states may set their own standards; (2) "Obscene" material is not protected by the First Amendment right of free speech; (3) It is not necessary to prove that obscenity is harmful in order to prohibit it; and (4) To show that material has "redeeming social value" is not sufficient as defense against an obscenity charge.

In sum, concern for the legal control of sexually oriented materials is a relatively recent phenomenon in Western culture. However, as availability increased so have public concern, legal statutes, and judicial rulings. Today, the definition and control of pornography have become persistent public and political issues.

Types and Extent of Erotica

The production of sexually oriented materials is a testament to human ingenuity. Indeed, perusal of the average American urban "sex shop" reveals that erotica exist appealing to every one of the human senses. Only a partial shopping list includes books, pictures, magazines, movies, live shows, records, tapes, lotions, creams, prophylactics in a wide variety of colors and shapes, flavored douches, dildos, leather goods intended for bondage, and even inflatable life-size dolls complete with fake genitalia.

Although no accurate accounting exists to judge availability, the casual impressions of almost anyone must yield the conclusion that the number of retail and mail order outlets for erotica has increased substantially in the past ten years. The President's Commission on Obscenity and Pornography reported in 1970 that the sexually oriented materials business in the United States may have grossed as much as two and one-half billion dollars. In all likelihood, the figure is much greater today.

Effects of Sexual Materials

The Commission on Obscenity and Pornography undertook, in 1967, the most comprehensive research program ever to provide information on the effects of exposure to explicit materials. The research procedures included surveys, experiments, and studies of rates and incidence of sex offenses at the national level. The summary report of the Commission's findings, in its own words, is reproduced below.

Psychosexual Stimulation. Experimental and survey studies show that exposure to erotic stimuli produces sexual arousal in substantial portions of both males and females. Arousal is dependent on both characteristics of the stimulus and characteristics of the viewer or user.

Recent research casts doubt on the common belief that women are vastly less aroused by erotic stimuli than are men. The supposed lack of female response may well be due to social and cultural inhibitions against reporting such arousal and to the fact that erotic material is generally oriented to a male audience. When viewing erotic stimuli, more women report the physiological sensations that are associated with sexual arousal than directly report being sexually aroused.

Research also shows that young persons are more likely to be aroused by erotica than are older persons. Persons who are college educated, religiously inactive, and sexually experienced are more likely to report arousal than persons who are less educated, religiously active, and sexually inexperienced.

Several studies show that depictions of conventional sexual behavior are generally regarded as more stimulating than depictions of less conventional activity. Heterosexual themes elicit more frequent and stronger arousal responses than depictions of homosexual activity; petting and coitus themes elicit greater arousal than oral sexuality, which in turn elicits more than sadomasochistic themes.

Satiation. The only experimental study on the subject to date found that continued or repeated exposure to erotic stimuli over 15 days resulted in satiation (marked diminution) of sexual arousal and interest in such material. In this experiment, the introduction of novel sex stimuli partially rejuvenated satiated interest, but only briefly.

Effects Upon Sexual Behavior. When people are exposed to erotic materials, some persons increase masturbatory or coital behavior, a smaller proportion decrease it, but the majority of persons report no change in these behaviors. Increases in either of these behaviors are short-lived and generally disappear within 48 hours. When masturbation follows exposure, it tends to occur among individuals with established but unavailable sexual partners. When coital frequencies increase following exposure to sex stimuli, such activation generally occurs among sexually experienced persons with established and available sexual partners. In one study, middle-aged married couples reported increases in both the frequency and variety of coital performance during the 24 hours after the couples viewed erotic films.

In general, established patterns of sexual behavior were found to be very stable and not altered substantially by exposure to erotica. When sexual activity occurred following the viewing or reading of these materials, it constituted a temporary activation of individuals' preexisting patterns of sexual behavior.

Other common consequences of exposure to erotic stimuli are

increased frequencies of erotic dreams, sexual fantasy, and conversation about sexual matters. These responses occur among both males and females. Sexual dreaming and fantasy occur as a result of exposure more often among unmarried than married persons, but conversation about sex occurs among both married and unmarried persons. Two studies found that a substantial number of married couples reported more agreeable and enhanced marital communication and an increased willingness to discuss sexual matters with each other after exposure to erotic stimuli.

Attitudinal Responses. Exposure to erotic stimuli appears to have little or no effect on already established attitudinal commitments regarding either sexuality or sexual morality. A series of four studies employing a large array of indicators found practically no significant differences in such attitudes before and after single or repeated exposures to erotica. One study did find that after exposure persons became more tolerant in reference to other persons' sexual activities although their own sexual standards did not change. One study reported that some persons' attitudes toward premarital intercourse became more liberal after exposure, while other persons' attitudes became more conservative, but another study found no changes in this regard. The overall picture is almost completely a tableau of no significant change.

Several surveys suggest that there is a correlation between experience with erotic materials and general attitudes about sex: Those who have more tolerant or liberal sexual attitudes tend also to have greater experience with sexual materials. Taken together, experimental and survey studies suggest that persons who are more sexually tolerant are also less rejecting of sexual material. Several studies show that after experience with erotic material, persons become less fearful of possible detrimental effect of exposure.

Emotional and Judgmental Responses. Several studies show that persons who are unfamiliar with erotic materials may experience strong and conflicting emotional reactions when first exposed to sexual stimuli. Multiple responses, such as attraction and repulsion to an unfamiliar object, are commonly observed in the research literature on psychosensory stimulation from a variety of nonsexual as well as sexual stimuli. These emotional responses are short–lived and, as with psychosexual stimulation, do not persist long after removal of the stimulus.

Extremely varied responses to erotic stimuli occur in the judgmental realm, as, for example, in the labeling of material as obscene or pornographic. Characteristics of both the viewer and the stimulus influence the response: for any given stimulus, some persons are more likely to judge it "obscene" than are others; and for persons of a given psychological or social type, some erotic themes are more likely to be judged "obscene" than are others. In general, persons who are older, less educated, religiously active, less experienced with erotic materials, or feel sexually guilty are most likely to judge a given erotic stimulus "obscene." There is some indication that stimuli may have to evoke both positive responses (interesting or stimulating), and negative responses (offensive or unpleasant) before they are judged obscene or pornographic.

Criminal and Delinquent Behavior. Delinquent and nondelinquent youth report generally similar experiences with explicit sexual materials. Exposure to sexual materials is widespread among both groups. The age of first exposure, the kinds of materials to which they are exposed, the amount of their exposure, the circumstances of exposure, and their reactions to erotic stimuli are essentially the same, particularly when family and neighborhood backgrounds are held constant. There is some evidence that peer group pressure accounts for both sexual experience and exposure to erotic materials among youth. A study of a heterogeneous group of young people found that exposure to erotica had no impact upon moral character over and above that of a generally deviant background.

Statistical studies of the relationship between availability of erotic materials and the rates of sex crimes in Denmark indicated that the increased availability of explicit sexual materials has been accompanied by a decrease in the incidence of sexual crime. Analysis of police records of the same types of sex crimes in Copenhagen during the past 12 years revealed that a dramatic decrease in reported sex crimes occurred during this period and that the decrease coincided with changes in Danish law which permitted wider availability of explicit sexual materials. Other research showed that the decrease in reported sexual offenses cannot be attributed to concurrent changes in the social and legal definitions of sex crimes or in public attitudes toward reporting such crimes to the police, or in police reporting procedures.

Statistical studies of the relationship between the availability of erotic material and the rates of sex crimes in the United States present a more complex picture. During the period in which there has been a marked increase in the availability of erotic materials, some specific rates of arrest for sex crimes have increased (e.g., forcible rape) and others have declined (e.g., overall juvenile rates). For juveniles, the overall rate of arrest for sex crimes decreased even though arrests for nonsexual crimes increased by more than 100%. For adults, arrest for sex offenses increased slightly more than did arrests for nonsex offenses. The conclusion is that, for America, the relationship between the availability of erotica and changes in sex crime rates neither proves nor disproves the possibility that availability of erotica leads to crime, but the massive overall increases in sex crimes that have been alleged do not seem to have occurred.

Available research indicates that sex offenders have had less adolescent experience with erotica than other adults. They do not differ significantly from other adults in relation to adult experience with erotica, in relation to reported arousal or in relation to the likelihood of engaging in sexual behavior during or following exposure. Available evidence suggests that sex offenders' early inexperience with erotic materials is a reflection of their more generally deprived sexual environment. The relative absence of experience appears to constitute another indicator of atypical and inadequate sexual socialization.

In sum, empirical research designed to clarify the question has found no evidence to date that exposure to explicit sexual materials plays a significant role in the causation of delinquent or criminal behavior among youth or adults. The Commission cannot conclude that exposure to erotic materials is a factor in the causation of sex crime or sex delinquency. (Report of the Commission on Obscenity and Pornography, 1970, pp. 24–27)

Explanations of Pornography

Functionalism. Polsky (1967) has argued that the same functionalist theory applied by Davis (1937) to prostitution can be used to explain the persistence of pornography. Recall that Davis sees prostitution as a necessary outlet for the expression of disapproved sexual activities that are impersonal, transitory, and nonfamilial. Under certain conditions, Polsky simply sees pornography as a *functional alternative* to prostitution.

> Prostitution and pornography occur in every society large enough to have a reasonably complex division of labor; and although pornography develops in only a rudimentary way in preliterate societies (by means of erotic folktales and simple pictoral or sculptural devices), whenever a society has a fair degree of literacy and mass–communication technology then pornography becomes a major functional alternative to prostitution.
>
> In saying that prostitution and pornography are, at least in modern societies, functional alternatives, I mean that they are different roads to the same desired social end. Both provide for the discharge of what society labels antisocial sex, i.e., impersonal, nonmarital sex: prostitution provides this via real intercourse with a real sex object, and pornography

provides it via masturbatory, imagined intercourse with a fantasy object. (p. 185)

In addition, pornography can function as a sexual outlet in situations where people are isolated from the opposite sex, such as prisons or the military. Some of the most famous works in erotic literature by the Marquis de Sade and Jean Ganet were written, apparently for their own entertainment, while in prison.

Finally, true to the functionalist theoretical tradition beginning with Durkheim, Polsky suggests that judging, labeling, and stigmatizing pornography and pornographers is part of the process helping to define the moral boundaries that distinguish a community. The interactions between pornographers and those who seek to control them help to serve notice as to the limits that community standards of behavior will tolerate. A social function of the pornographer and his products, in other words, is to explore, discover, map, and publicize the outer limits of acceptable sexual conduct.

Guilt, Sexism, and Violence. Most erotica is directed toward a male audience. Even casual observation reveals that most patrons of X-rated movies and adult book stores are white, middle-class, middle-aged men. We might fruitfully ask what draws these particular men to the forbidden sights, sounds, and fantasies depicted in contemporary erotica?

The answer appears to lie in the dominant themes of erotica, the setting in which they are viewed, and the psychosexual histories of the viewers. First, the sexual activities portrayed in most contemporary erotica are, generally, deviant. That is, they sharply diverge from the normative ideal that sex be confined to marriage and in that setting only a limited repertoire of activities (ideally, coitus) should be performed. Typically, X-rated movies or adult books revolve around non-marital sex, multiple partners, oral-genital activity, homosexual contacts, sadism, bondage, and so on. Above all, the appeal is to male sexual gratification devoid of interpersonal commitment. Women are displayed as playthings—lustful, insatiable, ever ready and eager to satisfy the orgasmic urge of the man. The world of erotica is oriented toward male sexual fantasies inhabited by an endless population of forbidden women.

Of course, for most white, middle-class males the fantastic domain of erotica and their actual sexual lives bear little resemblance. Genuinely desirable women are taught to withhold or at least be discreet in dispensing sexual favors. Indeed, for many middle-class adolescents, especially 20 years ago, the most prevalent sexual activity was masturbation—often with the aid of erotica as a stimulant. As Polsky (1967) has put it, "people given to using pornography do so for the most part as a means of facilitating masturbation. This is the primary use of pornography. It is summed up in the classic description of pornographic books as 'the book that one reads with one hand' " (p. 187).

Yet, masturbation, particularly to the mental fantasies provoked by the lust–filled world of erotica, is an anxiety–, guilty–laden activity. A pattern of social gratification through masturbation facilitated by erotica forges a link between the guilt of forbidden sexual fantasies and sexual stimulation. As Gagnon and Simon (1967) claim, guilt and anxiety may become closely associated with sexual behavior. As a result, contemporary erotica may be especially arousing to middle–class males for whom anxiously sneaking into an X–rated movie, or smuggling home a dirty novel may provide for making the guilt and anxiety often associated with the consumption of erotica aphrodisiacs with strong appeal.

Shortly after the Commission on Obscenity and Pornography published its report, a curious contradiction was pointed out by James Q. Wilson (1971). He noted that the National Commission on the Causes and Prevention of Violence had concluded that media violence, especially in movies or television, was apt to have the adverse effect of stimulating violent behavior while the Commission on Obscenity and Pornography concluded that pornography does not contribute to individual "harms." How can we account for the apparent discrepancy between the two findings? Wilson is careful to allow that part of the problem is due to the immense difficulties in doing valid, accurate research on problems such as the effects of media violence or pornography. However, in the end he argues that social science may never be able to provide evidence sufficient to be the sole basis for social policy.

> In the cases of violence and obscenity, it is unlikely that social science can either show harmful effects or prove that there are no harmful effects. It is unlikely, in short, that considerations of utility or disutility can be governing. These are moral issues and ultimately all judgment about the acceptability of restrictions on the various media will have to rest on political and philosophical considerations. (Wilson, 1971, p. 243)

In short, Wilson believes that social scientific evidence can never be adequate to resolve what are, essentially, political issues. McCormack (1978) has taken Wilson's observation of the contradictory findings of the two commissions a step further to suggest that the very research on which the conclusions are based is a reflection of female subordination in a male–dominated society. In studies of the effects of media violence the primary violent themes involve men against men. Such themes, which frequently include homosexual undertones as in boxing films in which "two male boxers slugging it out in the ring, periodically locked in embrace, bare body touching bare body, moving steadily toward a climax in which the loser is subdued and prone on the floor" (McCormack, 1978, p. 551), produce, in male viewers, anxiety about their sexual identity. On the other hand, the predominant themes of erotica portray powerless women satisfying the narcissistic virility of superpotent men. Thus, media violence themes are anxiety producing and threatening to males while pornographic themes reinforce male self-images of superiority and machismo.

> The humiliation of women and insecurity about sexual identity match the two conclusions merging from the areas of research examined, one condoning pornography as an innocent pleasure without serious social consequences; the other condemning media violence as leading to senseless and brutal acts in everyday life. The contradiction which seemed so puzzling and which we attempted unsuccessfully to resolve in favor of one or the other now turns out to be the central fact. On a deeper level, the contradiction disappears. The unifying variable is machismo. (p. 352)

It follows then, according to McCormack's reasoning, that in a male-dominated society the themes of media violence would be disapproved while the themes of erotica would be judged harmless. In a sexually stratified society, that which causes harm to men is to be condemned while that which portrays women as powerless sex objects is judged harmless.

Status Politics. The public display and availability of erotica has, on occasion, become a major political issue in a community. The rallying cry of those who seek severe restrictions usually amounts to "Pornography is leading us to our downfall." On the other side are those who insist upon the right of adults to see, hear, or read whatever they please under the protection of the First Amendment freedoms. However, like most inflammatory political issues in American history, from the temperance movement that culminated in the Prohibition amendment to the present right-to-life movement, antipornography crusades are largely symbolic of more farreaching differences of opinion and life-style.

Following the logic of Gusfield's (1963) analysis of the American temperance movement, Zurcher and Kirkpatrick (1976) argue that antipornography campaigns are most likely to arise in communities where what has long been regarded as middle-class respectability is threatened by social change. People who are "established, stable and solid" are being challenged by "the new, the upstart and the sophisticated." In a word, those who believe in the old way of life and its values feel their status slipping as the new way of life and its values gain prestige.

Naturally, those who feel their status ebbing wish to fight back. The most efficient, effective way to do so is to focus attention on a single, narrow issue that becomes symbolic of the broader divergence of beliefs. Thus, an antipornography crusade is a symbolic defense of a traditional way of life that encompasses religiosity, antiliberalism, belief in the weakness of human nature and the need to reverse a trend of moral decline.

Zurcher and Kirkpatrick found antipornography crusaders to be "status discontents" who were struggling to maintain the prestige of their lifestyle in a battle of status politics.

> ... The traditional life-style with which they were comfortable and to which they were committed was increasingly being challenged by social change. Conporns (antipornography crusaders) felt strongly that the prestige and power of their style of life was being undermined and was not being represented, particularly by the mass media, as viable. The issue of pornography had become, for the Conporns, a suitable summary symbol of the challenges and a focus for resistance to them. (p. 275)

Of course, struggles for recognition and status are not limited to traditionalist versus modernist or conservative versus liberal. Almost never are the lines of interest clearly drawn. Exemplifying this fact is the position of some women in the feminist movement concerning pornography. The viewpoint of these women closely parallels McCormack's hypothesis concerning why erotica has been found harmless by predominantly male social researchers. Pornographic themes designed to appeal to males are alleged to support, in fantasy, male self-images of superiority and machismo. Susan Brownmiller (1979), a leading feminist, puts it this way:

> We are not opposed to sex and desire and we certainly believe that explicitly sexual material has its place in literature, art, science and education. No, the feminist objection to pornography is based on our belief that pornography represents hatred of women, that pornography's intent is to humiliate, degrade and dehumanize the female body for the purpose of erotic stimulation and pleasure. We are unalterably opposed to the presentation of the female body being stripped, bound, raped, tortured, mutilated and murdered in the name of commercial entertainment and free speech. (p. 9A)

Both prostitution and pornography have been characterized as victimless crimes by some social scientists and social policy makers. Such a characterization should not be taken lightly or uncritically. It is true that these activities do involve willing customers who are unlikely to make a formal complaint to law enforcement authorities. Thus, the client or customer could hardly be called a victim. However, the sexist and often violent themes frequently running through relationships involving prostitution or images portrayed in pornography suggest a more general victimization of women in our sexually stratified society. Moreover, prostitutes or the porn actors are often no more than poorly paid bit players in much larger money-making schemes despite the fact that they have the most to lose in terms of personal danger or damaged reputation. Here are cases in which we might properly consider the deviant as the victim.

HOMOSEXUALITY

Historical And Cultural Attitudes

Homosexual behavior has been reported quite frequently in primitive societies by Western observers and, in many cultures, high status is attached to those who fulfill roles associated with homosexual behavior. Evidence from a survey of 76 primitive societies shows that in 64% of them "homosexual activities of one sort or another are considered normal or at least socially acceptable for certain members of the community" (Ford & Beach, 1951, p. 130).

In general, the most common acceptable form of homosexuality is the *berdache*. This is a male who dresses like a woman, performs women's tasks, and adopts the feminine role in sexual behavior with male partners. For example, among the Siberian Chuckch, a *berdache* is not only acceptable, but he is regarded by others as a prestigious shaman believed to be endowed with supernatural powers. In other societies such as the Tanala of Madagascar or the Mohave Indians of California and Arizona, the man-woman *berdache* is regarded by others in the community without ridicule or praise.

The other frequently occurring pattern of homosexual activity in primitive cultures is a liaison between men or boys who are otherwise heterosexual. "Among the Sivans of Africa, for example, all men and boys engage in anal intercourse. They adopt the feminine role only in strictly sexual situations and males are singled out as particular if they do not indulge in these homosexual activities.... Both married and unmarried males are expected to have both homosexual and heterosexual affairs" (Ford & Beach, 1951, pp. 131-132). Sometimes, as among the Aranda of Australia or the Koraki of New Guinea, older men engage in anal intercourse with young boys. Such a practice may be a temporary arrangement in lieu of a heterosexual marriage or part of initiation rites from puberty into manhood. Among women in primitive cultures, approved forms of homosexual relations appear to be far less common than for men.

While acceptable forms of homosexual behavior clearly do occur with some frequency in folk societies, such acceptance is not universal. Ford and Beach (1951) say that in 28 of the 76 societies they surveyed, "homosexual activities on the part of adults are reported to be totally absent, rare, or carried on only in secrecy." (p. 129) In numerous cultures (for example, the Cuna, Trukese, Chiricahua, and Sampoil) children who show any inclination toward homosexuality are harshly punished. In some others, such as the Rivala Bedouins, homosexuality is sufficient cause for the death penalty.

In Western culture, the situation is equally complex with themes of approval and disapproval existing both at the same and different times. The Hebrew moral code strongly condemns homosexuality. In classical Greece it appears that homosexuality and homosexual prostitution were fairly widespread and accepted, among intellectuals especially (Licht, 1955). At the same time, the attitude of the general public in Greece was far less favorable. A similar situation of elite acceptance and public disfavor seems to have existed in the Roman empire.

The extent of homosexual behavior during the Middle Ages is unknown, although there is some evidence that it may have been commonly practiced among some clergy (McIntosh, 1968, p. 187) and medieval rulers (Rowse, 1977) while still being generally condemned, in accordance with church doctrine, by the masses. Indeed, from ancient times to the present one can construct an impressive list of men avowedly homosexual or strongly suspected of homosexual conduct who have made their mark on history, including Socrates, Plato, Julius Caesar, Alexander the Great, Michaelangelo, Marlowe, and Shakespeare. It must be remembered that these famous examples from the past exemplify those who engaged in some (although not necessarily exclusively) homosexual behavior. They generally did not correspond to the stereotyped homosexual role associated with homoerotic behavior today because such a role did not emerge until the end of the 17th century in England (McIntosh, 1968, p. 189).

Since the 18th century in Western societies public attitudes toward homosexual behavior have tended to be hostile with some grudging tolerance, especially in some occupational categories such as artists. Indeed, it appears that Western governments, sometimes stemming the tide of popular opinion, have been leading the way in relaxing laws against homosexual behavior by consenting adults in private. England, West Germany, and Canada have instituted such reforms. The United States remains, among Western societies, the most severe in its legal and public condemnation of homosexual behavior.

Summing up this brief cultural and historical review, a majority of primitive societies recognize and tolerate, and some even encourage, limited amounts of homosexual behavior. At the same time, in no case is it ever the predominant mode of sexual activity among adults. In complex Western societies a certain amount of homosexual behavior seems to have existed (even as the object of literary praise) while most of the populace has not been very tolerant at all.

Defining Homosexuality

Homosexual acts are fairly easily defined. They are sexually oriented physical contacts between same-sex individuals which may include kissing, body rubbing, mutual masturbation, oral-genital stimulation, or anal intercourse. Defining a person as homosexual is another matter not as easily done. For instance, is it reasonable to classify a person a homosexual if only once or twice in their lives they engage in a homosexual act and, otherwise, their sexual activity is heterosexual? If not, how many homosexual acts are required to label someone a homosexual person? Clearly, these questions suggest that homosexuality and heterosexuality are not either-or categories. In fact, the most sophisticated researchers in the field have concluded that human sexuality is best conceived as lying along a continuum from exclusively heterosexual to exclusively homosexual, with a recognition that a great many people fall somewhere in between.

The difficulty inherent in classifying human sexuality into either-or, homo-or heterosexual categories, is demonstrated by Alfred Kinsey, (1948) in a frequently cited finding that 37% of all white American males and 13% of females had at least one homosexual experience to the point of orgasm between adolescence and old age. Should one then conclude that over a third of the American males in this survey were homosexual? And if not, what frequency of homosexual experiences or other criteria should be the defining characteristics of a homosexual? This and related issues led Kinsey to devise a seven-step continuum of human sexual preferences ranging from 0 which means that a person has never had any overt homosexual experience to 6, an individual who has had no history of overt heterosexual experience.

According to Kinsey's (1948, pp. 650–656) estimates, about three-quarters of men in any given year are exclusively heterosexual (0) and about half will be so throughout their lives. At the other extreme, about 5% will rate exclusively homosexual (6) in any given year and about 4% will be in this category throughout their lives. Thus, nearly half of American males actually fall somewhere between exclusively heterosexual (0) and exclusively homosexual (6).

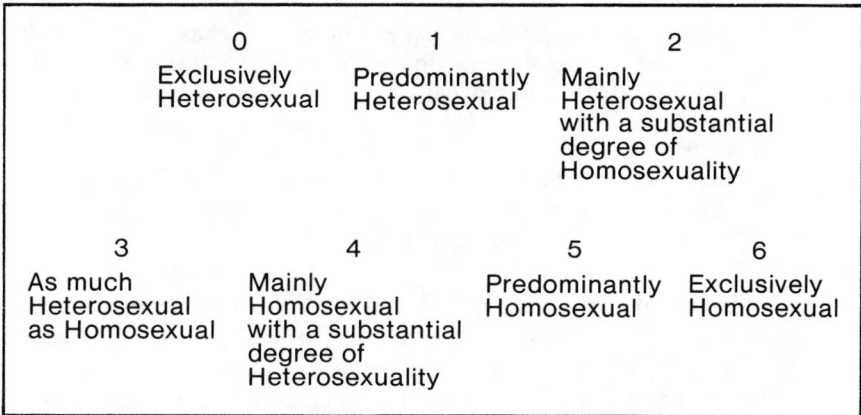

FIGURE 2.1. THE KINSEY HETEROSEXUAL – HOMOSEXUAL CONTINUUM

The viability of the Kinsey continuum has been recently reaffirmed through its enlightening use in major studies of the physiology of homosexual behavior by Masters and Johnson (1979) and homosexual life-styles by Bell and Weinberg (1978).

Masters and Johnson: Homosexual Physiology

After 14 years of clinically studying hundreds of males and females engaging in homosexual behavior in their institute laboratory, Masters and Johnson have produced an excellent base for comparison with their previously well-known findings on heterosexual activity. Generally speaking, they found no differences between homosexuals and heterosexuals in their physiological capacity to respond to similar sexual stimuli.

> ... there is no statistically significant difference between sexually experienced male homosexual and male heterosexual study subjects in facility to respond to orgasmic levels to stimulate techniques of masturbation, partner manipulation, and fellation. Similarly ... there is no statistically significant difference in facility or orgasmic attainment between sexually experienced female homosexual and heterosexual study subjects in response to masturbation, partner manipulation, and cunnilingus. (Masters & Johnson, 1979, pp. 205–206)

The most important difference observed when comparing homosexual and heterosexual technique was the apparent tendency for homosexual partners to be slower, more relaxed, and involved in their sexual relations.

> There was one dominant pattern of sexual behavior consistently observed in the sexual interaction of committed male or female homosexual couples that was infrequently present in the sexual activity of committed heterosexual couples. Usually, the committed homosexual couples *took their time* in sexual interaction in the laboratory.... They appeared to be more relaxed and gave the impression of more complete subjective involvement in the sexual activity than did their heterosexual counterparts. (Masters & Johnson, 1979, p. 64)

Masters and Johnson speculate that one reason for this apparent enhanced sexual communication between attached homosexual couples may be the effect of public hostility. In a hostile environment, partners may place great value on their established relationship—a fact that increased communication both in matters nonsexual and sexual. This conclusion is certainly compatible with the suggestion by labeling theorists that harsh societal reactions tend to solidify the relationships between members of a group who are the objects of public opprobrium or disgrace.

In dealing with sexual problems, there were also remarkable similarities between heterosexuals and homosexuals. Masters and Johnson conclude their clinical discussion by saying:

> Over the past 15 years, it has become apparent that the individual's sexual orientation does not significantly alter his or her problem of sexual dysfunction. Impotence and anorgasmic states have just as devastating an effect on homosexual as on heterosexual men and women. Fears of performance and spectator roles can make a sexual cripple of any sexually dysfunctional individual, homosexual or heterosexual. Sexual fakery is freely practiced by representatives of both sex preferences. (p. 406)

Overwhelmingly, then, this research underscores that "from a functional point of view homosexuality and heterosexuality have far more similarities than differences" (p. 403).

Bell and Weinberg: Homosexual Diversity

In this 1978 study of almost 1,000 men and women with homosexual orientations (Kinsey 5 or 6) compared with almost 500 heterosexuals (Kinsey 0 or 1), a number of common, uniform beliefs are challenged. Bell and Weinberg find in their study, for example, that:

- A majority of the men and women with homosexual preferences are not "out of the closet," but keep their sexual orientation covert.

- Homosexual men and women cannot be sexually stereotyped as either hyperactive or inactive.
- Search for sexual contacts is infrequent among lesbians and among homosexual men who "cruise" in public places, most conduct their sexual activity in the privacy of their homes.
- Over one-third of the homosexual women and about one-fifth of the men had been married at least once.
- Above all, homosexual men and women exhibit great diversity in their life-styles and personal adjustment, not at all unlike the diversity found among those whose sexual orientation is predominantly heterosexual.

To underscore the range of sexual experience among the men and women in their sample, Bell and Weinberg (1978) devised a typology with five categories.

Close–coupleds. · These individuals had close relationships in two senses. First, they were closely bound to a partner. Second, the pair tended to look to each other rather than outsiders for interpersonal and sexual gratification. The fact that many more homosexual women (39%) than men (14%) fall into this category is consistent with the widely established observation that lesbians tend to form more stable, enduring attachments than their male counterparts. Close–coupleds had the fewest reported sexual problems, the fewest difficulties at work, and generally had attained a very high level of personal adjustment and well-being.

Open–coupleds. These people lived with a special sexual partner, but also sought satisfactions with people outside the partnership. Both men and women did more than the average amount of cruising. Open–coupleds were less happy, less self-accepting, and more worried, tense, or depressed than close–coupleds.

TABLE 2.1. A TYPOLOGY OF SEXUAL EXPERIENCE

Type	Men	Women
Close–coupleds	14%	39%
Open–coupleds	25	24
Functionals	21	14
Dysfunctionals	18	8
Asexuals	23	16
	101[a]	101[a]
Total number	(485)	(211)

Source: Adapted from Bell and Weinberg, 1978.
[a]Total percentages exceed 100 due to rounding.

Functionals. "If close- and open-coupled respondents are in some respects like married heterosexuals, the functionals come closest to the notion of 'swinging singles' " (p. 223). Sex plays a large part in the lives of these men and women as reflected in their high level of sexual activity with many partners. They were least likely to regret being homosexual, cruised frequently, and were involved in the gay subculture. While their adjustment is characterized as cheerful, self-reliant, optimistic, and comfortable with their sexuality, Bell and Weinberg concluded that the close-coupleds surpassed them in overall well-being.

Dysfunctionals. This group "most closely accords with the stereotype of the tormented homosexual" (p. 225). They reported more sexual problems, difficulties with the law, and emotional instability than any other group. Although males spent a fair amount of time cruising and had a relatively high number of sex partners, sexual anxiety and performance failures were quite frequent. As Bell and Weinberg put it, "If we had numbered only dysfunctionals among our respondents, we very likely would have to conclude that homosexuals in general are conflict-ridden social misfits" (p. 226).

Asexuals. Both men and women in this group showed a lack of involvement with others. Of all the groups they had the lowest levels of sexual activity, number of partners, and ratings of their sex appeal. They had narrow sexual repertoires and had a fair number of sexual problems. Their life-style is solitary and, despite complaints of loneliness, they seem not very interested in establishing a stable relationship. Overall, they were moderate in their psychological adjustment and the extent to which their homosexuality caused them difficulty.

The findings of this study, then, show clearly that homosexual adults are a very diverse group. Indeed, one is probably justified in concluding that the types of relationships and personal adjustment found among homosexuals parallel quite closely those among heterosexuals. There is no question that the chief difference between heterosexuals and homosexuals is the nature of their sexual preference. The Masters and Johnson research reinforces this point in regard to physiology by emphasizing that *other than sexual preference,* heterosexual and homosexual function and dysfunction are remarkably similar. Likewise, any simplistic picture of homosexual life-style and personal adjustment is no more accurate or acceptable than such an image of heterosexuals would be. Of course, living in a hostile environment places significant social and psychological burdens on homosexuals and one can only imagine how most heterosexuals would adapt under the same handicaps. All of the evidence suggests that in the absence of widespread stereotypes, fear, prejudice, and discrimination, homosexuals are the equals of heterosexuals in their potential for satisfying social relationships and psychological adjustment. In the words of Bell and Weinberg, "... homosexual adults who have come to terms with their homosexuality, who do not regret their sexual orientation, and who can function effectively sexually and socially, are no more distressed psychologically than are heterosexual men and women" (Bell & Weinberg, 1978, p. 216).

Subcultural Patterns

Just as there is no single set of personality traits characterizing all homosexual men and women, there is not a typical life-style. A large number of homosexual men and women lead quiet, unassuming lives pursuing their work and their careers with no outward sign of their sexual preferences or relationships. Numerous others assume a double persona, playing conventional work and family roles when on the job or in the presence of relatives and reserving for their leisure hours the overt identification with the mannerisms, dress, language, and gathering places of the gay subculture (Warren, 1974). Unattached males who have "come out of the closet" are the most frequent participants in the gay world.
Coming out. As our previous discussion has indicated, having engaged in homosexual activity does not necessarily mean that one will identify him- or herself as a homosexual. Indeed, the homosexual role is neither universal nor ancient. McIntosh (1968) points out that "... the role does not exist in many societies, that it only emerged in England towards the end of the 17th century, and ... although the existence of the role in modern America appears to have some effect on the distribution of homosexual behavior, such behavior is far from being monopolized by persons who play the role of homosexual" (p. 192). Many people (probably most) who experience homosexual desires, fantasies, and even activities do not thereby decide that they are homosexual. Adoption of a homosexual identity is a process that, beyond attraction to same-sex people, requires neutralizing the common negative stereotype of the homosexual role and recognizing that despite hostile public images, homosexuality can be seen as neither sick nor evil but even a positive, desirable role.

Coming out, the assumption of a homosexual identity, is not likely to take place immediately upon being physically attracted to someone of the same sex. Dank (1971) found in a survey of 180 self-identified homosexuals that on the average there was a six-year interval between recognizing homosexual feelings of attraction and deciding that they were homosexual. Often the necessary component in identifying oneself as homosexual was positive interaction with people who had already assumed the homosexual role. Contact with such people could occur in a number of social contexts. Dank asked his respondents the context(s) in which they "came out" and he found the distribution shown in Table 2.2. The ordering of social contexts suggests that an intense, personal relationship with a homosexual and contact with the gay subculture often precipitates coming out.

> I knew that there were homosexuals, queers, and what not; I had read some books, and I was resigned to the fact that I was a foul, dirty person, but I wasn't actually calling myself a homosexual yet.... I went to this guy's house and there was nothing going on, and I asked him, "Where is some action?" and he said, "There is a bar down the way." And the time I really caught myself coming out is the time I walked into this bar and saw a whole crowd of groovy, groovy guys. And I said to myself, there was the realization, that not all gay men are dirty old men or idiots, silky queens, but there are some just normal-looking and acting people, as far as I could see. I saw gay society and I said, "Wow, I'm home." (Dank, 1971, p. 187)

TABLE 2.2. SOCIAL CONTEXTS IN WHICH RESPONDENTS "CAME OUT"

Social Contexts	%	(N)*
Having a love affair with a homosexual man	30	(54)
Frequenting gay parties and other gatherings	26	(46)
Frequenting parks	24	(43)
Frequenting gay bars	19	(35)
In the military	19	(34)
Read for the first time about homosexuals and/or homosexuality	15	(27)
Having a love affair with a heterosexual man	12	(21)
Living in all-male quarters at a boarding school or college	7	(12)
Seeing a psychiatrist or professional counselor	6	(11)
Just arrested on a charge involving homosexuality	4	(7)
Patient in a mental hospital	2	(3)
Living in a YMCA	1	(2)
Just fired from a job because of homosexual behavior	1	(2)
Was not having any homosexual relations	20	(36)

Source: Dank, 1971: 184.
*Total N of social contexts is greater than 180 (the number of respondents) because there was overlap in contexts.

Coming out, then, depends both upon a person's internal sexual feelings *and* the definitions and explanations of those feelings available in his or her social environment. For example, if homosexuality is commonly seen by friends or acquaintances as a mental illness (a negative definition or explanation), development of a homosexual identity will be inhibited. If, on the other hand, people important to one define homosexuality more as an alternative way of life, the problems of accepting a homosexual identity will be decreased. Goode (1978) nicely summarizes the combination of things that frequently precipitate adoption of a gay self-concept.

> One is *a persistent lack of erotic and/or emotional interest in the opposite sex*. Second: the continuing failure of one's ability to explain away one's homosexuality. Third: having a deep, significant, meaningful homosexual experience with someone whom one respects and loves. Fourth: having an intimate, particularly one who is gay, explain to one that one *is*, in fact, gay. And lastly: dramatically realizing that there are many attractive, desirable, "normal" men and women—who don't fit one's preconception of the homosexual—who are gay. (pp. 380–381)

Meeting Places: Bars, Baths and Tearooms. Among homosexuals, men are more apt than women to socialize in relatively overt homosexual gathering spots. Multiple temporary liaisons are the more frequent pattern of sexual activity among young male gays and the settings in which this interaction occurs constitute an important slice of the gay subculture. Bars and steam baths are a primary locus for the male homosexual community in many cities, providing an opportunity to get together during leisure hours to seek out partners for sexual encounters. The gay bar has been described, rather tamely, by one observer as "... the homosexual equivalent of the USO or the youth club, where the rating and dating process may unfold in a controlled and acceptable manner" (Achilles, 1967, pp. 231–232). The gay bar scene, itself, is divided into several subtypes which emphasize the patrons' particular sexual tastes.

> Bars then attract typified identities—especially in large metropolitan areas where large populations of homosexuals support specializing staging establishments. Boston, Chicago, San Francisco, and Washington, D.C., to name a few of many cities, have special bars that include western, leather, S–M, dance, and "piss–elegant" bars.[2] When the patron decides to go to a bar, he makes a conscious statement as to which population . . . he chooses to identify. He expects to find this population at the chosen bar. The piss–elegant patron does not expect leather people at his bar. Both consider the presence of the other ludicrous. Communi-

cations and interaction are seriously impeded by the appearance of incongruous identities. After all, the patron wishes to socialize with individuals with whom he can interact and relate to in a comfortable, taken-for-granted way....

Names of bars frequently suggest a "typified" identity. The Eagle, Ramrod, Spike, Boot Hill, Roadhouse, and Ty's imply a firm, masculine imagery, stressing western to leather gear; the Candy Store, Coat of Arms, and Regents Row, the piss-elegant set; and Piano Bar and Goldbug, the drag and dance set.

Light is universally dark in bar settings except those that present a nongay façade due to windows directly accessible to outside viewing, e.g.; Julius' Bar. Subtle light enhances the "virtual" appearance of the individual. Red and orange light seem the standard interior hue. Heavy layers of smoke also help blur the hard lines of physical appearances.

The stand-up, cruising bar is spartanly equipped. Aside from the stools surrounding the bar, the ubiquitous and necessary jukebox, an occasional pool table, the cigarette machine, and the toilet, the only other decorations are accessories that make some kind of identity statement about the population of the bar.

Physical aspects of the bar focus attention on cruising. Spacious empty areas not only accommodate large numbers of patrons, but permit enough "runway" space to allow the continual flow of individuals to incessantly ply back and forth among the crowd, exhibiting and posturing physical virtues while searching for the desired, erotic object of the evening. In a popular bar such as Kellers, for example, the pool table is covered on weekends to conserve desperately needed space. It also adds another surface on which to lean (and posture). A narrow bar at best, Kellers becomes so crowded that even getting inside the bar is difficult. Bodies mash tightly against each other, encouraging touch even if by accident. Squeezing through the throng, touching as one goes, is a crucial input in Kellers' popularity. The compactness of the bar and the fact that the patron is physically pressed against several other men generate sensuousness and a feeling of belonging, in spite of a lack of verbal intercourse. (Delph, 1978, pp. 113–116)

The gay bath offers a near-perfect setting for male impersonal sex being "devoted exclusively to immediate sexual gratification" (Delph, 1978, p. 135). Usually unpretentious on the outside as a shield against undue attention, inside the basic establishment usually includes a locker room, towels for hire, steam room, and private bedroom cubicles (also for hire). More elaborate ones may include a snack bar, restaurant, television room, discotheque, and shop purveying cosmetics and sexual devices. This environment provides nearly ideal conditions for impersonal sex: "protection; ample accessible opportunities; a known, shared, organized reality; bonding of experience; congeniality; and a comfortable physical setting" (Weinberg & Williams, 1975, p. 124).

Impersonality and anonymity are carried to an extreme. Upon entrance, all identity pegs, including clothing and jewelry (with a few exceptions described below), are replaced by a singular towel. The uniformity in staging areas standardizes any idiosyncratic claims of individuals: rooms and lockers are minimally furnished. No unique feature exists by which an individual can mold some personal, extraordinary claim about himself. Claims to interest narrowly devolve on the physicality of the individual, creative use of the towel, attitude, and self-presentation brought out in physical grooming, style of walk, and mannerisms. This anonymity frees the individual from inhibitions that prevail in less controlled, less safe, more ambivalent settings. Communications preceding liaisons are briefer and more to the point. Physical contact occurs without much ritualistic foreplay although successful transactions usually involve a brief period of courting and mutual exchanges of consent. Rejection, always possible, is not felt as keenly as in other public settings. (Delph, 1978, pp. 135–136)[3]

Tearooms are public toilet facilities, such as those in parks or subways, where impersonal, transitory homosexual encounters frequently take place. "Public restrooms are chosen by those who want homoerotic activity without commitment for a number of reasons. *They are accessible, easily recognized by the initiate, and provide little public visibility*" (Humphreys, 1975, pp. 2–3). In the tearoom, one may have sex with a variety of partners quickly, anonymously, and without any social obligation beyond the immediate physical exchange. Moreover, just as the case with many heterosexual partners, the dangers of being caught and exposed when having sex in a public place acts as a powerful aphrodisiac magnifying the psychological payoff.

The types of participants in tearoom activity tell us some about their probable motives and about the diversity among those who seek homoerotic activity—many of whom, it should be emphasized, do not participate in the more overt homosexual subculture. Humphreys (1975) divided the tearoom visitors in his study into four types. The most common participants (38%), known in the gay subcultural argot as "trade," were or had been married and worked at jobs which would be threatened if their homosexual activity should be unmasked. Often these men found sexual relations with their wives curtailed and unsatisfactory. Thus, to protect both their marriages and their jobs, they apparently find the quick, impersonal sex of the tearoom an acceptable form of release. Humphreys found ". . . .no indication that these men seek homosexual contact as such; rather they want a form of orgasm-producing action that is less lonely than masturbation and less involving than a love relationship" (p. 115).

"Ambisexuals" (24%), the second type, are also likely to be married.

However, unlike the trade, they "recognize their homosexual activity as indicative of their own psychosexual orientations. They think of themselves as bisexual or ambisexual ..." (p. 121). These men effectively lead two lives—one straight and the other gay—which they keep separate "much as a surreptitious gambling habit might be hidden from ... family and neighbors" (p. 122).

The "gay" are men who are strongly attached to uniquely homosexual institutions. They are unmarried with no pretense of living straight lives like the ambisexuals or trade.

> Although these men correspond most closely to society's homosexual stereotype, they are least representative of the tearoom population, constituting only 14% of the participant sample.... That any of them patronize the tearooms at all is the result of incidental factors: they fear that open cruising in the more common homosexual market places of the baths and bars might disrupt a current love affair; or they drop in at a tearoom while waiting for a friend at one of the "watering places" where homosexuals congregate in parks. They find the anonymity of the tearooms suitable for their purposes, but not inviting enough to provide the primary setting for sexual activity. (Humphreys, 1975, p. 125)

Finally, the "closet queens" (24% of Humphreys' sample) earn their appellation in the gay world argot because they feel their same-sex orientation strongly but feel an equal pressure to avoid exposure—often related to their jobs—not to come out into the homosexual subculture. They are socially isolated and often unhappy. Their situation amply demonstrates how the stigma of being identified openly as homosexual can drive some people into misery and further underground in the deviant activity. Sometimes the closet queens cruise the streets to pick up young boys for furtive, one-night stands.

> Although painfully aware of their homosexual orientations, these men find little solace in association with others who share their deviant interests. Fearing exposure, arrest, the stigmatization that might result from participation in the homosexual subculture, they are driven to a desperate, lone-wolf sort of activity that may prove most dangerous to themselves and the rest of society. (Humphreys, 1975, p. 129)

Discussion of these meeting places for homosexual encounters should alert us to at least three themes. First is the wide diversity of both the participants in homosexual behavior and the variety of settings in which it takes place. Many homosexuals lead very quiet lives consisting mainly of ordinary socializing with friends at home. Of those who do frequent the "sexual marketplaces," not all identify themselves as homosexual. Over 60% of Humphreys' tearoom participants did *not* identify with the gay subculture. Put simply, not all homosexual activity takes place within the gay subculture and all who engage in homosexual activity do not identify themselves as gay.

Second, the stigma attached to gay identity by a substantial proportion of people in the society all too often pressures those with homosexual feelings into temporary, impersonal contacts to secure sexual satisfaction. Fear of being labeled a homosexual is, for some, a powerful deterrent against coming out. Driven underground by this fear, they become traders in the most transitory, anonymous, and silent of public sexual marketplaces. The settings and circumstances of deviant behavior can only be adequately understood as they relate to the wider culture's norms and values.

Third, these meeting places are marvels of highly ordered, complex systems of nonverbal interaction. To be sure, the cues of body language, dress, gesturing, positioning and the like play a significant role in most heterosexual encounters. However, when guarantees of anonymity and speed become prime motivators for bringing sexual activity to its conclusion, silent interaction emerges as a surprisingly efficient means of communication.

One–Sex Environments: Prisons and the Military. "Total" institutions are places like prisons, mental hospitals, or monasteries which separate their inhabitants from the outside, controlling much of the daily round of life. "Their encompassing or total character is symbolized by the barrier to social intercourse with the outside and to departure that is often built right into the physical plant, such as locked doors, high walls, barbed wire, cliffs, water, forests, or moors" (Goffman, 1961, p. 4). Frequently, as in the case of prison or military training camps, the institutional setting is total and inmates (or recruits) are strictly segregated by sex for prolonged periods. Under such conditions the potential and pressures for homosexual behavior are heightened.

In prisons, the alternative sexual patterns for inmates are reduced to three: abstinence, masturbation, and homosexual activity. Although there are no precise estimates of how many male prisoners rely on each of these, a reasonable guess would suggest that 30 to 45% of inmates engage in homosexual activity (Buffum, 1972, p. 13). The patterns of homosexual behavior in the male prison constitute a subculture within a subculture in which there are rather clearly defined rules and roles creating a definite hierarchical structure.

At the top, in the words of the prison argot, are "wolves" or "jockers"—aggressive, frequently older men, who always take the inserter role. They do not see themselves as homosexual, but view their activity as a transitory substitute for heterosexual relations. Indeed, their aggressive activity is taken as a confirmation of their masculine identity and an enhancement of their status in the prison stratification system. The "punks" are pressured into the homosexual receptor role by force and fear, or they turn to it as a form of homosexual prostitution for monetary gain. In either case, the "punk" role is usually taken by young, slightly built inmates and carries with it the low status accorded its association with feminine weakness. Finally, "queens" or "fags" are those who partake of preferential homosexuality. They usually have homosexual experience prior to incarceration and are subject to the same stigma their sexual preference would arouse in the culture outside the prison.

Clearly, two of the prison roles revolving around homosexual activity, wolves and punks, are a product of the unique prison environment. In neither case did the men who assumed them have a homosexual identity prior to imprisonment. It is reasonable to ask, then, what the long-term effects of their prison-situated homosexual activity are after release. In a detailed study of nine men directed at this question, Sagarin (1976) found that of aggressive participants "who actively sought a homosexual experience and not only had willingly entered into it but also had inflicted it on others, all returned to heterosexuality. On the contrary, all of those who had been forced and subdued into homosexuality, who insisted that it had hurt and disgusted them and that they had entered it most unwillingly, continued the pattern and pursued it in their post-prison years" (p. 254).

This finding again emphasizes the importance of distinguishing homosexual behavior and homosexual identity.

> For the aggressors, the subduing of another was not primarily a search for sexual outlet, affection, or even release from tension. It was a means for the reaffirmation of masculinity in a subculture in which few other methods were available for such expression . . . For aggressors, the prison homosexuality was a temporary expedient, and because they always thought of it in that fashion, they could emerge with their heterosexuality untouched, their masculinity undiminished, their normalcy unquestioned, their self-image untarnished. (Sagarin, 1976, p. 254)

Clearly, the social and psychological importance of the homosexual act is not intrinsic to it; rather, the important thing is how the act is defined by others and by oneself.

As for the subdued, Sagarin finds no evidence of latent homosexuality in their pasts that might explain their post-prison persistence. Instead, it appears that homosexuality can be a learned way of life and that the learning may take place even under conditions of active unpleasantness. It takes place through adaptation and accommodation, through an effort to suppress fear and disgust in order to make the act less repugnant, and it is reinforced by the definitions of others and by the concepts of latency that are today widely known even in relatively less educated groups. Furthermore, the experience of going from heterosexual to homosexual identification and life pattern can take place after the onset of maturity: it need not be during adolescence, as has frequently been suggested. (Sagarin, 1976, p. 256)

Female penal institutions generally differ physically from those containing males. Women's prisons often have no walls, use dormitories as opposed to cells and are smaller than those for men. These structural differences account, in part, for the pattern of sexual relationships common in women's prisons. Unlike the male situation, prison lesbianism rarely takes the form of forcible subjugation. Rather, relatively stable inmate "family" systems tend to develop in which "married" couples are represented by homosexual pairings. In some cases, these "pseudofamilies" extend beyond the husband and wife roles to daughter or grandmother roles as well. Apparently, this pattern of attachments is consistent with the widely diffused feminine ideal of linking sexuality with affection and maintenance of nurturing, emotionally supportive relationships. However, one recent study (Propper, 1982) found that not all make-believe family participation by imprisoned girls involves overt homosexual behavior; nor does all lesbian activity take place within pseudofamily roles.

Both male and female patterns of homosexual behavior in prisons tend to be adaptations for creating structure in the absence of other symbols of status and identity. The pattern in women's prisons emphasizes affectionate stability akin to the typical family while men in prison create, sometimes coercively, a hierarchical stability revolving around strict sexual role assignment and patterns of domination. One retains his or her sexuality regardless of the loss of personal identifiers such as unique clothing or family and work relationships that are removed in the identity stripping process and isolation of imprisonment. It should be no wonder that, when deprived of alternative bases for the creation and maintenance of social structure, homosexual activity becomes one focal point around which to build social organization.

The military is another single-sex environment in which particular concern about homosexuality has been expressed by authorities. Legally, in line with federal employment policies, the U.S. military regards a homosexual as unfit to serve. However, during periods of conscription especially, a substantial number of male homosexuals are inducted and most, like homosexuals in any other form of employment, do their jobs well with their sexual orientations never leading to disciplinary attention. One study of male homosexuals (Saghir and Robins, 1973) found that 16% who were called were not drafted because they identified their sexual preference; 4% were rejected due to prior arrests; and the great majority who entered the service experienced no problems. Six % of those inducted did, eventually, receive less than honorable discharges. One estimate places the frequency of less than honorable discharges from the U.S. military for reasons connected with homosexuality at around 3,000 per year (Williams and Weinberg, 1971).

When the draft is in effect, homosexuals are placed in a difficult double bind. If one admits his or her homosexuality at induction, the result will be a deferment and a stigmatizing blotch on one's record that will likely mar future employment opportunities. If, fearing such an outcome, the homosexual goes into the military, there remains the risk of discovery which usually brings with it a less than honorable discharge. Such a separation from the military renders one ineligible for veterans benefits and also threatens future job possibilities. Williams and Weinberg (1971) conclude:

> The majority of homosexuals who serve do so with honor, and it seems foolish to pursue this group with the ardor that authorities exhibit. If an individual's sex life does not interfere with his service activities, it should be of no concern to military authorities. If it is of such a type that causes problems, then homosexuals should be separated but not necessarily in a way that is punitive. Punitiveness should be based on the nature of the offense without regard to the serviceman's sexual orientation. The automatic use of less than honorable discharges in the military's disposition of homosexuals is in our eyes immoral. (p. 187)

Explanations of Homosexuality

Heredity and Hormones. If it could be found, the identification of a homosexual gene would provide the most elegant explanation possible. The probabilities of one being homosexual would be statistically calculable just as hair or eye color are based upon genetic endowment. The crucial difference, however, is that hair and eye color are relatively fixed physical characteristics while homosexuality is a complex, emergent mix of attitudes and patterns of behavior. To be sure, there is some evidence from twin studies that among identical twins if one is homosexual the other is quite likely to be (Kallman, 1952a, 1952b; Heston & Shields, 1968). However, numerous problems of the research on homosexual twins—including selective samples and small sample size—do not permit definite conclusions. It remains possible that a hereditary factor may play some part in some types of homosexual behavior. But even in these cases, the outcome of any predisposition must depend upon its interaction with the individual's social environment.

A very similar situation holds in regard to studies of hormonal differences between homosexuals and heterosexuals. Masters and Johnson (1979) ask:

> What conclusions or inferences can be drawn from the available evidence? First, it is apparent that all of these reports are significantly handicapped by methodological limitations ranging from relatively small sample size to problems in sampling intervals. Until these problems are remedied, it is difficult to assess the evidence with any security. Second, it is apparent that homosexuality is no more a unitary phenomenon than is heterosexuality: Until it is possible to separate specific subgroups of homosexuals and heterosexuals by precise classification criteria, the heterogeneity that cuts across the basic lines of homosexual versus heterosexual—supported by the heterogeneity found in the physiologic and clinical studies reported in this text—complicates the identification of significant hormonal differences even if these exist. Third, until more is known about the origins of heterosexuality, it is difficult to believe that meaningful insights will be reached regarding the origins of homosexuality. Finally, in view of the current lack of secure information in this field, we must maintain an intellectually open stance acknowledging that in at least some instances—though clearly not in most cases—hormonal predispositions may interact with social and environmental factors to lead toward a homosexual orientation. (p. 411)

Psychoanalytic Perspectives. These explanations generally assume that homosexuality is symptomatic of pathology or sickness. The detailed dynamics of scenarios that produce the alleged abnormality vary, but from this perspective homosexuality is viewed as an illness to be treated and, hopefully, cured. In males, fear of castration (castration anxiety) is thought, in some cases, to be heightened with the sight of a sexual partner without a penis. Thus, certain men are revulsed by women and attracted to men. Another alternative proposes that an overbearing mother and a weak, unassertive father can combine to alienate a son from masculine identification (Bieber, 1962).

Among females, a variation of the male's castration anxiety forms the foundation for psychoanalytic theories of homosexuality. Lacking a penis, the female may suffer from "penis envy" and the trauma of realizing that she may have already been castrated or at least not have been born fully equipped. One possible consequence might be that a girl would identify so closely with her father that she fails to incorporate a feminine orientation. Generally speaking, in the case of boys or girls, the psychoanalytic perspective hypothesizes that if there is a too–intense attachment to the parent of the opposite sex, guilt and fear associated with the incest taboo create revulsion against all heterosexual contacts. The result may be homosexuality.

Criticism of psychoanalytic theories has been intense. Of the many problems we will only briefly mention three. First, the explanations are *post hoc*; that is, they are derived by examining case studies of homosexuals and then piecing together possible reasons for sexual orientation. However, there is rarely any attempt to compare homosexuals to heterosexuals or studies to test the theories by predicting sexual orientation given certain conditions. Second, just how the personalities of homosexuals are "disordered" or "sick" is very unclear. In one famous study (Hooker, 1957), for example, a panel of psychiatrists and clinical psychologists was unable to distinguish homosexuals from heterosexuals on the basis of personality tests. Finally, psychiatric case studies of homosexuals are usually based upon people who have gone to a psychiatrist precisely because they are troubled. It would not be surprising to find evidence of personality or social maladjustment among people who place themselves in a psychiatrist's care whether they were homosexual *or* heterosexual. Certainly the majority of homosexuals and heterosexuals never come to the attention of psychiatrists. In a word, psychiatric conclusions regarding sexuality in general, and homosexuality in particular, are probably based upon very biased samples of cases.

Learning. Implicit in the physiological or psychoanalytic explanations is the assumption that some sort of disorder, either in the person's body chemistry or psyche, motivates his or her homosexuality. The fundamental imagery of the homosexual portrayed in these theories is that of a person driven into deviance by an abnormal condition. In sharp contrast, explanations relying on learning theory assume that homosexual behavior can be learned and reinforced like any other behavior. The initial homosexual experience, according to this viewpoint, is not usually the result of some drive or need, but often instead a matter of chance. For example, the preadolescent sex play common between boys or between girls may provide an experience or attachment that is pleasurable and rewarding. At the same time, learned fears or inhibitions regarding heterosexual relations may make a person more receptive to homosexual activity.

The effect of rather isolated but pleasurable homosexual experiences can be reinforced and enlarged through fantasies imagined during self-masturbation.

> Through both direct reinforcement and reinforcement through masturbatory imagery, then, the homosexual experience may be repeated.

> Each time that it results in positive outcomes, the probability of repeating it increases. Rewarded repetition and practice enhance the ability to attain pleasure from the homosexual acts of mutual masturbation, fellatio, and anal intercourse. Inhibitions toward homosexuality continue to decrease. Depending on how frequent and how pleasurable simultaneous heterosexual experiences are, each succeeding successful homosexual episode increases the probability of further homosexual involvement. (Akers, 1973, p. 160)

Beyond learning the techniques and learning to enjoy homosexual behavior, individuals may (but not necessarily) learn to play homosexual or gay roles. In the process of coming out, persons learn to organize their lives around their alleged deviant images. In interaction with others who share their homosexual identification, subcultural participants learn how best to manage their shunned status, how to rationalize their behavior to themselves and others, and how to get along with others in a hostile world.

Societal Reaction. This approach, sometimes called labeling theory, emphasizes the consequences of negative sanctions directed against deviants. Weinberg and Williams (1974) have found that "for the majority of homosexuals in the societies we studied (the United States, Denmark, and the Netherlands) the impact of the legal situation is not *direct*. Instead, we believe the most universal (though not necessarily the most serious), effect of legal repression is to symbolize society's rejection of the homosexual. This rejection seems to be a major source of the homosexual's problems" (p. 268). Widespread adaptations to this rejection include development of the homosexual subculture to provide social support and the emergence of militant homophile movements which attempt to confront directly and politically the laws symbolizing the rejection.

The Politics of Definition. In December 1973 the American Psychiatric Association (APA) officially declared that homosexuality "by itself does not necessarily constitute a psychiatric disorder." From 1951 to 1973 homosexuality had been categorized in the APA's *Diagnostic and Statistical Manual* in the context of "sexual deviation." The APA Board of Trustees' action was accompanied by a "Position Statement on Homosexuality and Civil Rights" which clearly recognized the power of society's most potent official "labelers," especially psychiatrists, to influence the lives of their "clients." In the Position Statement,

> ... the board deplored all public and private discrimination against homosexuals and urged the enactment of civil rights legislation to protect homosexuals and the repeal of all discriminatory legislation against homosexual behavior. It further deplored the use of "pejorative connota-

tions derived from diagnostic or descriptive terminology used in psychiatry" as the basis for such discrimination. (Spector, 1977, p. 53)

Almost immediately, opposition led by psychoanalysts Irving Beiber and Charles Socorides mobilized to the change in nomenclature. This group circulated a petition, gathering the 200 APA members' signatures required to throw the board's decision open to a referendum of the entire APA membership. A vote was scheduled for April 1974 with both sides campaigning strenuously during the three months preceeding the vote. The issue of whether officially to classify homosexuality as a mental disorder was being politically decided by the members of a prestigious professional society in a hotly contested "election" on the issue. Over ten thousand of the APA's 18,000 members voted in the referendum with the Board of Trustees' decision being upheld by 58%.

One might rightfully ask: What's so important about a definition? Some thought on the question necessarily leads to the realization that deviance, and the theoretical images concocted to explain it, are very much pure matters of definition arrived at by far from unanimous agreement through intensely political struggles. Likewise, this episode directs our attention to the pivotal position of the professions concerned with human behavior, especially those like psychiatry, psychology, sociology, and medicine, as battlegrounds for issues of social control in a modern society.

SWINGING

During the 1960s and early 1970s there was a flurry of attention from social scientists and the popular press directed towards an apparent increase in mate swapping as an alternative to strictly monogamous marriage. The phenomenon that aroused this interest went beyond simple marital infidelity to situations in which husband and wife had sexual relations with other people at the same time and usually in the same place. The sexual activity itself might involve only one other couple or more than a half dozen. In some cases, partners have sex in one another's presence while in others they might retire to separate rooms. However, aside from their comarital character (that is *both* marital partners engaging in extramarital relations at the same time with each other's knowledge), swinging was noteworthy because of two characteristics possessed by its most frequent participants—their conventionality in other aspects of their lives and their middle-class status. Summarizing numerous studies, Fang (1976) says that the "majority of swingers are in their twenties and thirties and can be characterized as white, middle-class, suburban, highly educated, and highly mobile, both geographically and socially. These people are often considered as dull homebodies, with few interests, excluding watching television and reading the newspaper (Bartell, 1970). According to the Smiths (1974) they rate as 'uninterestingly normal' on the Minnesota Multiphasic Personality Inventory" (p. 221).

Meeting, Motives, and Manipulation

Probably the most common mode of entry into the swinging scene is through personal reference from another like-minded couple. Less common are swinger bars, night clubs, or special social functions like open parties in hotel ballrooms. Some swingers also make contacts through advertisements in magazines such as *Swingers Life, Kindred Spirits, Select,* and the *National Registry*. Indeed, the emergence of specialized publications devoted to the activity suggests that for a time it was gaining the momentum of a small-scale social movement.

Some of the more common motives people cited behind their decision to swing include: "boredom and restlessness; a need for new experiences; tired of cheating covertly; need of an 'ego lift;' restriction of marital exclusivity; a means for patching up a failing marriage; and a desire for more sex than the partner gives" (Fang, 1976). Usually a couple enters swinging on the husband's initiative and wives are more often the ones to insist on dropping out. It appears that curiosity and relief from boredom may be the most common motivations to swing. Once the uniqueness of the experience wanes, reasons to quit, especially jealousy, became more important.

Swinging has been interpreted very positively by some commentators (e.g., Smith & Smith, 1974, and Palson & Palson, 1972) who have hailed the virtues of swinging ("reromanticizing" marriage) as part of the sexual revolution. Implicit in this viewpoint is the assumption that swinging represents a breakdown of the sexual double standard thereby contributing to the genuine equality of men and women. However, others question this proposition. Henshel (1973) found that husbands, rather than wives, were overwhelmingly the first to learn of swinging; the first to suggest it; and dominated the final decision to try it. She concludes that "in the context of marital decision making, swinging can be viewed as a male institution, and confirmations of the advent of a 'sexual revolution' and of the abolition of the double standard should be reconsidered" (p. 128). Denfeld (1974) is equally forthright. "The results of reports from marriage counselors also challenge the argument that swinging demonstrates the realization of equality of the sexes. Husbands often force wives into swinging and wives were more dissatisfied with swinging and more frequently initiated dropping out. Rather than being egalitarian, swinging is more likely to be a truly 'sexist' activity" (pp. 48-49).

The Sociological Significance of Swinging

Students of deviance should find swinging of theoretical interest first because it challenges our ability to explain middle-class deviance among people who otherwise appear to be rather ordinary and conventional. One researcher (Walshok, 1971) suggests that three distinct points offer a valuable perspective. (1) The high personal and social value placed on sexuality among middle-class Americans provides a receptive social atmosphere for the emergence of swinging. (2) The insecure, marginal status of individuals new to the middle-class from more sexually restrictive lower- or working-class backgrounds makes them very responsive to intense forms of experience. And (3) the highly organized, routinized character of swinging—through clubs, ads, or cocktail parties—emphasizes sex without emotional attachment or commitment. This would allow for a minimal threat to the marriage and maximal opportunity to separate participation in this deviant activity from the other roles of the person's more conventional life-style. "Participation in the deviant subculture thus becomes a functional alternative to potentially deviant commitments in other role spheres" (Walshok, 1971, p. 494). In a word, these conditions are almost ideal for secret deviance.

Swinging was thought by some, at one time, to be part of a trend that might soon make it a very widespread marital practice. This has not come to pass and, in retrospect, must lead us to ask just what might account for its short-lived existence. The possibilities are instructive when considering the apparent sudden rise and fall of any deviant activity. Is the increase real?—that is, are substantially more people actually doing it? Or, have the media, police, social scientists, or other agents of social control simply started for some reason (often political) to pay greater attention to the phenomenon, making it appear as if there is a great increase? Sagarin (1977) suggests that the mass media may have been largely responsible for the spread of swinging, got tired of it, and then moved on to other more exotic phenomena.

> It is not known whether the entire swinging scene disappeared, remained more or less as it had been but received less attention, or had never amounted to much at all. . . . If one limits the figure to the legally married, it is doubtful whether more than 1 percent of all married couples in the United States ever participated. Of those who did, some did so for a very short period—one evening or one weekend—and then abandoned the activity; others found that they were unable to continue with their marriages. In short, most reports indicate that married couples who

became involved in the activity either left the scene with some haste or did not remain together as husband and wife. This author has no report of a married couple whose marital difficulties were alleviated by such performances. The swinging seems to have been a fad that hit America at a time when people had not yet tired of the sexual revolution. It was the subject of widespread publicity, it remained an exotic curiosity, and it never ceased to be the subject of scorn and hostility (not merely in Middle America), while at the same time it satisfied some vicarious excitement in readers and television viewers who both envied and condemned the participants. (Sagarin, 1977, pp. 448–449)

This should remind us that deviance is, significantly, in the eye of the beholder and, moreover, social scientists and the media often color the lens through which our eyes view the world.

SUMMARY

In this chapter we have presented research findings and explanations concerning prostitution, pornography, homosexuality, and swinging. At the sociological level of explanation, functionalist theory has been frequently drawn upon to account for the widespread prevalence of both prostitution and pornography. Prostitution is thought to provide for men's alleged need to have relatively noncommittal sexual outlets outside the family. It "functions" as a sexual safety valve. Likewise pornography, from the functionalist's perspective, is an alternative to prostitution that fulfills similar needs. Also at the sociological level of explanation, we considered various cultural themes including sexism, the double standard, guilt, violence, and machismo that contribute to the flourishing of prostitution and pornography. At the social–psychological level, in respect to prostitution, we described common patterns of family background, peer relationships, learning, labeling, and development of self-concept that help explain a woman's movement into this life-style. And again at the sociological level, we considered how prostitution is integrally entwined with America's economic, political, and legal system.

Explanations of homosexuality included the biogenetic (heredity and hormones), psychological (sexual identification), social psychological (learning and development of self-concept), and sociological (the politics of labeling homosexuality as deviance). One central theme in the discussion of homosexuality was that sexuality runs along a continuum between pure heterosexuality and pure homosexuality. Most people's lives do not represent a strict "either/or" pattern. Another important thread was the great diversity of homosexual life-styles that are too often overlooked in stereotypical thinking. Likewise, within the broad category of prostitutes is a tremendous range of relative statuses, risks, independence, and economic success. In respect to both prostitution and pornography we considered how the female deviant can properly be conceived of as the victim in a sexually stratified society.

Finally, our brief discussion of swinging alerted us to the role of the media in the emergence and decline of deviance. What we see in the world depends heavily upon what we are shown in the media and what the official "labelers" (police, psychiatrists, psychologists, sociologists, and medical doctors) tell us are important at the time. To be sure, deviance is not merely a figment of our imaginations. However, we should never underestimate the ease with which our uncritical images of deviance can be intentionally or unintentionally manipulated.

NOTES

1. Gagnon and Simon (1967) originally introduced the following typology.
2. "Piss-elegance" refers to a style of presentation that is seen as "pseudo" authentic and thus false. The style emphasizes conservative attire and formal manners. The image is closely associated with the "closeted" homosexual and middle-class virtues. The style is also associated with pecuniary success, which many participants have not attained. "Elegance"—meaning monied manners— is pretended and hence labeled "piss." Patrons of these bars do not refer to themselves as "piss-elegant" although they employ the term when referring to others whom they wish to derogate.
3. Of course, settings like gay bars and baths provide the means for men to have numerous sexual contacts. Such a life-style, sometimes involving hundreds of different partners, is not without its medical risks. Recently, for example, public health specialists have observed an increase in rates of Karposi's sarcoma and *Pneumocystis* pneumonia—often fatal diseases that appear to be concentrated among men whose life-styles include a large number of homosexual relationships. In general, the greater the number of sexual partners, the greater the incidence of sexually transmitted diseases of all sorts. (Ismach, 1981; Darrow, Barrett, Jay, & Young, 1981).

REFERENCES

Achilles, N.
    1967   The development of the homosexual bar as an institution. In J. H. Gagnon & W. Simon (Eds.), *Sexual Deviance.* New York: Harper and Row.

Akers, R. L.
    1973   *Deviant behavior: A social learning approach.* Belmont, California: Wadsworth.

Atkinson, M., & Boles, J.
    1977   Prostitution as an ecology of confidence games: The scripted behavior

of prostitutes and vice officers. In C. D. Bryant (Ed.), *Sexual Deviancy in Social Context.* New York: New Viewpoints.

Bartell, G. D.
   1970   Group sex among mid-Americans. *Journal of Sex Research,* 6, 113–130.

Bell, A. P., & Weinberg, M. S.
   1978   *Homosexualities: A study of human diversity.* New York: Simon and Schuster.

Bieber, I.
   1962   *Homosexuality: A psychoanalytic study of male homosexuals.* New York: Basic Books.

Brownmiller, S.
   1979   *Philadelphia Inquirer,* August 1:9A.

Buffurn, P. C.
   1972   *Homosexuality in prisons.* Washington, D.C.: U.S. Government Printing Office.

Bullough, V., & Bullough, B.
   1978   *Prostitution: An illustrated social history.* New York: Crown.

Dank, B. M.
   1971   Coming out in the gay world. *Psychology 34:*180–197.

Darrow, W. W., Barrett, D., Jay, K., & Young, A.
   1981   The gay report on sexually transmitted diseases. *American Journal of Public Health, 71:* 1004–1011.

Davis, K.
   1937   The sociology of prostitution. *American Sociological Review, 2*:744–755.

Davis, N.
   1971   The prostitute: Developing a deviant identity. In J. M. Henslin (Ed.), *Studies in the sociology of sex.* New York: Appleton-Century-Crofts.

Delph, E. W.
   1978   *The silent community: Public homosexual encounters.* Beverly Hills, Calif.: Sage.

Denfeld, D.
   1974   Dropouts for swinging. *The Family Coordinator, 23*:45–49.

Fang, B.
   1976   Swinging: in retrospect. *Journal of Sex Research, 12*:220–237.

Federal Bureau of Investigation
   1981   *Uniform Crime Reports.* Washington, D.C.: U.S. Department of Justice.

Flexner, A.
   1920   *Prostitution in Europe.* New York: Century.

Ford, C. S., & Beach, F. A.
   1951   *Patterns of sexual behavior.* New York: Harper and Row.

Gagnon, J. H., & Simon, W.
   1967   *Sexual deviance.* New York: Harper and Row.

Gandy, P., & Deisher, R.
  1970 Young male prostitutes. *Journal of the American Medical Association, 212*:1661–1666.
Gebhard, P. H.
  1969 Misconceptions about female prostitutes. *Medical Aspects of Human Sexuality, 3*:28–30.
Geis, G.
  1972 *Not the law's business? An examination of homosexuality, abortion, prostitution, narcotics and gambling in the United States.* Washington, D.C.: National Institute of Mental Health.
Goffman, E.
  1961 *Asylums: Essays on the social situation of mental patients and other inmates.* Garden City, N.Y.: Anchor.
Goode, E.
  1978 *Deviant behavior: An interactionist approach.* Englewood Cliffs, N.J.: Prentice–Hall.
Gray, D.
  1973 Turning-out: A study of teenage prostitution. *Urban Life and Culture, 1*:401–425.
Greenwald, H.
  1970 *The elegant prostitute.* New York: Ballantine.
Gusfield, J. R.
  1963 *Symbolic crusade. Status politics and the American temperance movement.* Urbana: University of Illinois Press.
Hall, S.
  1972 *Gentleman of leisure: A year in the life of a pimp.* New York: New American Library.
Henshel, A. M.
  1973 Swinging: A study of decision making in marriage. In J. Huber (Ed.), *Changing women in a changing society.* Chicago: University of Chicago Press.
Heyl, B. S.
  1979 *The madam as entrepreneur: Career management in house prostitution.* New Brunswick, N.J.: Transaction.
Heston, L. L., & Shields, J.
  1968 Homosexuality in twins: A family study and registry study. *Archives of General Psychiatry, 18*:149–160.
Hooker, E.
  1957 The adjustment of the male overt homosexual. *Journal of Projective Techniques, 21*:18–31.
Humphreys, L.
  1975 *Tearoom trade: Impersonal sex in public places.* Chicago: Aldine.
Hunt, M.
  1974 *Sexual behavior in the 1970s.* Chicago: Playboy Press.
Hyde, H. M.
  1964 *A history of pornography.* New York: Dell.

Ismach, J. M.
   1981   Health hazards of homosexuals. *Medical World News, 23*:56–67.
James, J.
   1977   Prostitutes and prostitution. In E. Sagarin and F. Montanino (Eds.), *Deviants: Voluntary actors in a hostile world.* Morristown, N.J.: General Learning Press.
Kallman, F. J.
   1952a Comparative twin study of the genetic aspects of male homosexuality. *Journal of Nervous and Mental Disease, 115*:283–298.
Kallman, F. J.
   1952b Twin sibships and the study of male homosexuality. *American Journal of Human Genetics, 4*:136–146.
Kinsey, A. C., Pomeroy, W. B., & Martin, C. E.
   1948   *Sexual behavior in the human male.* Philadelphia: W. B. Saunders.
Lemert, E. M.
   1951   *Social pathology.* New York: McGraw-Hill.
Licht, H.
   1955   Male homosexuality in ancient Greece. In D. W. Corey (Ed.), *Homosexuality: A cross cultural approach.* New York: Julian Press.
Masters, W. H., & Johnson, V.
   1979   *Homosexuality in perspective.* Boston: Little, Brown.
McCormack, T.
   1978   Machismo in media research: A critical review of research on violence and pornography. *Social Problems, 25*:544–555.
McIntosh, M.
   1968   The homosexual role. *Social Problems, 16*:182–192.
Muedeking, G. D.
   1977   Pornography and society. In E. Sagarin & F. Montanino (Eds.), *Deviants: Voluntary actors in a hostile world.* Morristown, N.J.: General Learning Press.
Palson, C., & Palson, R.
   1972   Swinging in wedlock. *Society, 9*:28–37.
Polsky, N.
   1967   *Hustlers, beats and others.* Chicago: Aldine.
President's Commission on Obscenity and Pornography
   1970   *Report of the president's commission on obscenity and pornography.* New York: Bantam Books.
Propper, A. M.
   1982   Make-believe families and homosexual activity among imprisoned girls. *Criminology 20*:127–138.
Roby, P. A.
   1969   Politics of criminal law: Revision of the New York State penal law on prostitution. *Social Problems, 17*:83–109.
Rosenblum, K. E.
   1975   Female deviance and the female sex role: A preliminary investigation. *British Journal of Sociology, 26*:169–185.

Rowse, A. L.
   1977   *Homosexuals in history: A study of ambivalence in society, literature and the arts.* New York: Macmillan.
Sagarin, E.
   1976   Prison homosexuality and its effects on post-prison sexual behavior. *Psychiatry, 39*:245-257.
Sagarin, E.
   1977   Sex deviance: A view from the window of middle America. In E. Sagarin & F. Montanino (Eds.), *Deviants: Voluntary actors in a hostile world.* Morristown, N.J.: General Learning Press.
Saghir, M. T., & Robins, E.
   1973   *Male and female homosexuality.* Baltimore: Williams and Wilkins.
Sheehy, G.
   1973   *Hustling: Prostitution in our wide-open society.* New York: Delacorte Press.
Smith, L. G., & Smith, J. R.
   1974   Co-marital sex: The incorporation of extramarital sex into the marriage relationship. In J. R. Smith & L. G. Smith (Eds.), *Beyond monogamy: Recent studies of sexual alternatives in marriage.* Baltimore: The Johns Hopkins University Press.
Spector, M.
   1977   Legitimizing homosexuality. *Society, 14*(5):52-56.
Walshok, M. L.
   1971   The emergence of middle-class deviant subcultures: The case of swingers. *Social Problems, 18*:488-495.
Warren, C. A. B.
   1974   *Identity and community in the gay world.* New York: Wiley.
Weinberg, M. S., & Williams, C. J.
   1974   *Male homosexuals: Their problems and adaptations.* New York: Oxford.
Weinberg, M. S., & Williams, C. J.
   1975   Gay baths and the social organization of impersonal sex. *Social Problems, 23*:124-136.
Williams, C. J., & Weinberg, M. S.
   1971   *Homosexuals and the military: A study of less than honorable discharge.* New York: Harper and Row.
Wilson, J. Q.
   1971   Violence, pornography and social science. *The Public Interest, 22*:45-61.
Winick, C., & Kinsie, P. M.
   1971   *The lively commerce: Prostitution in the United States.* New York: Quadrangle.
Zurcher, L. A., Jr., & Kirkpatrick, R. G.
   1976   *Citizens for decency: Antipornography crusades as status defense.* Austin: University of Texas Press.

Chapter 3
MENTAL DISORDERS

IMAGES OF MADNESS
  Mental Disorder in Western History
  Cross–Cultural Perspectives
DEFINITION OF MENTAL DISORDERS
TYPES OF MENTAL DISORDERS
THE DISTRIBUTION OF MENTAL DISORDERS
  Counting Cases
SOCIOCULTURAL FACTORS AND MENTAL DISORDERS
  Age
  Sex
  Race
  Rural–Urban Settings
  Social Class
EXPLANATIONS OF MENTAL DISORDER
  Nature Versus Nurture: The Genetics–Environment Issue
  Social Disorganization: The Ecological Approach
  Social Structural Strain
  Family Dynamics
  Labeling
REACTIONS TO MENTAL DISORDER
  Public Attitudes
MENTAL HOSPITALS
PUBLIC POLICY
  Deinstitutionalization and Community Mental Health
MENTAL DISORDER AND THE LAW
  Involuntary Commitment
  Incompetency to Stand Trial
  The Insanity Defense
POLICY SUGGESTIONS
SUMMARY

IMAGES OF MADNESS

Mental Disorder in Western History

Throughout most of Western civilization magic or demonic possession have dominated as popular images of the reasons for especially bizarre behavior. The ancient Greeks believed that madness was due to possession by malignant demons or gods. Even the gods themselves were subjected to possession, as when Hercules went insane from possession by Lyssa, the goddess of madness, or Orestes' madness was ascribed to the Furies.

Contemporaneously with these views, Hippocrates, the Greek physician, proposed an organic theory of madness in a treatise entitled "On the Sacred Disease." Dealing primarily with epilepsy, Hippocrates attacked explanations relying on diabolical possession and, in a more modern manner, claimed than an organic disturbance in the brain caused madness. In contrast to Hippocrates' organic emphasis, Plato emphasized the psychological biography of a person. His concern was how family relationships and education in a person's formative years explained adult behavior. Hippocrates' theory emphasizing organic dysfunction and Plato's social–psychological one still represent viable alternative hypotheses for contemporary researchers who try to understand the cause of mental disorders.

In the Middle Ages (roughly from the collapse of the Roman Empire in the 5th century A.D. through the beginning of the Renaissance in the 14th century) the Church was the primary institution presiding over a difficult era dominated by wars, famine, plague, and pestilence. Madness often expressed itself in mass hysteria, flagellants, and dance manias which were popularly attributed to demonic possession. The Renaissance (roughly the fourteenth through the sixteenth centuries) saw continued emphasis on demonology, especially witchcraft, as an explanation of madness. In the face of great opposition, a few like Johann Weyer, who is today considered to be the father of modern psychiatry, tried to counter the accusation and vicious treatment of alleged witches by offering psychological reasons for their behavior. However, his views would have to wait several centuries before receiving popular support.

In the 17th and 18th centuries the insane were increasingly placed in the same institutions with the poor, crippled, and delinquent. In an age of Enlightenment, madness, along with other social problems, was believed subject to conquest by reason, even if the insane had to be captured, caged, and forced into submission. In the United States, asylums specifically for the insane emerged during a period of idealistic reform in the 1800s (Rothman, 1971). In England in the 1800s theories of madness moved from what Skultans (1975) describes as "psychiatric romanticism," in which the moral force and will of the individual were called upon to combat insanity, to "psychiatric Darwinism," which cited inherited character and constitution flaws as root causes of madness.

Analysis of the internal dimensions of the mind (ego, superego, and id) and the individual's relationship to an external social context are both embodied in twentieth-century Freudian psychology. Researchers have discovered organic causes and treatments for numerous mental disorders such as Hippocrates' "Sacred disease," epilepsy. Physicians, psychiatrists, psychologists, and sociologists continue to seek explanations and effective treatments for functional mental disorders which have no apparent organic causes.

Images of madness have not historically followed a smooth path from the primitive to the enlightened. However, despite occasional halts and temporary reversals the supposed causes of madness have generally moved from an emphasis on (1) the sacred (possession by gods, demons, witches) to the secular; (2) from the moralistic search for flaws in the individual to naturalistic explanations emphasizing scientific research findings; and (3) from locating the causes within the person (internal) to an accounting of the impact of a person's external social environment.

Cross-Cultural Perspectives

The most obvious outward sign or symptom of mental disorder is odd behavior. However, not everyone who behaves oddly at one time or another is diagnosed mentally ill. Moreover, a person can get away with acting very strangely in some situations without any particularly incriminating outcome. In fact, under certain circumstances behaving oddly is considered normal. For example, people dress and cavort during New Orleans' Mardis Gras week in a way that would bring a very negative response at other times of the year. Behavior is rarely, if ever, evaluated out of its situational context.

In New Orleans, the standards for judging behavior change rather dramatically from time to time during the year. Likewise, people's activities are differently evaluated from place to place—that is, in different cultures. The idea that behavior can only be understood in the context of a particular situation or culture is called *cultural relativity*. According to the principle of cultural relativity any behavior may be viewed as normal in one culture but as aberrant, even as a sign of mental disorder, in another. From a cultural relativist's position, the reason why a person's behavior is labeled crazy or mad may be in the culturally filtered eye of the beholder rather than in the malfunction of the physiology or psyche of the person whose behavior is being judged. It appears, from this viewpoint, that there are no absolute standards or symptoms for determining the presence or absence of mental illness. Indeed, taking cultural relativity to its logical extreme, one might even legitimately ask: Is there such a thing as mental illness? We will return to this question shortly.

People in various cultures *do* evaluate similar behaviors differently, a fact which supports the cultural relativist position. As mentioned previously, numerous American Indian tribes are known to have adopted a special social role called the *berdache*. These were "men–women" who "at puberty or thereafter took the dress and occupations of women" (Benedict, 1934, p. 263). This special role provided a socially acceptable outlet for homosexuals who in another culture might either be persecuted or prosecuted. Likewise, the shaman (medicine man) of some American Indian, Siberian, African, and other cultures may exhibit trancelike states, hallucinations, seizures, and violent behavior dangerous to themselves and others. However, the shaman in these cultures is held in esteem for his special powers while the same behavior would not be tolerated in many other cultures.

Anthropologists have also found that a certain type of deviant behavior sometimes appears to be unique to a specific culture. For example, a person running *amok* in Malaysia indiscriminantly kills anyone in his path. Some people of the Chippewa and Cree Indian tribes of Canada are said to have been afflicted with the *windigo psychosis* in which under conditions of extreme deprivation and isolation the victim would cannibalize his own family and rampage wildly until hunted down. Haiti has its magical death or *voodoo*. Numerous cultures including Navajo, Mexican Zapotec, medieval Western Europe, and colonial New England have had their versions of witchcraft.

It is tempting to conclude from this sort of ethnographic evidence that mental disorder is a phenomenon so relative to any particular culture that we cannot possibly discover sufficiently common symptoms to classify it as a definite type of "illness" found in all human populations. However, experts on culture and personality like Anthony Wallace (1970, 1972) do not interpret cultural differences in the reaction to similar behavior or the tremendous variety of symptoms among different cultures as denial of a common mental disease process to which human beings are generally vulnerable. We can sum up the prevailing weight of anthropological opinion.

1. Different cultures do encourage different styles of mental disorders. Symptoms vary according to the individual's cultural experience and symbolic mode of presenting them. Paranoid delusions expressed as fear of devils, demons, and other supernatural spirits in a primitive culture are replaced by radio, radar, and voices from outer space in modern Western society. Nevertheless, the major categories of mental illness (organic psychoses, functional psychoses, neuroses, personality disorders, etc.) seem to be universal.
2. There are no societies in which mental disorders are unknown, but societies do vary in overall frequency and relative frequency of various types of mental disorder. Explaining these differences is one of the more interesting questions for anthropologists and sociologists.
3. The causes of mental disorders, whether rooted in genes, psychic experience or social interaction seem to be ubiquitous in human groups. Despite what appear to be common underlying causes, explanations of mentally disordered behavior and reactions to it vary widely. Depending on the culture, reactions to bizarre behavior may include continued integration in the group by assignment to a special role; enforced exclusion through institutionalization; intensive magical, psychological, or medical therapy; and even total indifference.

DEFINITION OF MENTAL DISORDERS

Until recently in our culture, the stigmatizing labels of "mad," "crazy," "lunatic," "idiot," "insane," "mentally defective," and so on, were reserved for rather severe exhibitions of abnormal behavior. In many other cultures today, the mentally disordered are distinguished only after the most obvious demonstration of a person's incapacity to function normally in day-to-day living with others. However, 20th century Western civilization is characterized by a broadening definition of mental disorders to the point where behaviors only mildly disturbing to the flow of everyday life, such as minor neuroses or psychosomatic disorders, have become a significant concern among those who diagnose and treat psychopathology.

While the definition of mental disorder has varied over time and among different cultures, the modern tendency has been for more types of disorders to be included in diagnostic manuals and for a broadening of the definition of previously included types. Given shifting standards among different times and cultures, a brief, precise definition of mental disorder is difficult. However, in most times and places a person has been classified as mentally disordered when he or she exhibits what seems to be uncontrolled, irrationally motivated behavior considered by most others to be sufficiently abnormal and irresponsible in its sociocultural context to require special treatment, isolation, or social control.

In this definition, mental disorder is recognized through the way a person behaves—the distinguishing symptom of mental disorder is how a person acts. Beyond that, the definition takes into account the apparent motivation for the behavior, the context in which it occurs, and a judgment or reaction on the part of others. Mentally disordered behavior is usually distinguished from criminal behavior on the basis of motive and responsibility. In the case of the criminal, the motive is usually rather clear and the individual is held accountable. A criminal is thought to be responsible for his violation of the law, and punishment is, therefore, the appropriate response. The mentally deranged behave with unclear motives and, being judged irresponsible, require treatment or, at worst, exclusion from everyday social situations in which their behavior is upsetting or dangerous to others.

TYPES OF MENTAL DISORDERS

The accepted standard for classifying mental disorders is the *Diagnostic & Statistical Manual of Mental Disorders,* 3rd ed. (1980), published by the American Psychiatric Association (DSM,III).This recent reclassification divides mental disorders into the 17 major categories listed in Figure 3.1. The main change in the DSM,III as compared to its forerunners is that neuroses and their various subtypes, which were a major category in the past, are no longer listed separately. The former neurotic subtypes are now included with affective, anxiety, somatoform, and dissociative disorders. Naturally, because DSM, III is very new, most research on mental disorders is based upon the older classification scheme. Thus, our discussion in this chapter will necessarily rely upon the earlier, and for our purposes still valid, DSM, II system.

Traditionally, mental disorders have been divided into two major categories: (1) organic brain syndromes and (2) functional disorders not attributable to physiological changes in the brain. The symptoms in

1. Disorders usually first evident in infancy, childhood, or adolescence (e.g., hyperactivity, anorexia nervosa, stuttering)
2. Organic mental disorders (e.g., senility, substance – induced damage)
3. Substance use disorders (e.g., abuse of alcohol, barbiturates, opioids, etc.)
4. Schizophrenic disorders
5. Paranoid disorders
6. Other psychotic disorders not elsewhere classified
7. Affective disorders (depression, mania)
8. Anxiety disorders (e.g., phobias, anxieties, compulsive behavior)
9. Somatoform disorders (psychogenic pain, hypochondriasis)
10. Dissociative disorders (hysterical neuroses, dissociative type)
11. Psychosexual disorders (e.g., gender identity, fetishism, exhibitionism, etc.)
12. Factious disorders
13. Disorders of impulse control not elsewhere classified (e.g., pathological gambling, kleptomania, pyromania, etc.)
14. Adjustment disorders
15. Psychological factors affecting physical condition
16. Other conditions
17. Personality disorders (e.g., narcissistic, antisocial, etc.)

FIGURE 3.1. THE MAJOR CATEGORIES OF MENTAL DISORDERS ACCORDING TO THE DSM, III CLASSIFICATION

both of these major categories may be similar and include hallucinations, impairment of memory and judgment, lowered intellectual function, and social failure. The major distinction between the two is whether or not the disorder is clearly related to physical brain damage. The origin of functional disorders is generally assumed to be psychosocial. Indeed, the use of the word "functional" implies that these mental disorders arise from a person's attempts to adjust to psychological or social stresses and strain. Abnormal behavior "functions" as a form of adaptation to a difficult situation.

Organic brain syndromes are further divided into subtypes according to the agent which produced the brain damage. Included among organic disorders are senile or old-age psychoses, *paresis* or dementia paralytica caused by syphilis infection, alcoholic psychoses, drug addictions, and syndromes caused by various infections (encephalitis, meningitis, typhoid fever), physiological disturbances (uremia, tumors, vitamin deficiency) or congenital cranial anomalies (Mongolism, birth trauma). Table 3.1 shows that organic brain syndromes, exclusive of alcoholic and drug disorders, comprise about 17% of resident state and county psychiatric patient disorders in the U.S. Adding to this percentage those patients with alcoholic and drug disorders, plus a portion of those classified as mentally retarded, the total of people diagnosed as having organic disorders account for about one third of resident patients in the United States.

Because functional disorders are presumed to have psychosocial causes, this major psychiatric category has received the most attention from social scientists. Functional disorders are further divided into subcategories: psychoses, neuroses, personality disorders, psychophysiologic disorders, transient situational personality disorders, and behavior disorders of childhood and early adolescence. Neuroses are distinguished from psychoses by being less socially debilitating and rarely requiring long-term institutionalization. Compulsive behavior; phobias; hysteria; amnesia; disturbances of speech, hearing, and sight; and hypochondria are usually classified under neurosis. Psychoses, on the other hand, are apt to be more severe and intense and likely to lead to institutionalization.

Psychoses are subdivided into two major types: schizophrenia and affective disorders (manic–depression). Schizophrenia is characterized by withdrawal, disorientation in time and place, inability to perform expected roles, hallucinations, occasionally incomprehensible speech, and other inappropriate social behaviors such as unwarranted laughing

TABLE 3.1. NUMBER AND PERCENT DISTRIBUTION OF RESIDENT PATIENTS BY DIAGNOSIS, STATE AND COUNTY MENTAL HOSPITALS, UNITED STATES, 1978

Major diagnostic categories	Number	Percent
Organic		
Organic brain syndromes*	25,230	17.1
Alcoholic disorders	8,019	5.4
Drug disorders	1,527	1.0
Mental retardation	13,685	9.3
Functional		
Schizophrenia	72,606	49.3
Depressive (affective) disorders	8,766	6.0
Personality disorders	3,348	2.3
Other psychoses	1,471	1.0
Other		
Undiagnosed	6,890	4.7
All other	5,741	3.9
Total	147,283	100.0

Source: U.S. Department of Health and Human Services, 1981, p. 48.
*Excludes organic brain syndromes associated with alcoholism and drug addiction.

or odd gestures. Schizophrenia is the most frequent diagnosis of institutionalized mental disorder comprising about half of the patients in U.S. public facilities. (See Table 3.1.)

The other major category of psychosis, manic–depression, is usually more transitory with a better prognosis than schizophrenia. Manic-depressives may be extremely agitated and excited in the manic stage or withdrawn and guilt-ridden in the depressive stage. The person with this disorder may vacillate between mania and depression, or he may remain in only one state. As Table 3.1 shows, depressive disorders, which make up about 6 percent of institutionalized patients, are far less frequently diagnosed than schizophrenia. One should note, however, that depression is more frequently diagnosed among the well-to-do and, since the data in Table 3.1 come from public facilities whose patients come mostly from the lower classes, the total proportion of depressive disorders may be underrepresented while the total proportion of schizophrenia may be overrepresented. We will return to this point shortly when we discuss explanations of mental disorder.

The remaining subcategories of functional disorders cover a very broad range of behaviors which are diagnosed to affect only a small percentage of institutionalized mental patients. Personality disorders may be diagnosed for behaviors ranging from stuttering and nail biting to aggressive, antisocial acts like arson or murder. Psychophysiologic disorders include conditions that affect single organ systems such as weight loss, cramps, asthma, and other physical problems which are caused by emotional upset. Transient situational personality disorders are reactions to extreme situations such as a major disaster. Finally, childhood and early adolescent disorders include behavioral problems specific to this age category.

THE DISTRIBUTION OF MENTAL DISORDERS

Counting Cases

Our discussion of the types of mental disorders and their institutionalized rates should not leave the impression that we have accurately estimated the extent of mental disorder in the U.S. To begin, while the diagnostic categories may appear exhaustive and mutually exclusive in the abstract, in practice psychiatric diagnosis has been shown to be weak in reliability and validity. In one review of six studies that compared the agreement rates of psychiatric diagnosis, agreement on the diagnosis varied from 56 to 88 percent (Conover, 1972). In another well-known study by Rosenhan (1973) eight sane people gained admission to psychiatric hospitals by faking minor, nondescript symptoms.

In each case the pseudopatient was diagnosed as schizophrenic and after admission each gave no further evidence of symptoms. The eight remained hospitalized an average of nineteen days until discharged with a diagnosis of schizophrenia "in remission." In no case was the pseudopatient discovered by the hospital staff and, in a subsequent experiment, it was demonstrated that members of the hospital staff's would frequently identify genuine patients as pseudopatients when told that a pseudopatient would attempt to gain admission.

To discover the extent of mental disorder in a population then, one must first evaluate the problem of unreliable, invalid diagnosis. No definite solution exists to counter this difficulty. The best one can usually do is to examine carefully the criteria that were used to determine a case to see how closely they conform to one's own working definition.

Researchers have long recognized that institutionalized patients in mental hospitals do not account for the total number of people afflicted with mental disorders in a population. Restricting the definition of a case to patients admitted to institutionalized psychiatric treatment excludes those who may have symptoms but who have not received care. An extensive psychiatric survey of midtown Manhattan showed that only about one fourth of those judged to resemble psychiatric cases had ever been in treatment (Srole et al, 1962, p. 147). Furthermore, the use of treatment facilities varies with their availability and public attitudes toward their use (Dohrenwend & Dohrenwend, 1969, pp. 5–7). Thus, while enumeration of treated cases is important for planning psychiatric services, institutionalized patient census data do not estimate accurately the occurrence or distribution of mental disorders throughout a population. For information on the "true" prevalence of mental disorder we must turn to surveys of general populations or communities designed to uncover untreated cases.

A review of 24 North American "true" prevalence studies in both rural and urban areas (Dohrenwend, 1975) leads to unsettling conclusions about our ability to grasp the overall extent of functional psychiatric disorder. In some communities, rates of less than two percent were reported while in others the rates exceeded 50%. Analysis reveals that these vast differences are due primarily to contrasting data collection procedures, especially definitions of what constitutes a case of psychiatric disorder. In the end, the "true" prevalence of mental disorders remains an elusive statistic clouded by methodological inconsistency in definitions and data collection. It is, however, safe to conclude that only a portion of treatable psychiatric cases in a population ever receive treatment and, therefore, statistics based on institutionalized rates underestimate the true prevalence of mental disorder.

SOCIOCULTURAL FACTORS AND MENTAL DISORDER

Age

In most studies which report the relationship between age and rates of mental disorder, the young have shown the lowest rates of psychopathology. This fairly clear pattern of findings with regard to minimum rates of disorder is not matched by an equally definitive age at which maximum rates of mental disorder are likely. In an exhaustive review of evidence (Dohrenwend & Dohrenwend, 1969), it was found that in twenty-four different studies the maximum rates of mental disorder were reported five times in adolescence, twelve times in the middle years, and seven times in the oldest group.

A further analysis of results by age for psychosis, neurosis, and personality disorders does not add any more useful information. No age group consistently shows a higher rate for any of these types of mental disorder. While some very specific types, such as senile psychosis in the elderly, are obviously related to age, we can conclude that no consistent relationship between age and mental disorder emerges from current findings.

Sex

Comparisons of numerous studies reveal no consistent sex differences in rates of functional psychoses (Dohrenwend & Dohrenwend, 1976). Overall, men and women are equally prone to mental disorders in general, and they appear to be similarly susceptible to being diagnosed schizophrenic. There are, however, differences between men and women on other major subtypes. Manic–depressive psychosis is generally higher among women as are rates of neurosis. In contrast, rates of personality disorder are consistently higher for men.

In their discussion of these findings, Dohrenwend and Dohrenwend raise an important issue for future research.

> These results cannot easily be explained by role theories arguing that at some time and place one or the other sex is under great stress and, hence, more prone to psychiatric disorder in general. Instead, the findings suggest that we should discard undifferentiated, unidimensional concepts of psychiatric disorder and with them false questions about whether women or men are more prone to "mental illness." In their place we would substitute an issue posed by the relatively high female rates of neurosis and manic–depressive psychosis, with their possible common

denominator of depressive symptomatology, and the relatively high male rates of personality disorders with their possible common denominator of irresponsible and antisocial behavior. The important question then becomes, What is there in the endowments and experiences of men and women that pushes them in these different deviant directions? (1976, p. 453)

Race

Relatively few studies allow for comparison between white and black rates of mental disorder. The evidence from eight studies which do permit analysis of the data by race show no consistent pattern at all. Four studies reported higher rates for whites and an equal number reported higher rates for blacks (Dohrenwend & Dohrenwend, 1969). Neither race is more prone to mental disorder.

Rural–Urban Settings

Many people suppose that, due to the stresses and pressures of urban life, mental disorder is more prevalent in cities than rural areas. This belief is further enhanced by the fact that rates of *hospitalized* mental disorder are greater in urban areas. Yet, recall that rates of institutionalized disorder probably reflect the availability of treatment facilities and community attitudes toward abnormal behavior more than the true prevalence of disorder in the general population. For example, researchers have found that rural populations are more resistant to use of treatment facilities and are more apt to retain in the community a person who behaves oddly (Eaton & Weil, 1955; Mott & Roemer, 1948; Eaton, 1974).

The evidence from community surveys attempting to estimate true prevalence in rural and urban settings shows that urban rates tend to be higher, but only slightly so. More interesting are the findings for subtypes of disorder. Manic–depressive psychoses appear to be clearly more prevalent in rural areas; schizophrenia, personality disorder, and neurosis rates are higher in urban settings. Explanations for these differences are suggested when we subsequently discuss sociological theories of mental disorder. The evidence must be considered cautiously, however, because no studies have adequately accounted for the possibility that higher urban rates might be due, in part, to migrants from rural to urban areas who bring with them certain types of psychopathology.

Social Class

No finding in psychiatric epidemiology is more consistent and clear-cut than the highest rates of overall mental disorder appearing in the lowest social class. The most widely cited study confirming this relationship is Hollingshead and Redlich's 1950 survey of *Social Class and Mental Illness* (1958) in New Haven, Connecticut. Using a five-step index of social class comprised of a person's area of residence, occupation, and education, they analyzed all patients in public and private psychiatric hospitals plus all who were undergoing treatment but were not institutionalized. In the general population the lowest social class (Class V) made up about 18% of the total, but about 38% of the patients were in this social class. Seriousness of the mental disorder was also related to social class in the New Haven study. As Figure 3.2 shows, neurosis is far more likely to be the diagnosis for patients in the two higher classes (I and II) and psychosis is the more frequent type in the lower classes.

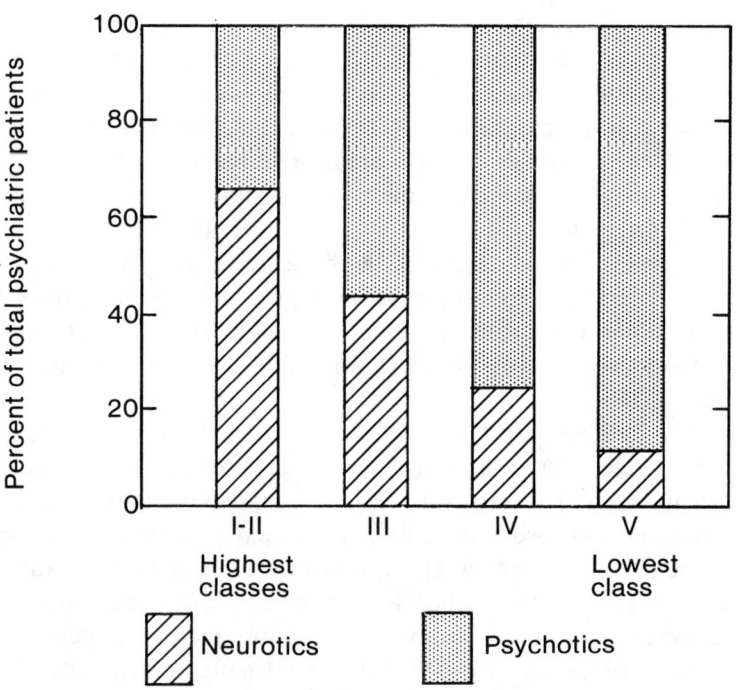

Percentage of Neurotics and Psychotics among Total Psychiatric Patients—by Class (Age and Sex Adjusted).

FIGURE 3.2. CLASS POSITION AND TYPES OF MENTAL ILLNESS
Source: Adapted from Hollingshead and Redlich, 1958, p. 223.

Certain aspects of Hollingshead and Redlich's findings are replicated using more recent national data on the incidence of admissions to public and private psychiatric hospitals.[1] As one examines Table 3.2 it seems reasonable to assume that public hospitals are more likely to receive patients from the lower social classes while private hospitals will handle more affluent patients. Concordant with the 1950 data from New Haven, all of the organic disorders, especially those associated with alcohol, are more frequently diagnosed in public institutions while depressive disorders and neuroses are higher among private psychiatric patients. Schizophrenia is also the more likely diagnosis in public institutions.

True prevalence studies of noninstitutionalized populations also agree with the evidence presented above. A review of these studies (Dohrenwend, 1975) reveals that:

The highest rates of overall psychiatric disorder have been consistently found in the lowest social class.

The highest rates of schizophrenia and personality disorders are generally found in the lowest social class.

The rates of neurosis and manic–depressive psychosis are not as consistent, but there is a tendency for these disorders to be more prevalent in the higher social classes.

TABLE 3.2. TOTAL ADMISSIONS TO STATE AND COUNTY MENTAL HOSPITAL INPATIENT SERVICES AND TOTAL ADMISSIONS TO PRIVATE MENTAL HOSPITAL INPATIENT SERVICES BY PRIMARY DIAGNOSIS, UNITED STATES, 1975 (%)

Diagnostic category	State and county mental hospitals	Private mental hospitals
Organic		
Organic brain syndromes	5.3	4.0
Alcoholic disorders	27.7	8.3
Drug disorders	3.7	2.4
Functional disorders		
Schizophrenia	33.6	21.8
Depressive disorders	11.7	42.5
Personality disorders	6.8	5.1
Neuroses	1.5	5.6
All others	9.7	10.3
Total	100.0%	100.0%
(N)	(385,237)	(129,832)

Source: Adapted from Rosenstein and Milazzo-Sayre (1981; pp. 46–47).

In sum, then, the evidence shows that:

1. There is no consistent relationship between age and overall rates of mental disorder.
2. Men and women are equally prone to mental disorder. However, women have higher rates of affective disorders and neuroses while men consistently have higher rates of personality disorders.
3. There is no relationship between race and rates of mental disorder.
4. Rates of mental disorder tend to be slightly higher in urban areas. Schizophrenia, personality disorder, and neuroses rates are higher in urban areas while depressive psychosis rates are higher in rural areas.
5. Overall, the highest rates of mental disorder are in the lower class. Lower-class patients are more likely to be diagnosed as schizophrenic or as having personality disorders while higher class patients are more likely to be diagnosed as depressive or neurotic.

EXPLANATIONS OF MENTAL DISORDER

Nature Versus Nurture: The Genetics-Environment Issue

There is undeniable, impressive evidence pointing to the role of heredity in the etiology (the causation) of mental disorders. In early studies of schizophrenia by a geneticist, it was found that over 68 percent of children whose parents were both schizophrenic later developed schizophrenia (Kallman, 1938). If only one parent was schizophrenic, the chances dropped to about one in six and the odds continued to decline as schizophrenic relatives became more distant (Kallman, 1946). Subsequent genealogical studies (Book, 1953) and investigations of twins (Gottesman & Schields, 1972; Heston, 1966) add further to the evidence of hereditary factors even when social conditions in the home of schizophrenic parents have been controlled in the research design. Although less extensive, there is support for the role of genetics in other types of psychoses, neuroses, and personality disorders (Essen-Moller, 1965).

Whereas at one time the genetics-environment issue centered on the either-or question of which one was *the* cause of mental disorder, most investigators now agree that a person's genetic endowment and his or her social experiences in the environment interact in precipitating mental disorder. Certain genotypes clearly appear to be more prone to disorders, but the actual occurrence of psychopathology in the individual's life also depends upon environmental factors. Still to be settled are questions about the relative weight of heredity or the environment, especially differences in various types of mental disorders, and questions about precisely how the genetic transmission operates and is stimulated to produce disorders.

Social Disorganization: The Ecological Approach

A pioneering sociological study called *Mental Disorders in Urban Areas* was published in 1939 by Faris and Dunham. They collected data on admissions to all public and private mental hospitals in Chicago and then plotted on maps the rates of mental disorder for various areas of the city. Using this "ecological" technique they discovered, as in Figure 3.3, that overall rates of mental disorder were highest in the poor, transient areas near the center of the city and the rates declined as one moved out to the more affluent, stable suburbs. This is, of course, consistent with the findings of subsequent researchers already presented in our discussion of social class. Perhaps more important than the basic empirical findings are the issues Faris and Dunham raised as they posed possible explanations for their results. The alternatives they offer remain fundamental concerns in the sociology of mental disorder and, indeed, the entire field of deviant behavior.

In any study it is possible that the findings one observes happened by chance. Thus, Faris and Dunham first confront the alternative that the distribution of rates they found in Chicago was a peculiar occurrence. However, based on evidence from another city and the degree and consistency of differences, they reject the *chance hypothesis*. As we have noted, the weight of almost all studies since supports their rejection of this alternative.

The second possibility, called the *selection hypothesis,* states "that the patterns of rate distribution represent only a concentration of cases of mental disorder which have been institutionalized because of poverty" (p. 161). It could be that mental disorders are really evenly distributed throughout all areas of the city, but only the poor, because they are relatively powerless, are institutionalized. The suggestion has also been made that the visibility of and tolerance for bizarre behavior varies among different communities making institutionalization more likely in some than in others. Faris and Dunham reject the selection hypothesis on the grounds that they managed to cover most cases in their survey of both public and private hospitals. However, the selection hypothesis remains a viable alternative favored by many sociologists today. In fact, Dunham (1964) displays considerable scientific

100 UNDERSTANDING DEVIANCE AND CONTROL

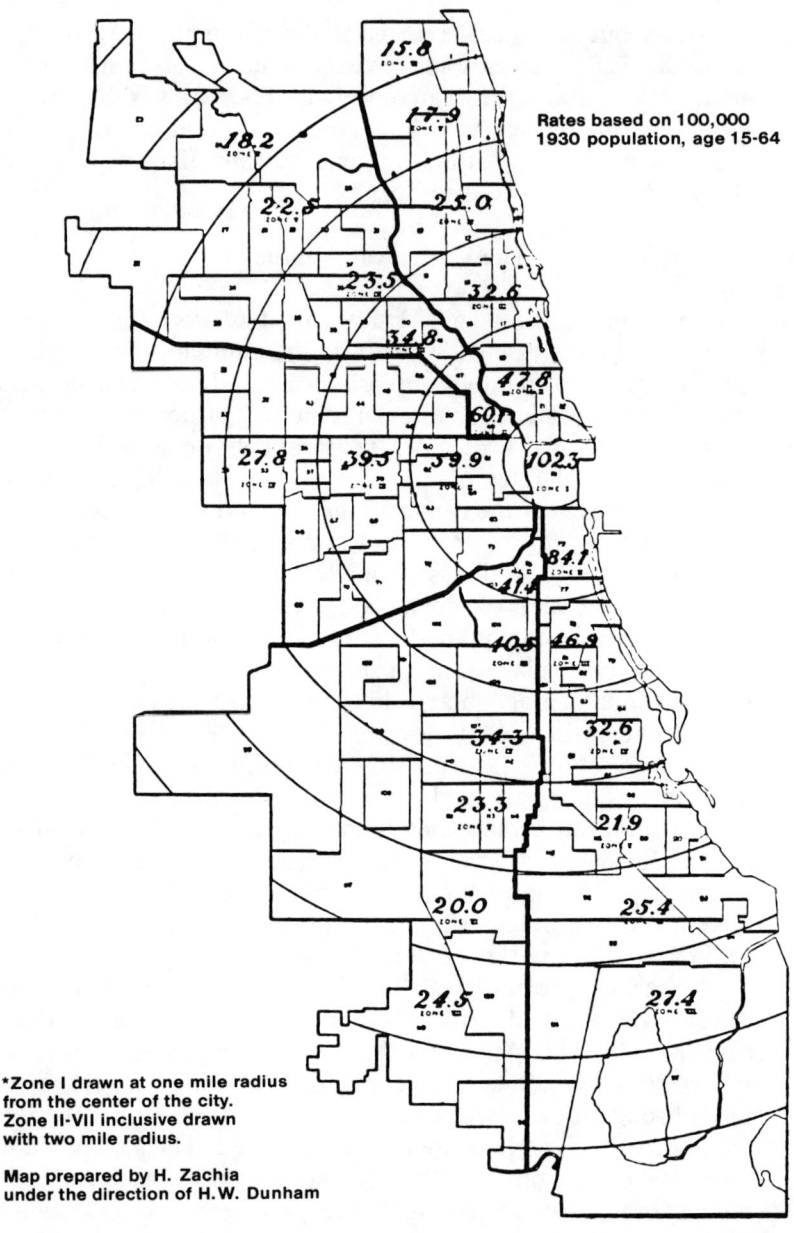

FIGURE 3.3. SUB-COMMUNITIES BASED ON CENSUS TRACTS OF CHICAGO

Insanity Average Rates, 1922-1934.
By Zones and Divisions of the City.

Source: Adapted from Faris and Dunham, 1939, p. 53.

integrity when critiquing his own classic work and, reversing his earlier position, declares the likely validity of the selection hypothesis. The selection hypothesis continues to provide a focus for contemporary theoretical debate (Dohrenwend, 1975).

Faris and Dunham next considered the *drift hypothesis.*

> An interpretation frequently made of the concentration in the center of the city of insanity rates, and the schizophrenic rates particularly, is that persons who are mentally abnormal fail in their economic life and consequently drift down into the slum areas because they are not able to compete satisfactorily with others (p. 163).

A more recent variation suggests that in a society where upward mobility is highly valued, the healthy and competent are able to work their way out of the slum leaving behind a residue of less able people among whom a relatively high proportion have psychiatric disorders. While Faris and Dunham rejected the drift hypothesis in their 1939 study because it appeared that most cases of mental disorder were not downwardly mobile but instead had been long-term residents of lower-class areas, the drift hypothesis—especially its residue variation—remains an alternative today favored by some theorists.

The possibility finally accepted by Faris and Dunham is the *social and life conditions* or *stress* hypothesis. Stated in its more general form, the greater stress and strains of life in the lower class are assumed to increase the chances for mental breakdown and thus caused the higher rates of mental disorder in the central city. More specifically, they hypothesize that in socially disorganized parts of the city interpersonal contacts are most likely to be disrupted which, in turn, leads to greater social isolation and higher rates of schizophrenia. Because rates of manic-depressive psychoses do not decrease as one moves out from the city's center, it is suggested that the etiology of this disorder, in contrast to schizophrenia, might be found in extremely intimate and intense social contacts more characteristic of rural settings. A later study (Eaton & Weil, 1955) of the Hutterites—a very close-knit, communal, family-oriented, rural sect living in the northwestern United States and southwestern Canada—revealed unexpectedly high rates of depression, thus supporting this hypothesis.

Having begun their study in Chicago and strongly influenced by social disorganization theorists located there, it is not surprising that Faris and Dunham concluded by favoring the social and life conditions hypothesis. It best reflects the social disorganization tradition of which they were a part. However, each of the alternatives they raised remains a viable explanation and provides the stimulus for much research and theoretical debate today. Whenever evaluating the results and interpretations from any study of rates of mental disorder, or any deviant behavior, one should carefully consider the applicability of the *selection, drift* or *stress* hypotheses.

Social Structural Strain

Condition of the Economy. As we have seen, the highest rates of mental disorder generally are found in the lower socioeconomic strata of American society. If one accepts the stress hypothesis, it seems reasonable to propose that some of the unique conditions of lower-class life eventually lead to greater mental disorder. Following this line of reasoning, sociologist M. Harvey Brenner has conducted several studies exploring the hypothesis that as the state of the economy worsens, rates of mental hospitalization will increase. An analysis of the relationship between the employment index and fluctuations in mental hospital admissions rates in New York over a 127-year period supported the hypothesis (Brenner, 1973). Periods of low employment were consistently followed by higher rates of mental hospital admissions.

A subsequent study using national data from 1940 to 1973 showed that increases in the unemployment rate were followed by increases in mental hospital admissions (Brenner, 1976). Using a sophisticated technique for making estimates, Brenner concludes that a one percent increase in the unemployment rate sustained over a period of six years has been associated (during the past three decades) with an increase of over 4,000 state mental hospital admissions (pp. 5–6).

While the basic relation that mental hospitalization will increase during economic downturns and decrease during upturns seems irrefutable, how that relation should be interpreted is open to question. Brenner's own theory is similar to the stress and social life conditions explanation of Faris and Dunham. Brenner states:

> This hypothesis assumes that social disorganization, reflected in turn in symptoms and intolerance of deviance, will result from the inability of individuals to perform socially designated roles. Inability to fulfill one's social role frequently results from downward shifts in economic activity, during which more people are losing than are gaining income, prestige, and power. The economy provides the fundamental means whereby the individual fulfills the majority of his aspirations, as well as the more immediate social obligations he faces. His inability to maintain his usual or intended life-style and social position indicates that he is unable to meet the requirements of other people who form the network of his social relations, responsibilities, and requirements. (1973, p. 11)

Nevertheless, Brenner's use of the term "intolerance of deviance" in the above quote suggests that the *selection hypothesis* is also a plausible explanation. The selection hypothesis implies that higher hospital admission rates following economic downturns occur because admission standards change or unusually high frustration is directed at those who behave oddly. Brenner also notes, correctly, that the state of the economy has considerable impact on people's abilities to fulfill their aspirations—particularly those associated with improving their social status. This idea relates closely to anomie theory which focuses on the possible effects of a discrepancy between people's aspirations and the avenues open for achieving them.

Anomie. In his famous essay "Social Structure and Anomie," Robert K. Merton (1938) shows how social conditions exert pressure on certain people to engage in deviant behavior. Briefly, he argues that anomie (or normlessness) arises when a culture encourages its members to value goals which they are actually unable to attain under its accepted laws or norms. Thus, anomie is present when members of the lower class are constantly informed through the popular culture that material rewards such as home ownership and fancy cars are positively valued, while at the same time experience tells them that the legitimate means for achieving these goals, such as good educations and well-paying jobs, are not readily accessible to them. A likely result of this anomic condition—the discrepancy between means and ends—is for individuals to maintain their desires to achieve the culturally valued goals but to reject the legitimate means for achieving them in favor of illegitimate ones. Merton labels the adaptation to this situation "innovation," which in fact usually amounts to what we more commonly call crime.

In contrast to innovation, Merton refers to mental disorders as a "retreatist" form of adaptation. Retreatist behavior is also likely when a person desires culturally valued goals but is denied the means to attain them—a situation which calls for "innovative" rule breaking to reach the goals. But what if a person has so thoroughly internalized prohibitions against breaking the law that he or she simply cannot illegally "innovate"? In this case the individual is trapped in a double bind. They desire the goals but neither legitimate nor illegitimate means are available. The result, says Merton, is a rejection of *both* the culturally valued goals and the legitimate means. The person escapes the conflict of discrepant goals and means by retreating into the alien, privatized world of psychosis. Thus, Merton conceives mental disorder as an escapist adaptation akin to chronic drunkenness, drug addiction, isolation, or the ultimate retreat, suicide.

Subsequent studies (Kleiner & Parker, 1963), guided by Merton's insights, show that psychopathological groups usually have larger discrepancies between achievements and aspirations than normal control groups. Indeed, Parker and Kleiner (1966) found that the discrepancy between aspirations and achievements, which they called goal–striving stress, was significantly higher in the institutionalized mentally ill population than in the community population; higher among psychotic patients than neurotics; and higher among people in the community with a greater incidence of psychoneurotic symptoms.

It appears than when avenues to achievement are blocked, the resulting frustration may become manifest in greater incidence of mental disorder. There is some evidence that depression is the type of disorder most likely to arise from blocked opportunities. Linsky (1969) designed a study to explore the relationship between depression and opportunities available for occupational success relative to aspirations. He found that depression was highest in communities where relative opportunities were the least. He concludes that "It appears that chronic stress attendant on life in communities with opportunity structures incapable of satisfying the aspirations of the residents increases the frequency of depression" (p. 131).

Family Dynamics

As noted in our brief discussion of the role of heredity in the cause of mental disorders, there is some evidence that people who develop mental disorders are more likely to have a psychopathological parent. Those favoring genetic transmission theory accept these findings as support for their position. Alternatively, some theorists suggest that the higher incidence of mental disorders among children from a home in which a parent is mentally ill may be due to maladaptive patterns of adjustment learned in this situation. For example, in his analyses of how people in families interact, British psychiatrist R. D. Laing (1969) shows how patterns of interaction and methods of dealing with everyday problems seem to be learned and passed on from parents to children. Therefore, in addition to genetic transmission in families he raises the equally plausible possibility of social–psychological transmission through socialization.

Other researchers have found certain modes of socialization which seem to be especially prevalent among those who are later diagnosed as schizophrenics. Parents, especially the mother, tend to be unstable, domineering, and demanding (Weinberg, 1967). Myers and Roberts (1959) found that patients had close attachments to the parents of the opposite sex, but hostile relationships to parents of the same sex. There is not clear evidence that mental disorder is related to birth order of children in the family. However, the preschizophrenic child tends to be isolated from other siblings because of age, physique, or some other factors. While tendencies such as these appear, there is no single family type or pattern of socialization which inevitably produces or inhibits the later development of psychopathology.

The picture of family dynamics given us by researchers who have studied families in which one member develops schizophrenia portrays an overwhelming series of difficulties which exceed the person's ability to cope. In their study of poor families in San Juan, Puerto Rico, Rogler and Hollingshead (1965) describe the interrelated crises the schizophrenic persons experienced during the 12 months preceding the perceived onset of the disorder.

> Systematic comparisons of the six types of perceived personal problems reported by the sick persons (and families) with those of the well persons (and families) demonstrate that each of the diagnostic family types in the sick group encountered many more problems than the well families during the problematic year. There are more economic difficulties and more severe physical deprivation in the sick than in the well families. There are far more interspouse conflicts among the sick families than the control families; difficulties with members of the extended family are more frequent and more severe. The sick families report more quarrels and fights with their neighbors. There are more physical illnesses in the schizophrenic families. Finally, more sick persons than well persons, male as well as female, note a disparity between their own perception of the difficulties they encountered and the ways they think their spouses viewed these same problems. Stated otherwise, the schizophrenic men and women think their spouses do not understand the personal difficulties they face, as well as the men and women in the control group do. In general, the person who is diagnosed as suffering from schizophrenia perceives himself as bombarded by a multiplicity of personal and family problems he is not able to handle. The behavioral evidence shows, however, that he struggles to solve them by every means available to him. (pp. 409–410)

It is difficult to say with assurance which of these difficulties are causes and which are consequences of the mental disorder. However the authors of this study do feel that in contrast to childhood and adolescent experiences, "a rash of insoluble, mutually reinforcing problems" which trap the person in the period prior to onset of the disorder clearly distinguish those who become schizophrenic.

Despite serious problems which arise in the family because of failure on the part of a disturbed person successfully to perform his or her social roles, family members have been found to be remarkably resistant to seeking professional help (Yarrow et al., 1955). Thus, while in certain cases family dynamics may contribute to the precipitation of mental disorder, at the same time families frequently have a very high tolerance for deviance which permits them to avoid contact with professionals until the disturbed person's behavior becomes very disruptive to family life (Sampson et al., 1962).

Labeling

A contemporary sociological theory of mental disorder introduced by Scheff in his book *Being Mentally Ill* (1966) has generated much controversy and debate. Scheff states that there is very little verified theory about the causes of functional mental disorders and that a major deficiency in most current explanations is a failure sufficiently to incorporate the role of social processes. Scheff's goal is to explain stable, recurring, functional mental disorders—as opposed to isolated, idiosyncratic episodes or organic pathology—by emphasizing the effects of the reaction of others on a person's odd behavior.

The theory begins by defining mental illness in terms of rule-breaking behavior. Many kinds of rule-breaking in our culture are given specific labels such as crime, perversion, drunkenness, and the like. However, there are numerous other forms of rule-breaking which have no explicit label. Frequently, this type of rule-breaking involves violation of everyday norms which define how to courteously interact and get along with others. Thus, while constantly interrupting the conversation of others, or refusing to speak when spoken to, may not be against the law, such actions do constitute a form of rule-breaking behavior. Odd, annoying behavior of this sort Scheff calls *residual rule-breaking*. He argues further that much of what commonly becomes labeled mental illness falls into the category of residual rule-breaking. Put another way, residual rule-breaking, under certain circumstances, may be defined by others as symptomatic of mental illness.

The nine propositions of Scheff's theory follow with a brief example of the sort of evidence which seems to support them.

1. *Residual rule-breaking arises from fundamentally diverse sources.* People may violate everyday interaction norms for many reasons. Scheff discusses four: organic (e.g., drug ingestion or lack of food or sleep), psychological (e.g., childhood trauma or peculiar upbringing), external stress (e.g., battle fatigue, disaster, or exam period) and volitional acts of innovation or defiance (e.g., "avant-garde" works of art or civil disobedience). It is important to bear in mind that the precise reasons why residual rule-breaking first occurs are less important to Scheff's theory than how others do or do not react to it.

2. *Relative to the rate of treated mental illness, the rate of unrecorded residual rule-breaking is extremely high.* Many people who engage in residual rule-breaking are never labeled mentally ill either by themselves or others. Odd behaviors such as withdrawal, aggressiveness, or hallucinations often go unrecognized, ignored, or rationalized. Furthermore, there is evidence, such as that we have already discussed, that communities frequently contain many "psychiatrically impaired" persons who have never been hospitalized or treated.
3. *Most residual rule-breaking is "denied" and is of transitory significance.* This proposition is closely linked to the preceeding one. When someone behaves strangely in the dorm it might be rationalized as due to the stress of exams. The behavior passes and not much is made of it. The behavior does not form the basis for the person becoming labeled mentally ill. The critical question for the rest of the theory is: Under what conditions does residual rule-breaking become officially labeled mentally illness?
4. *Stereotyped imagery of mental disorder is learned in early childhood.* Underlying this proposition is the assumption that being mentally ill is a social role which can be learned and imitated like any other role such as that of mother, father, or teacher. Evidence for this assumption may be often seen among children in school yards who are apt to "play crazy" just as they "play house."
5. *The stereotypes of insanity are continually reaffirmed, inadvertently, in ordinary social interaction.* Mental disorder as depicted in the media is generally an image of violence, bizarre facial expressions or physical movements, and incoherent speech. Negative references such as "Ex-Mental Patient Kills Six" frequently appear as headlines or in news broadcasts. Even our everyday speech is laced with clichés ("You're nuts," "Are you out of your mind?") which reinforce stereotyped images of insanity.
6. *Labeled deviants may be rewarded for playing the stereotyped deviant role.* Once a patient, a person often gets positive reactions when displaying insight into the causes of the illness during psychiatric interviews. This is not unlike the notion that "The first step to a 'cure' is to recognize that you are sick." Patients who thoroughly subordinate themselves to the hospital officials and staff—patients who make the least trouble and keep their place—are apt to receive the most favorable, albeit condescending, responses.

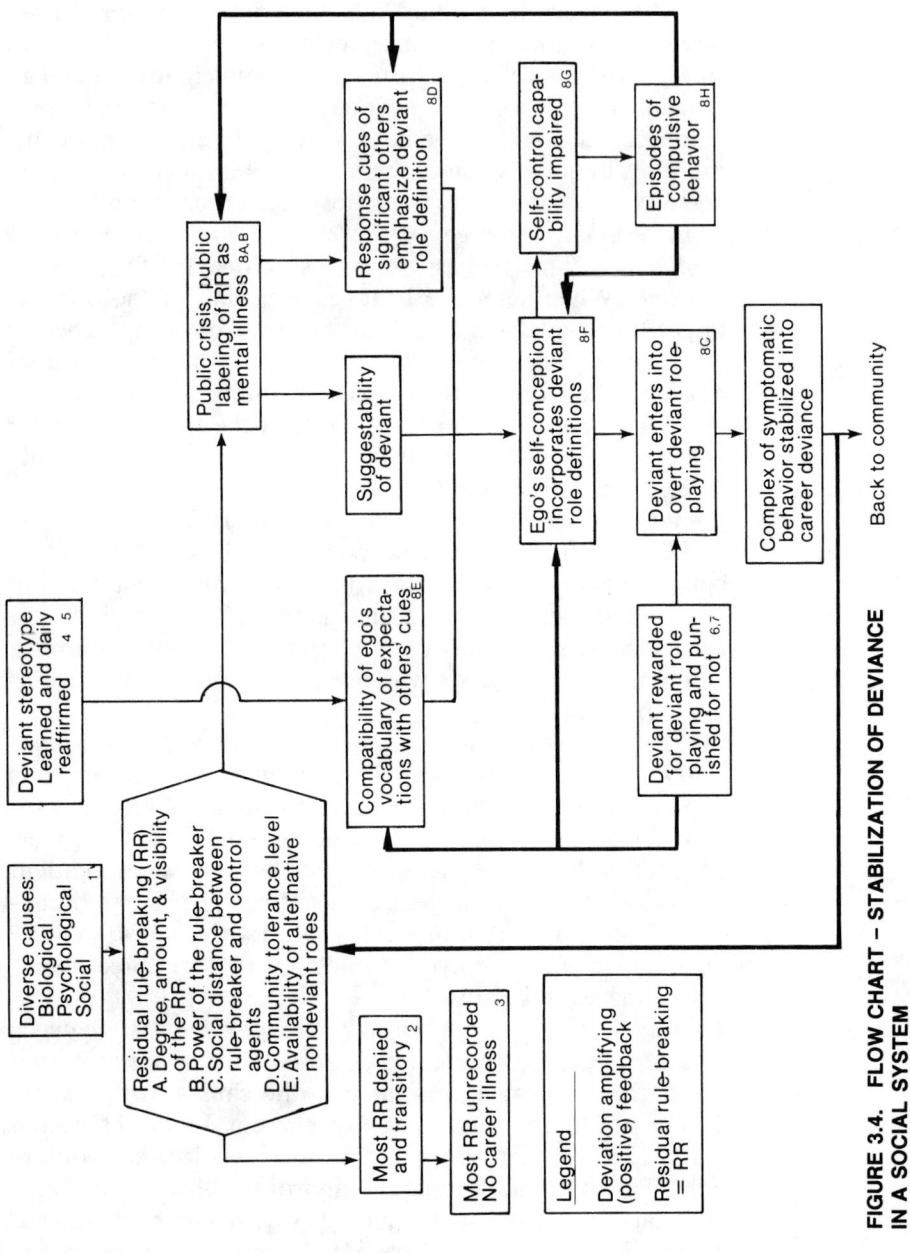

FIGURE 3.4. FLOW CHART – STABILIZATION OF DEVIANCE IN A SOCIAL SYSTEM

Source: Adapted from Scheff, 1966, p. 100.

7. *Labeled deviants are punished when they attempt to return to conventional roles.* The stigma of being an "ex-mental patient," regardless of past diagnosis and treatment or present condition, is a difficult burden. Prior mental hospitalization virtually guarantees that one will be rejected for certain jobs. The most publicized case in recent history is the dropping of Senator Thomas Eagleton from the 1972 Democratic vice-presidential ticket after his brief period of mental hospitalization several years before became public knowledge.
8. *In the crisis occurring when a residual rule-breaker is publicly labeled, the deviant is highly suggestible, and may accept the proffered role of the insane as the only alternative.* Most people become confused, anxious, and easily manipulated when under a great deal of stress. Imagine your own feelings when you are unexpectedly called upon in class. Magnify these feelings to suit the gravity of an accusation that you are out of your mind. At this point you may very well begin to agree with the accusation as you begin to experience more anxiety, confusion, and loss of self-control.
9. *Among residual rule-breakers, labeling is the single most important cause of residual deviance.* Put otherwise, this proposition states that the labeling reaction of others to residual rule-breaking is the most critical factor in a person being viewed by others and himself as mentally ill.

In Scheff's theory, the likelihood of being labeled a mental patient depends upon how severe the societal reaction is to the residual rule-breaking. The severity of the societal reaction depends on: (1) the degree, amount, and visibility of the rule-breaking; (2) the power of the rule-breaker and the social distance between him and agents of social control (police, doctors, psychiatrists); and (3) the tolerance level of the community and the availability in the culture of the community of alternative nondeviant roles which help to rationalize residual rule-breaking.

Figure 3.4 is designed to show the relationships among the propositions of the theory. It begins in the upper left-hand corner with residual rule-breaking arising from diverse causes (proposition 1). While most residual rule-breaking is denied and transitory (proposition 3) you can follow the sequence of events proposed to occur when public labeling (proposition 9) does take place. Note that some of the relationships take the form of a vicious circle. For example, in the lower right-hand corner of the chart, as the person begins to believe himself deviant (8F), becomes anxious, loses self-control (8G), and engages in episodes of compulsive behavior (8H) which in turn reinforce his own developing belief that he is indeed deviant. Similar "deviation-amplifying feedback" loops can be seen at various points in the diagram.

Labeling theory does, of course, have its detractors. Following a lengthy, detailed survey of the present evidence which bears on Scheff's propositions, Gove (1975) reaches the following conclusion.

> The labeling perspective does not view the deviant as someone who is suffering from an intrapersonal disorder, but instead as someone who, through a set of circumstances, becomes publicly labeled a deviant and who is forced by societal reaction into a deviant role. In essence, they view the deviant as someone who is victimized. The available evidence, however, indicates that the societal reaction formulation of how a person becomes mentally ill is substantially incorrect. There is very little evidence of victimization. The evidence shows that a substantial majority have a serious disorder quite apart from any secondary deviance that may be associated with the mentally ill role. Furthermore, persons in the community do not view as mentally ill someone who happens to act in a bizarre fashion. On the contrary, they persist in denying mental illness until the situation becomes intolerable. Even after prospective patients come into contact with public officials, a substantial screening occurs, presumably sorting out persons who are being railroaded or who are less disturbed. It is only in the last stages of the commitment process that some ritualization appears to occur, and even here a discernible proportion of persons is sorted out. Perhaps the most telling evidence is that, to the extent to which the individual societal attributes do seem to have an effect on the hospitalization process, their effect is in the opposite direction from that posited by the labeling perspective—that is, controlling for level of disorder, it is the individuals with the most resources who are the most likely to enter the role of the mentally ill. The evidence also indicates that the societal reaction theorists have overstated the degree to which secondary deviance is associated with mental hospitalization: (1) there appear to be many restitutive processes associated with hospitalization, (2) patients treated in the modern mental hospital typically do not spend enough time in the hospital to become truly institutionalized, and (3) in most cases the stigma of having been a former mental patient does not appear to greatly affect one's performance in the community. In summary, the studies reviewed, while in no way denying the existence of the processes outlined by the labeling theorists, suggest that mental hospitalization, in our present society, does not typically lead to a prolonged occupancy of the mentally ill role. Furthermore, the available evidence indicates that, when former patients continue to have difficulties, these difficulties are generally due to the person's confronting a troubled situation or to some psychiatric disorder, and not to the social expectations of others. (pp. 67–68)

Central to Gove's critique is the idea that both public attitudes toward mental illness and approaches to institutionalization and treatment have changed considerably since the 1950s. Scheff's theory was developed on the basis of data from this period and, while the evidence appeared to support its propositions then, there is far less support today. With this in mind, we can turn to a brief discussion of public reaction to mental disorders.

REACTIONS TO MENTAL DISORDER

Public Attitudes

Studies of attitudes toward mental disorders have attempted to measure public knowledge of various aspects of mental illness, responses to statements about the mentally ill, and the desire to maintain social distance from the mentally ill. The earliest of these studies seem to indicate that fear, stigmatization, and rejection characterized public feeling about the mentally ill and knowledge about types of mental disorder; optimism about treatment, and opinions of psychiatrists were quite low (Star, 1955, 1961; Bingham, 1951). Two other well-known studies done during the 1950s, one in Canada (Cumming & Cumming, 1957) and the one in the United States (Nunnally, 1961) concluded that public attitudes were dominated by denial, isolation, and insulation of mental illness and that the public was largely uninformed about mental illness. The Nunnally study included a large scale content analysis of television, radio, newspapers, and magazines which demonstrated that mental patients were heavily stereotyped as dangerous and unpredictable. This study was very influential in support of Scheff's postulate about the stereotyped imagery of mental disorders.

Subsequent studies have generally reported greater public knowledge and more positive public attitudes toward mental illness. Summarizing this research, Gove (1975) says,

> For example, recent research shows that persons are now more knowledgeable about mental illness and are better able to identify the mentally ill (see Spiro et al., 1973; Crocetti et al., 1974, for a review of the evidence). Furthermore, as Aviram and Segal (1973, p. 127) and Crocetti et al. (1974) have shown, there has been a consistent decline over time in the extent to which the mentally ill are rejected. Most striking is the finding by Simmons (1969, p. 33) that, among 13 types of deviance, ex-mental patients were less likely to be rejected than eleven of the other types, including atheists, gamblers, beatniks, alcoholics, and adulterers. In fact, the only category of deviance that was even less likely to be

rejected was intellectualism. Thus, although the data from the 50s support the societal reaction view that those perceived as mentally ill are excluded from social interaction, the recent evidence suggests that this view now rests on a questionable empirical base. (pp. 38–39)

MENTAL HOSPITALS

In American society mental hospitalization has very different effects upon those who experience it from those felt by people who are hospitalized for physical illness. One need only recognize that when talking about a general hospital there are no equivalents to the terms "booby hatch," "nut house," or "funny farm" popularly used to describe mental institutions. Moreover, the patients in mental hospitals are frequently placed in them involuntarily. For example, in 1972 about 42% of the 404,000 patients admitted to state and county mental hospitals were involuntary commitments (Mitchell, 1975). Sociological interest in mental institutions seems to stem primarily from the stigmatizing effects they have on both inmates and staff combined with difficult multiple goals of custody, treatment, and rehabilitation.

Erving Goffman (1961) has described the mental hospital as a "total institution" similar in many important respects to prisons, bootcamps, boarding schools, or monasteries. The key fact of total institutions is "the handling of many human needs by the bureaucratic organization of whole blocks of people" (p. 6). Total institutions are "total" because they become virtually the entire physical and social environment for their inmates. Thus, the total institution is "a social hybrid, part residential community, part formal organization" (p. 12). As a total institution in the business of processing people, the mental hospital is characterized by a bureaucratic structure of its staff, great social distance separating the staff and patients, and, all too frequently, depersonalization and powerlessness as a routine in the patients' everyday experience.

Recall the study by Rosenhan (1973) in which eight researchers had themselves committed to twelve different mental hospitals around the United States. They feigned a relatively minor hallucinatory symptom and all but one were admitted with a diagnosis of schizophrenia. They remained undetected as pseudopatients in the hospitals an average of 19 days whereupon they were all released with a diagnosis of schizophrenia "in remission." During their stay, each of the pseudopatients carefully observed the interactions among patients and the staff. Their experiences as psychiatric patients support much of the previous sociological observation. For example,

> Consider the structure of the typical psychiatric hospital. Staff and patients are strictly segregated. Staff have their own living space, including their dining facilities, bathrooms, and assembly places. The glassed quarters that contain the professional staff, which the pseudopatients came to call "the cage," sit out on every dayroom. The staff emerge primarily for caretaking purposes—to give medication, to conduct a therapy or group meeting, to instruct or reprimand a patient. Otherwise, staff keep to themselves, almost as if the disorder that afflicts their charges is somehow catching. (Rosenhan, 1973, p. 254)

Those with the most power (e.g., psychiatrists) spent the least time and had least to do with patients while those with the least power (orderlies, nurses) were most involved with them. When patients attempted to interact with the staff, they were often totally ignored as though they didn't even exist. Powerlessness of the patient was evident from his loss of legal rights, lack of personal privacy, and restricted freedom of movement.

Rosenhan attributes the depersonalization of the mental patient primarily to negative attitudes toward the mentally ill and those who treat them and the hierarchical structure of the mental hospital we have described. In addition, he suggests that heavy reliance on psychotropic medication may also contribute to depersonalization by convincing hospital staff that pills or injections are sufficient treatment and further patient contact may not be necessary. The extensive use of physical treatment techniques including psychosurgery, insulin, electroshock, hydrotherapy, and drugs has been reported by others as well. For example Perrucci (1974) reports that,

> During the year in which Riverview (state hospital) was studied by this writer, the total patient population was approximately 2,400 persons. A total of 751 patients received 4,851 treatments of electroconvulsive therapy, and 131 patients received 2,337 treatments of hydrotherapy for a total of 4,724 hours. During the same year, a total of 368 hours of individual and group psychotherapy took place, with a maximum of 45 hours in a single month. There is no record of the exact number of patients involved in such "talk therapies" but it is clear that the number is very small. (pp. 33–34)

While the conditions in mental hospitals reported by researchers frequently strike us as inhumane and counter to a rehabilitative goal, we should take care not to ascribe these conditions entirely to the staffs who care for patients in these institutions. Indeed, as Perrucci (1974) suggests, staff themselves are frequently victims of stigmatizing public attitudes simply by virtue of working at the state hospital. For example, he ran into people in the community who wondered aloud if "the doctors and other staff at the state hospital weren't as crazy as the patients." This sort of stigma, coupled with problems wrought by dwindling resources, adds to the difficulty of working in a mental institution. The public attitudes within which the mental hospital must operate and the bureaucratic structure of the hospital's organization substantially account for the depersonalization and apparent callousness attendent with institutionalization.

PUBLIC POLICY

Deinstitutionalization and Community Mental Health

Over the past 20 to 25 years there has been a steady decrease in reliance upon mental hospitals in the treatment of mental disorders paralleled by increased utilization of community-based facilities. For example, in 1955 about half of the psychiatric patient care episodes in the United States were in state mental hospitals compared to about one-fifth in 1971. Outpatient services accounted for only 23% of psychiatric care episodes in 1955, but for 42% in 1971. Use of federally funded community mental health centers has risen dramatically since their beginning in 1963 (Bachrach, 1976).

In addition, the number of resident patients in state hospitals has declined since a peak of about 559,000 in 1955. As Table 3.3 shows, since 1970 a slight decline in the rate of admissions to psychiatric hospitals has combined with a dramatic reduction in the length of stay in psychiatric hospitals. Thus, the overall trend during the past twenty years has been toward shortened hospitals stays and greatly increased use of outpatient care in community-based facilities such as general hospitals and community mental health centers.

TABLE 3.3. PSYCHIATRIC HOSPITAL USE RATES, 1960–1981

Year	Admissions per 1000 population	Days in hospital per 1000 population
1960	2.3	1,491
1965	2.9	1,261
1970	3.3	862
1975	3.2	495
1977	3.0	390
1979	2.9	341
1980	2.8	326
1981	2.7	304

Source: *Statistical Abstract of the United States,* 1984, p. 117.

Much of the support for this changing philosophy in mental health care has come from the labeling theorists like Scheff and observers like Goffman who brought their sociological perspective to the problems of mental hospitalization. These researchers consistently concluded that hospitalization is stigmatizing and it sometimes leads to institutionalization of those who are committed whereby they become so integrated into the hospital routine that functioning outside the institution becomes impossible. Furthermore, hospitalization breaks the patient's family and community ties, frequently making return to the community difficult. Being the culmination of the process of labeling, many argue that hospitalization may in fact contribute to a person assuming a mentally ill role. Generally, there has been growing agreement among mental health professionals that retention of the patient in the community, away from the custodial environment of the mental hospital, has more therapeutic value. Broadened community acceptance of the mentally ill along with the widespread use of psychoactive drugs has made implementation of this philosophy possible. From a more critical perspective, some observers (Scull, 1977) persuasively argue that the real reason behind the "decarceration" or deinstitutionalization movement is the government's desperate need to cut the costs of social control, custodial care, and rehabilitation.

Despite the persuasive arguments in favor of community mental health care and statistical evidence cited above that deinstitutionalization is taking place, there are many problems to be faced. A few of the most significant issues can be presented as questions.

1. What patients should be selected for community care? With the advent of community mental health care, there has been a tendency for more attention to be given to those with less severe disorders. They are easier to care for in community-based facilities. Furthermore, it is likely that people from lower–class, minority communities are apt to return to an environment and facilities less conducive to their needs than nonminority patients.
2. How should treatment in the community be organized? This question has to do with the proper places, available hours, and personnel required for treatment. Critics have also pointed to the over reliance on psychoactive drugs as a treatment modality in community mental health.
3. How can patients be supported in the community? That is, are employment, housing, social activities, and other social resources available?
4. How can community resistance to the presence of the mental-

ly ill be reduced? There is evidence that patients discharged from mental hospitals are not welcomed back into the community with open arms. It is possible that return to a hostile community is no less detrimental than isolation in the hospital's back wards. There are also problems of pressure exerted on families who become responsible for the care and rehabilitation of a relative released from a hospital.

None of these issues, among numerous others, has been entirely resolved. Bachrach (1976) replaces the problems of the deinstitutionalization movement in a helpful theoretical context by employing a functionalist perspective. She argues that *"the deinstitutionalization movement in the United States represents a search for functional alternatives to the mental hospital"* (p. 19). In other words, the policy of moving patients out of mental institutions and back in their communities is guided by the assumption that the job of care and rehabilitation of the mentally ill can be done as well or better in a community setting. However, while the apparent, manifest functions of mental hospitals are care and rehabilitation, these institutions also serve some less obvious, latent functions. For example, mental hospitals in certain cases provide necessary long-term custodial care for the chronically disturbed; they sometimes remove the patient from a hostile environment thus serving as a haven or asylum in the most positive sense; they protect society from certain dangerous individuals; they provide a centralized place for research and for the training of mental health professionals. As a result, the large-scale dissolution of mental hospitals has met with resistance from the families of mental patients, the communities to which the mental patients must now turn for care, and the mental health professionals whose interests are tied to mental hospitals.

Thus, *"many of the problems confronting the deinstitutionalization movement result from the failure to provide functional alternatives for some basic functions served by the mental hospital.* The logical conclusion that follows from a functionalist point of view is that *mental hospitals must not and cannot be eliminated until alternatives for the functions of asylum and custodial care have been provided"* (Bachrach, 1976, p. 19).

We can conclude that deinstitutionalization and the community mental health movement have laudable goals that are consistent with much sociological theory and observation about the detrimental effects of mental hospitalization. At the same time, implementation of this movement, while occurring very rapidly, has met with resistance and occasional ineffectiveness. A functional analysis indicates that it would be an error to anticipate total elimination of mental hospitals until their functions are assumed adequately by alternative structures. In the end, it would seem that our best public policy would be the prudent implementation of community mental health care facilities while simultaneously improving the mental hospital to more ideally fulfill its role of humane custody, intensive treatment, and true asylum.

MENTAL DISORDER AND THE LAW

On a day-to-day basis, officials in communities must make decisions about what to do with people whose behavior is disruptive to others, sometimes clearly illegal, and occasionally even dangerous. At the same time that these officials are providing for the rights of the community to remain peaceful and safe, they are charged with assuring the individual rights of anyone accused of being disruptive or dangerous.

Simultaneous protection of the community's and individuals' rights underlie the public policy issues with which psychiatrists and lawyers must jointly deal. There are three kinds of decisions involving convergence of psychiatry and the law to be discussed here: (1) involuntary commitment, (2) incompetency to stand trial, and (3) the insanity defense.

Involuntary Commitment

Every state provides for the legal, involuntary commitment of certain persons to a psychiatric hospital. The underlying principle of such laws is the assumption that some people may pose a danger to themselves and others requiring their removal from the community. While this principle makes sense in theory, it is frequently very difficult to interpret in practice. How does one determine that a person is a danger to himself or others? In extreme cases such as clear physical threats to others or attempted suicide the determination may be straightforward. However, involuntary commitment frequently occurs with far less convincing evidence of threat. Complaints that lead to involuntary commitment frequently come from those who find the accused person's behavior disturbing, odd, or in disagreement with their own standards. The problem, then, is to be sure that simply being different is not grounds for removing a person's freedom and rights through involuntary hospitalization.

The process of involuntary commitment in many states has been severely criticized for ignoring individual rights, especially during a court hearing. Indeed, it is the legal hearing that is supposed to provide the setting for the protection of the individual's rights. However, as

Mechanic (1969) notes, judges are apt to accept routinely the advice of psychiatrists in commitment cases. "The court has other business to attend to, and judges frequently assume that a legal hearing would not be conducive to the patient's mental health" (Scheff, 1964a; 1964b). "Thus the commitment process often has had the form of due process of law but was actually vacuous because the decision was frequently predetermined" (Mechanic, 1980, p. 190).

In one study of court procedures it was found that medical examiners spent an average of ten minutes on each case and almost always recommended detention. Furthermore, court hearings were usually brief and perfunctory.

> In one urban court (the court with the largest number of cases) the only contact with the judge and the patient was in a preliminary hearing. This hearing was held with such lightning rapidity (1.6 minutes average) and followed such a standard and unvarying format that it was obvious that the judge made no attempt to use the hearing results in arriving at a decision. He asked three questions uniformly: "How are you feeling?" "How are you being treated?" and "If the doctors recommend that you stay here a while, would you cooperate?" No matter how the patient responded, the judge immediately signified that the hearing was over, cutting off some of the patients in the middle of a sentence. (Scheff, 1964b, p. 22)

There is no doubt that improvements to protect individual rights are needed. These include allocation of more resources for overloaded courts to make hasty commitment proceedings less likely; more serious attempts to encourage people to enter a hospital voluntarily when hospitalization is clearly necessary; and procedures for periodic review of involuntary commitment cases to ensure that the patient does not get lost in the institution's back wards receiving only custodial care.

Incompetency to Stand Trial

During the summer of 1977, New York City police undertook one of the biggest, most widely publicized manhunts in history. They were searching for a gunman known as "Son of Sam" who had used a handgun to shoot six young people in the head and also wounded seven others in a year's time. The shootings were apparently motiveless and random except that all the victims were attractive young women. Following his capture, David Berkowitz, the "Son of Sam" killer, was immediately described in the press as "completely wacko," "nutty as a fruitcake," "paranoiac," and "bizarre."

Public reaction to this case was particularly intense and people were frequently heard expressing the fear that Berkowitz might enter an insanity plea at his trial only to end up at a psychiatric hospital rather than a prison. In fact, the insanity defense at a trial is far less frequent than a decision *prior* to the trial that the person charged is incompetent to stand trial. Berkowitz, despite early media characterizations, was judged competent to stand trial and was later found guilty. However, similar psychiatric screening procedures have been used to bar trials for other famous cases such as the Boston Strangler or New York's "Mad Bomber" who set off 37 explosives over 16 years in a campaign against the city's electric and gas company. The incompetency ruling is not uncommon in less celebrated cases as well.

The rationale for the incompetency ruling is that a defendant must be able to cooperate in preparing the case for his own defense. If a person lacks the capacity to understand the charges and proceedings because of mental disease or deficiency, it would be unfair to go on with the trial because the right to an adequate defense would be denied.

While the incompetency ruling is clearly intended to guarantee an individual's right to a fair trial, it can also be used to deny a defendant's rights as well. Mechanic (1980) summarizes this argument.

> A judgment of incompetency to stand trial thus allows for the indefinite detention of persons believed to be dangerous, of those who cannot take care of themselves, and of those who are public nuisances . . . Many such defendants are clearly mentally ill, and lawyers and judges often feel that a determination of incompetence is in their best interest. Critics of the process feel that this legal provision effectively allows the community to deny persons their legal right to a trial, to determinate sentence, and to due process of law. (p. 207)

Judging from the public reaction to particularly brutal crimes, it appears that many people also criticize the incompetency procedure because they feel it denies the community an opportunity for retribution.

The Insanity Defense

When a case comes to trial, the law presumes that the person accused was aware of the wrongful behavior for which he is charged. The most widely used criterion to establish responsibility is the McNaghten rule stating that

> every man is presumed to be sane, and . . . that to establish a defense on the ground of insanity, it must be clearly proved that, at the time of

> committing the act, the party accused was labouring under such a defect of reason, from disease of the mind, as not to know the nature and quality of the act he was doing; or if he did know it, that he did not know he was doing what was wrong. (Goldstein, 1967:45.)

The legal issues surrounding interpretation of the insanity defense are too complex to outline here. There are, however, two aspects of the McNaghten rule which point to the difficulty of judging whether an insanity verdict is appropriate. First, as studies like Rosenhan's "pseudopatients" experiment have shown, diagnosis of insanity is a very inexact procedure. Indeed, at many trials where the insanity defense is used, eminently qualified psychiatrists called as expert witnesses for the prosecution and defense differ in their diagnoses of the defendant's sanity. In these cases it becomes obvious that diagnosing insanity is not the same straightforward procedure as is diagnosing many physical ills.

Second, even when it can be agreed that a defendant suffers from a psychiatric disorder, that does not constitute evidence that the psychiatric disorder caused the unlawful behavior. Mechanic (1969) summarizes this problem well.

> The judgment of whether it is reasonable to regard the defendant as responsible for his behavior cannot be made on technical or scientific grounds. If, for example, a schizophrenic patient is apprehended committing a crime and when arrested is seen to be in a hallucinogenic state, one would be tempted to attribute his unlawful behavior to schizophrenia. However, most hallucinating schizophrenics do not commit crimes, and many nonschizophrenics do. Thus, the fact the schizophrenia is a concomitant of the unlawful act in no sense establishes a causal relationship between them. In some cases, of course, the link is obvious, as when a mental patient hears voices which tell him to commit an irrational and meaningless offense. But in such circumstances one hardly needs a psychiatrist to make the necessary observations. (p. 142)

Finally, lawyers claim that the insanity defense is not an easy one to uphold successfully. Trial lawyer F. Lee Bailey has been quoted as saying, "Juries don't like the phraseology. The phrase 'not guilty' sticks in their craw when a jury is faced with colorful evidence. And jurors often say, 'I know this guy is nuts, but we're not going to put him in some institution where some psychiatrist can let him out" (Alpern & Agrest, 1977). On the other hand, the successful insanity defense of would-be presidential assassin John Hinckley, Jr. has raised a public outcry that may result in legal changes intended to alter the "not guilty by reason of insanity" verdict or make it still more difficult to attain.

POLICY SUGGESTIONS

Because of the ambiguities in diagnosis, the difficulties in determining responsibility, and an overriding principle of properly balancing community and individual rights, there is much public policy debate over points where psychiatry and the law merge. Most of these issues are a matter of social judgment which will not give way to scientific assessment. However, there are reasonable public policy suggestions which can be made and some have been implemented over the last few years in many states.

For example, involuntary commitment should be sought only as a last resort. When this procedure is used, a thorough review of the case by both physicians and judges should be mandatory. In all three proceedings just discussed—involuntary commitment, incompetency to stand trial, and the insanity defense—there should be explicit procedures to guarantee periodic review of the case to insure release or a speedy trial if or when the individual is declared so fit. Last, there should be every effort to guarantee that when a person is institutionalized for treatment that treatment is in fact available. This means the continued improvement of mental hospitals so those in them receive more than minimal custodial care.

SUMMARY

Mental illness presents especially difficult problems of definition and diagnosis that have been irksome to the development of theory, research, and social policy. This chapter began with a review of historical and cross-cultural evidence, concluding that in most times and places, apparently uncontrolled, irrationally motivated behavior has been classified as mentally disordered. According to contemporary American usage, mental disorders fall into two major types—organic (brain disease or damage, alcoholic psychoses, drug-induced psychoses) and functional (not attributable to any clear physiological impairment). Within the functional category are the psychoses (schizophrenia, manic-depression, and personality disorders) and the neuroses (phobias, anxieties, hysterias).

From our examination of findings on the distribution of mental disorders among various social categories, the major variable emerging was social class. The highest rates of mental disorder are in the lower class, and lower-class patients are more likely to be diagnosed as schizophrenic or with a personality disorder while higher-class patients are more likely to be diagnosed depressive or neurotic.

Biogenetic explanations of certain mental disorders, particularly schizophrenia, have received strong research support. Heredity, as a predisposing factor, and a person's social experiences probably interact in the precipitation of some mental disorders. At the sociological level, in respect to social environment, the stress of living under conditions of social disorganization was one of the earliest theories proposed and tested by Faris and Dunham (1939). They found that rates of mental disorder are highest in the urban center and decrease toward the periphery. Their work is also important because it clearly identified four alternative hypotheses that have guided the design and interpretation of many research studies since. The hypotheses are:

Chance: The distribution of highest rates of mental disorder in the city's center might merely be an odd occurrence.

Selection: Those who have the least power to resist being labeled (inner–city, poor residents) are more likely to be identified as mentally ill and institutionalized.

Drift: Those who are the least mentally competent move into the city center which tends to be a collecting point for social failures while those who are most able to, move away. The result is a higher density of the socially and mentally impaired who contribute to the high rates of mental disorders.

Stress: Social and life conditions aggravated by poverty and social disorganization in the central city are very stressful, causing higher rates of mental illness.

Largely consistent with the stress theory of mental disorders are findings that rates of mental hospitalization increase with downturns in the economy. Likewise, Merton's anomie theory suggests that blocked opportunities to reach goals may lead some people to retreat into the imaginary world of mental disorder, especially depression.

At the social–psychological level of explanation we considered family socialization and coping with problems of day–to–day life. Scheff's labeling theory is a social–psychological explanation arguing that influential others, like psychiatrists, in the process of officially designating a person mentally ill, can actually increase the person's aberrant symptoms, his self–conceptualization as mentally disordered, and the likelihood of more permanently taking on the mentally ill role.

Mental hospitals were considered both for their effects on patients and the people who work in them. The climate of negative public opinion and the bureaucratic structure of the modern psychiatric institution contribute to the difficult problems of depersonalization and largely custodial treatment modes. The recent national policy of deinstitutionalization for mental patients was analyzed from a functionalist perspective. In these terms, deinstitutionalization represents a search for functional alternatives to the mental hospital.

Finally, we considered the points at which psychiatry and the law meet in respect to public policies concerning involuntary commitment to a mental institution, incompetency to stand trial, and the insanity defense. Several principles were suggested to guide the formation of policies that both protect the rights of the accused while retaining the reasonable expectation that mentally competent people should be responsible and accept the legal consequences of their behavior.

NOTE

1. *Prevalence* refers to the number of cases in a population at any point in time. In contrast, *incidence* means the number or rate of new cases or admissions over a span of time, for example, during a given year or month.

REFERENCES

Alpern, D. M., & Agrest, S.
    1977 Will he stand trial? *Newsweek,* August 29:27-28.
American Psychiatric Association
    1980 *Diagnostic and statistical manual of mental disorders,* 3rd ed. Washington, D.C.
Aviram, U., & Segal, S.
    1973 Exclusion of the mentally ill: Reflection on an old problem in a new context. *Archives of General Psychiatry 29,* 126-131.
Bachrach, L. L.
    1976 Deinstitutionalization: An analytical review and sociological perspective. Mental Health Statistics Series D, No. 4. Washington, D.C.: National Institute of Mental Health.
Benedict, R.
    1934 *Patterns of culture.* Boston: Houghton Mifflin.
Bingham, J.
    1951 What the public thinks of psychiatry. *American Journal of Psychiatry, 107*:599-601.
Book, J. A.
    1953 A genetic and neuropsychiatric investigation of a north Swedish population. *Acta Genetica et Statistica Medica 4*:1-100, 133-139, 345-414.
Brenner, M. H.
    1973 *Mental illness and the economy.* Cambridge, Mass.: Harvard University Press.
Brenner, M. H.
    1976 *Estimating the social costs of national economic policy: Implications*

for mental and physical health, and criminal aggression. Washington, D.C.: U.S. Government Printing Office.

Conover, D.
   1972 Psychiatric distinctions: New and old approaches. *Journal of Health and Social Behavior, 13*:167–180.

Crocetti, G. M., Spiro, H. R., & Siassi, J.
   1974 *Contemporary attitudes toward mental illness.* Pittsburgh: University of Pittsburgh Press.

Cumming, E., & Cumming, J.
   1957 *Closed ranks: An experiment in mental health education.* Cambridge: Harvard University Press.

Dohrenwend, B. P.
   1975 Sociocultural and social–psychological factors in the genesis of mental disorders. *Journal of Health and Social Behavior, 16*:365–392.

Dohrenwend, B. P., & Dohrenwend, B. S.
   1969 *Social status and psychological disorder: A causal inquiry.* New York: Wiley.

Dohrenwend, B. P., & Dohrenwend, B. S.
   1976 Sex differences and psychiatric disorders. *American Journal of Sociology, 81*:1447–1454.

Dunham, H. W.
   1964 Anomie and mental disorder. In M. B. Clinard (Ed.), *Anomie and deviant behavior: A discussion and critique.* New York: The Free Press.

Eaton, J. W., & Weil, R. J.
   1955 *Culture and mental disorders.* Glencoe, Ill.: The Free Press.

Eaton, W. W.
   1974 Residence, social class and schizophrenia. *Journal of Health and Social Behavior, 15*:289–299.

Essen-Moller
   1965 Twin research and psychiatry. *International Journal of Psychiatry, 1*:466–475.

Faris, R. E. L., & Dunham, H. W.
   1939 *Mental disorders in urban areas.* Chicago: University of Chicago Press.

Goffman, E.
   1961 *Asylums.* New York: Doubleday–Anchor.

Goldstein, A.
   1967 *The insanity defense.* New Haven, Conn.: Yale University Press.

Gottesman, J. J., & Schields, J.
   1972 *Schizophrenia and genetics: A twin study vantage point.* New York: Academic Press.

Gove, W.
   1975 *The labeling of deviance: Evaluating a perspective.* New York: Halstead.

Heston, L. L.
   1966 Psychiatric disorders in foster home retarded children of schizophrenic mothers. *British Journal of Psychiatry, 112*:819–825.

Hollingshead, A. B., & Redlich, F. C.
  1958   *Social class and mental illness.* New York: Wiley.
Kallman, F. J.
  1938   *The genetics of schizophrenia.* Locust Valley, N.Y.: J. J. Augustine.
Kallman, F. J.
  1946   The genetic theory of schizophrenia. *American Journal of Psychiatry, 103*:309-322.
Kleiner, R. J., & Parker, S.
  1963   Goal striving, social status and mental disorder: A research review. *American Sociological Review, 28*:189-203.
Laing, R. D.
  1969   *The politics of the family and other essays.* New York: Vintage.
Linsky, A. S.
  1969   Community structure and depressive disorders. *Social Problems, 17*:120-131.
Mechanic, D.
  1969   *Mental health and social policy.* Englewood Cliffs, N.J.: Prentice-Hall.
Mechanic, D.
  1980   *Mental health and social policy,* 2nd ed. Englewood Cliffs, N.J.: Prentice-Hall.
Merton, R. K.
  1938   Social structure and anomie. *American Sociological Review, 3*:672-682.
Mitchell, W. J.
  1975   The insanity verdict: Who is dangerous, who is sick. *New York Times,* June 1, 1975, Section 4, p. 20.
Mott, F. D., & Roemer, M. I.
  1948   *Rural health and medical care.* New York: McGraw-Hill.
Myers, J. K., & Roberts, B. H.
  1959   *Family and class dynamics in mental illness.* New York: Wiley.
Nunnally, J. C.
  1961   *Popular conceptions of mental health, their development and change.* New York: Holt, Rinehart and Winston.
Parker, S., & Kleiner, R. J.
  1966   *Mental illness in the urban Negro community.* New York: Free Press.
Perrucci, R.
  1974   *Circle of madness: On being insane and institutionalized in America.* Englewood Cliffs, N.J.: Prentice-Hall.
Rogler, L. H., & Hollingshead, A. B.
  1965   *Trapped: Families and schizophrenia.* New York: Wiley.
Rosenhan, D. L.
  1973   On being sane in insane places. *Science, 179*:250-258.
Rosenstein, M. J., & Milazzo-Sayre, L. J.
  1981   *Characteristics of admissions to selected mental health facilities, 1975: An annotated book of charts and tables.* Washington, D.C.: National Institute of Mental Health.

Rothman, D. J.
    1971   *The discovery of the asylum: Social order and disorder in the new republic.* Boston: Little, Brown.

Sampson, H., Messinger, S. L., & Towne, R. D.
    1962   Family processes and becoming a mental patient. *American Journal of Sociology, 68*:88–96.

Scheff, T.
    1964a   The societal reaction to deviance. *Social Problems, 11*:401–413.

Scheff, T.
    1964b   Social conditions for rationality: How urban courts deal with the mentally ill. *American Behavioral Scientist, 8*:21–24.

Scheff, T. J.
    1966   *Being mentally ill: A sociological theory.* Chicago: Aldine.

Scull, A. T.
    1977   *Decarceration: Community treatment and the deviant, a radical view.* Englewood Cliffs, N.J.: Prentice-Hall.

Simmons, J. L.
    1969   *Deviants.* Berkeley: Glendessary.

Skultans, V.
    1975   *Madness and morals: Ideas on insanity in the nineteenth century.* Boston: Routledge and Kegan Paul.

Spiro, H. R., Siassi, I., & Crocetti, G.
    1973   Ability of the public to recognize mental illness: An issue of substance and an issue of meaning. *Social Psychiatry, 8*:32–36.

Srole, L., Langer, I. S., Michael, S. I., Opler, M. K., & Rennie, I. A. C.
    1962   *Mental health in the metropolis.* New York: McGraw-Hill.

Star, S.
    1961   *The dilemmas of mental illness cited in the joint commission on mental illness and health action for mental health.* New York: Science Editions.

Star, S.
    1955   The public's idea about mental illness. Paper presented at the National Association for Mental Health Meetings, Chicago, Ill.

U.S. Bureau of the Census
    1981   *Statistical abstract of the United States.* Washington, D.C.: U.S. Government Printing Office.

U.S. Department of Health and Human Services
    1981   *Additions and resident patients at end of year state and county mental hospitals by age and diagnosis, by state, United States, 1978.* Washington, D.C.: National Institute of Mental Health.

Wallace, A. F. C.
    1970   *Culture and personality,* 2nd ed. New York City: Random House.

Wallace, A. F. C.
    1972   Mental illness, biology and culture. In F. L. K. Hsu (Ed.), *Psychological anthropology.* Cambridge, Mass.: Schenkman Publishing.

Weinberg, S. K.
   1967   *The sociology of mental disorders.* Chicago: Aldine.
Yarrow, M. R., Schwartz, C. G., Murphy, H. S., & Deasy, L. C.
   1955   The psychological meaning of mental illness in the family. *Journal of Social Issues, 11*:11–24.

Chapter 4
SUICIDE

HISTORICAL AND CULTURAL ATTITUDES
VARIATIONS IN THE SUICIDE RATE
   International Rates
   Suicide in the United States
   Evaluating Official Statistics
SOCIAL CORRELATES OF SUICIDE
   Sex, Age, and Race
   Occupation, Marital Status, and Religion
   Adolescent and Young Adult Suicide
EXPLANATIONS OF SUICIDE
   Social Integration and Regulation
   Status Integration
   Social Disorganization
   Frustration and Aggression
   Suggestibility, Societal Reaction, and Social Meaning
   Suicide Notes
   A Basic Suicide Syndrome
SUICIDE PREVENTION AND SOCIAL POLICY
SUMMARY

Humans have been described as the most tragic of all creatures because they alone recognize their own mortality. Possessing this awareness, it should not be surprising that novelists, philosophers, and social scientists have long been fascinated with the question of why some people willfully end their own lives. Suicide is seemingly a decision that only humans can make; therefore, by understanding suicide we might better grasp the essentials of our humanity. This distinctly human aspect of suicide is reflected in the existentialist philosopher Camus' declaration that "There is but one truly serious philosophical problem, and that is suicide. Judging whether life is or is not worth living amounts to answering the fundamental question of philosophy" (Camus, 1955).

At the end of the 19th century sociologists were motivated to study suicide by Emile Durkheim's program to establish social reality as a distinct object of study. Durkheim began by contriving a foil. Why, he asked, might sociologists who are interested in collective social phenomena choose to study suicide, probably the most intensely individualistic and personal of human acts? His response was, of course, that even a highly personal decision such as taking one's life is, in part, the product of social and cultural conditions. As you will see in this chapter, suicide rates often follow quite regular patterns among various societies, subcultures, and social categories. Furthermore, it appears that the number and quality of a person's social relationships with others may frequently be central to the decision to choose death over life.

HISTORICAL AND CULTURAL ATTITUDES

Anthropological evidence seems to establish that in most small-scale, primitive societies suicide rates are relatively low (La Fontaine, 1975, p. 85). In many primitive societies suicide has been a tabooed subject accompanied by fear, superstition, and magic rituals. For example, Baganda women of Uganda are said to be afraid of the ghosts of suicides who might possibly impregnate them, so to ward off the evil they throw grass and sticks on the place where a suicide was buried. The

Gisu of Africa attribute suicide to the anger of the ancestors. Thus, they say that an immediate sacrifice to the ancestors is a necessary precaution following a suicide to rid the community of more evil. Also, the body of the suicide is not accorded the normal burial ritual, but instead is thrown in the thick brush to be forgotten (La Fontaine, 1960). In addition to taboo and fear, Farberow (1975, p. 3) suggests two other reasons for revulsion from suicide. First, the act may indicate a contempt for the community by rejecting further participation in it. Second, suicide is an economic loss to the society by depriving it of a useful mother, warrior, or worker.

Suicide is not, however, universally abhorred among primitive people. Indeed, in certain societies the act has been positively valued and encouraged under some circumstances. A Netsilik Eskimo is quoted as saying: "For our custom up here is that all old people who can do no more, and whom death will not take, help death to take them. And they do this not merely to be rid of life that is no longer a pleasure, but also to relieve their nearest relations of the trouble they give them" (Leighton & Hughes, 1955, p. 327). A similar recognition of the possible positive social functions of suicide is a significant aspect of the debate over euthanasia in contemporary Western societies.

Suicides or suicide attempts in some primitive societies also provide a means of symbolizing anger, unhappiness, unjust treatment, or protest. For example, Giddens (1971:156) notes that among the Trobriand Islanders, the Kuma and the Dobu of New Guinea, suicide attempts may be used as a way of registering displeasure with one's spouse. In this context, suicide or attempted suicide is a rational social act intended to pressure others to respond in a desired way. In general, then, when viewing suicide from a cross-cultural perspective, it becomes evident that suicide is not always an unreasoned act committed by a pathological individual.

Throughout the history of Western civilization, attitudes toward suicide have varied a great deal. Among Jews of the Old Testament, suicide was considered wrong except under very extreme conditions such as disgrace of capture or torture. Jewish law generally condemned suicide, and when it occurred, the victim and his family were not accorded the usual rites of burial and mourning. During the Greek and Roman periods, spanning the 5th century B.C. to the 4th century A.D., the lower classes found suicide repugnant while the upper classes developed an attitude of indifference and even approval under certain circumstances such as preserving one's honor, avoidance of pain or shame, expressing bereavement at the loss of a loved one, or dying for a patriotic cause (Farberow, 1975, pp. 4–5).

During the early Christian era, the Romans enacted laws against suicide to curb their financial losses when their soldiers or their slaves killed themselves. Punishments included forfeiture of estate when a person under arrest committed suicide. Again, this was to prevent lost revenues to the state. In the same historical period, Christians condemned suicide but, paradoxically, they became frequent and willing martyrs.

About the 4th century A.D., suicide became virtually unknown because of strong denunciation and punishment by the Church. Sanctions against suicide included confiscation of the victim's property, degradation of the corpse, and refusal of burial in consecrated ground. A common practice in England was to bury the suicide at a crossroad by night with a stake driven through the heart. In other parts of Europe, the corpse would be dragged through the streets and/or hanged on a gallows (Rosen, 1975, p. 14).

In the mid-18th century, intellectuals began to question some of the dogmatic attitudes toward suicide that characterized the Middle Ages. Three trends evident in the shift of opinion continue to the present day. First, there was opposition to the traditional Christian attitude that suicide is sinful and morally obnoxious. Second, writers became interested in how national character related to suicide, thus presaging the more contemporary interest in environmental factors such as climate, urbanization, and the like. Third, there was a tendency to consider self-destruction as a medical problem frequently associated with madness, hereditary psychopathology, or brain disease (Rosen, 1975, p. 21). The popular tendency to associate suicide with mental illness probably accounts for the fact that up to the present day, suicide is likely to be a stigmatizing social disgrace for the relatives of the victim.

VARIATIONS IN THE SUICIDE RATE

International Rates

Because of variations in reporting procedures and the unreliability of the data among countries, it would be unwise to draw conclusions from only slight differences in the national suicide rates. There is, however, a broad range in the suicide rates for various countries of the world, from less than one per 100,000 to almost fifty per 100,000 annually. In general, there is a tendency, with a few exceptions, for more highly industrialized societies to have higher rates while poorer developing countries tend to have lower suicide rates.

One might first be inclined to predict higher suicide rates for those who are poor and have the worst living conditions. The logic of this

TABLE 4.1. SUICIDE RATES OF SELECTED COUNTRIES (Rate per 100,000 population)

Developed Countries	Rate	Date	Developing Countries	Rate	Date
Hungary	43.2	1978	Cuba	17.7	1977
Denmark	25.8	1976	Singapore	11.4	1978
Finland	25.8	1976	Uruguay	10.5	1978
Austria	25.1	1979	Trinidad & Tobago	8.7	1977
Switzerland	24.5	1979	S. Africa (nonwhite)	7.3	1971
Federal Republic of Germany	22.2	1978	Cape Verde	6.1	1975
Czechoslovakia	21.4	1978	Chile	5.8	1979
Sweden	20.5	1979	Venezuela	4.6	1978
Belgium	19.1	1979	Guadeloupe	4.3	1978
Luxembourg	18.2	1978	Costa Rica	4.2	1978
Japan	17.7	1978	Barbados	3.4	1978
France	17.2	1978	Ecuador	3.1	1978
Canada	14.8	1978	Greece	2.9	1978
S. Africa (white)	14.5	1971	Paraguay	1.8	1977
Yugoslavia	13.9	1978	Mexico	1.7	1976
Bulgaria	13.6	1978	Panama	1.7	1978
Iceland	13.3	1979	Peru	1.3	1977
Poland	12.8	1979	Angola	1.2	1973
United States	12.5	1978	Jamaica	1.0	1971
Norway	12.1	1979	Kuwait	0.8	1978
Australia	11.2	1978	Philippines	0.8	1976
New Zealand	10.4	1978	Bahamas	0.5	1975
Netherlands	9.7	1978	Guatemala	0.3	1977
Portugal	8.5	1975	Guyana	0.3	1976
Scotland	8.5	1978	Egypt	0.3	1977
England & Wales	8.2	1978	Jordan	0.1	1976
Hong Kong	7.2	1978			
Italy	5.7	1976			
Israel	5.6	1978			
Ireland	4.6	1977			
N. Ireland	4.5	1978			
Spain	4.1	1978			

Source: United Nations (1982).

prediction might be that a dismal, downtrodden existence would make life seem less worth living; therefore, more suicides would occur. However, the data obviously do not support such an argument. Indeed, Durkheim noticed long ago that poverty seemed to offer some "protection" against suicide. In addition to international data, higher white than nonwhite suicide rates within the United States, South Africa, and other countries tend to support Durkheim's claim that poor groups will have lower suicide rates than the more affluent. Several theories to be discussed later in this chapter offer explanations for these findings.

Suicide In The United States

Some researchers have treated suicide and homicide as extreme types of aggressive, violent behavior (Henry & Short, 1954). In the case of suicide, it is proposed that violence is directed inwardly against the person's self while homicide is an extreme form of outwardly directed aggression. Because suicide and homicide can be conceptualized as alternative modes of aggressive behavior, their rates are frequently compared over time as in Figure 4.1. Over the past 25 years American suicide rates have remained remarkably stable with only a very slight tendency to rise. In contrast, homicide rates have risen dramatically with an apparent leveling off during the mid-1970s.

In general, homicide is an act committed by relatively young people between the ages of 15 and 35. It is likely that some portion of the rising homicide rate during this period is a result of a rising proportion of people in our population who, born in the 1940s and 1950s baby boom, have reached the age at which they are most likely to commit homicide. In contrast, suicide rates generally increase with increasing age. Until the mid-1970s the American population was growing proportionately younger and, therefore, while homicide rates increased, suicide rates remained quite stable. However, as we move into the 1980s and 1990s it is clear that as a result of the recently declining birth rate the United States will have proportionately fewer young people and proportionately more older people. Thus, we might expect over the next decade or so that homicide rates will stabilize and possibly even drop, while suicide rates will begin to rise.

The tendency for suicide rates to be higher among older people is not unique to the United States; it is a worldwide phenomenon. Most industrialized countries tend to have a much older age distribution of their populations than the less industrialized Third World nations which have high birth rates and relatively young populations. Thus, when accounting for the contrasting suicide rates among the countries in Table 4.1, age distribution of the population may be an important consideration. Countries with "young" populations tend to have low suicide rates while those with "older" populations have higher suicide rates.

Evaluating Official Statistics

During 1983 in the United States there were approximately 29,000 people who were officially recorded as suicides, a rate of 12.4 per 100,000. This made suicide the ninth-ranking cause of death among Americans

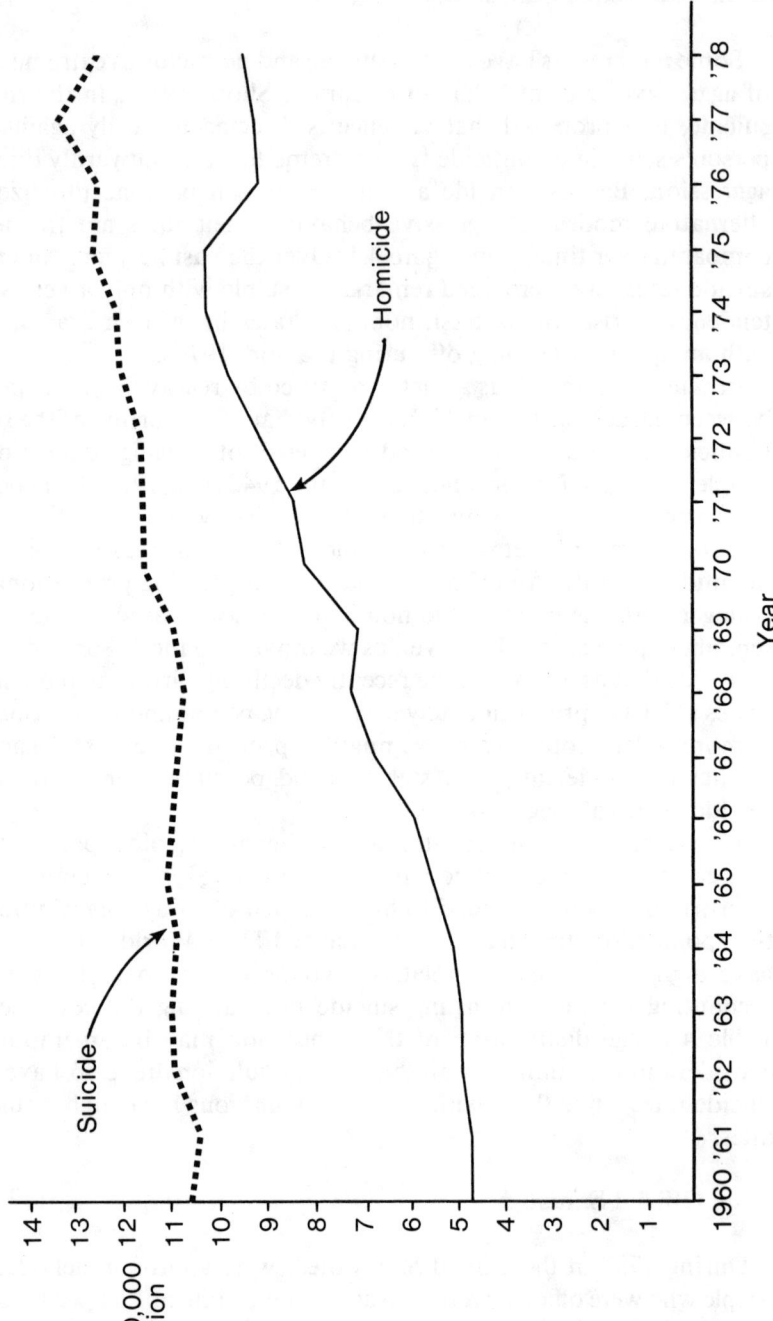

FIGURE 4.1. U.S. HOMICIDE AND SUICIDE RATES, 1960-1978
Source: *Statistical Abstract of the United States*, 1981.

according to the public record (*Monthly Vital Statistics Report,* 1984, p. 18). We should take care not to infer, however, that these statistics accurately reflect the true amount of suicidal behavior. The most obvious omission is the large number of attempted suicides, a number estimated to be around 200,000 per year. However, even if we concern ourselves only with completed suicides, we can justifiably be concerned with the validity and reliability of suicide statistics.

Official statistics on suicide, or any other social phenomenon, are the product of professionals' (police, doctors, coroners) decisions to define, classify, and record each individual case they observe. Statistics such as annual suicide rates are the collective result of a very large number of individuals' intuitions and interpretations with a correspondingly large possibility for unreliability and error. The first difficulty in deciding whether to classify a death as a suicide stems from the definition of the term. There is general agreement that "intention to die" is fundamental to suicide. But what are the grounds for inferring intent? As she or he examines a corpse, how can that medical examiner determine whether or not the person intended to take his or her own life? Should only the physical evidence such as the victim's wound or stomach contents be considered? Or should the medical examiner try also to account for the victim's psychological state prior to death?

A wide variety of behaviors may be reasonably defined as suicidal. For example, cigarette smoking has been described as a form of slow-motion suicide. It is clear that smoking significantly increases one's risk of life-threatening illness. While it is certainly not routinely done by coroners, a case might be made for classifying long-term cancer victims who were heavy smokers as suicides. At the other extreme, a coroner might argue that intent is clear only when a suicide note is left by the deceased. Studies have shown, however, that only a minority (one-sixth to one-third) of suicides leave notes. Thus, using the existence of a note as the only criterion for classifying a death as a suicide would seriously underestimate the actual number of suicides. In practice, coroners and medical examiners each have their own idiosyncratic working definitions which they apply to the cases they observe. In the absence of a suicide note, one medical examiner's suicide may be another's accident. This source of variation significantly contributes to the unreliability of official statistics.

Reporting systems also affect statistics. Naturally, the more standardized and efficient the reporting system, the more accurate the resulting summary rates will be. It is likely that urban areas and more technologically advanced societies have much better reporting systems for all sorts of social phenomena, including suicide, than rural areas and developing countries. This reason alone might account for some of the difference between developed urban areas, which tend to have higher official rates of suicide, as distinct from less developed rural areas, which tend to have lower rates. A thorough, efficient reporting system which includes every case recorded as a suicide will make official rates appear higher than an inefficient, slipshod system that fails to record many cases.

For many people, suicide of a family member is a social disgrace. Thus, it may be to the advantage of survivors to cover up any evidence that suicide was the cause of death or they may convince the medical examiner officially to classify a possible suicide as death by some other cause. It has even been suggested that religious sanctions might lead certain groups to underreport suicides. For example, the Catholic church condemns suicide and church law forbids burial of suicide victims with church sanction.

People who contemplate suicide are usually aware of how this method of death might represent a loss of face both to themselves and to friends or relatives close to them. Moreover, in addition to social embarrassment, suicide may lead to an economic loss on the part of the survivors because taking one's own life frequently negates the obligation of an insurance company to pay the policy holder's beneficiaries. For these reasons, researchers speculate that many suicides disguise their self-destructive intent by planning their death to look like an accident. It is likely, therefore, that a certain number of fatal falls, drownings, and automobile accidents are really suicides. With regard to auto accidents, Pokorny, et al. (1972) found that in a detailed examination of 28 auto crash fatalities, four were suicides. In another study the research suggested that about 20 percent of those involved in auto accidents might have certain depressive or self-destructive potentialities (Tabachnick & Gussen, 1973, p. 175). It appears that a significant number of the more than 55,000 annual auto fatalities in the U.S. could be added to the 27,000 who are classified as suicides if it were possible to understand the victim's intent in every case.

The conclusion we reach in this consideration of official statistics is that disagreements about definition, inconsistent working procedures, different reporting systems, and efforts by the suicide's relatives or the victim himself to mask his intent to die all contribute to the unreliability of official suicide data. Since it appears more likely that there are greater pressures to classify an ambiguous death as something other than a suicide, official statistics probably underestimate the true incidence of self-destruction.

SOCIAL CORRELATES OF SUICIDE

Sex, Age, and Race

Men and women differ in several respects with regard to suicidal behavior. Men in the United States kill themselves at a much higher rate than women, according to official statistics. The male suicide rate per 100,000 in 1980 was 18.6 while for females it was only 5.5. This difference in suicide rates generally repeats itself in other countries as well.

At the same time, although men *complete* suicide at a higher rate than women, women have a higher rate of *attempted* suicides. A likely explanation is to be found in the different suicidal methods used. Over half of U.S. male suicides in 1980 were with firearms and over a third of female suicides employed poisoning. Since using a gun is a far more swift and lethal method than, for instance, taking an overdose of sleeping pills, the more common male method is more likely to result in death.

There are a number of plausible explanations for the different choices of method by men and women. Men in American culture have been raised to identify firearms with strength and masculinity. Women, on the other hand, may choose poisoning most frequently, in part, as a matter of vanity, for having one's head split apart by a gun is not a very attractive image of oneself, even in death. Indeed, when women do shoot themselves, they tend more than men to shoot their bodies rather than their heads (Lester, 1972, p. 40). It also seems likely that women more frequently than men use suicidal threats or attempts as a means of manipulating others or as a cry for help (Farberow & Shneidman, 1965) to draw attention to their problems.

Overall, suicide rates rise with age. Among very young children, under 5 years old, suicide is virtually unknown. In 1978, the suicide

TABLE 4.2. U.S. SUICIDES, 1980, BY SEX AND METHOD (%)

Method	Sex	
	Males	Females
Firearms	63	39
Poisoning	15	38
Hanging and strangulation	15	11
Other	7	12
Total	100	100
N	20,505	6,364

Source: *Statistical Abstract of the United States*, 1984, 83.

rates in the United States ranged from 0.2 per 100,000 among 5–14–year–old females to a peak of 37.5 among white males 65 years of age and older. Generally speaking, those who *attempt* suicide are younger than those who *complete* suicide (Shneidman & Farberow, 1957) and older people tend to use more lethal methods than those who are younger (Lester, 1972). The reasons are probably much the same as those for similar differences between attempts and completions among men and women.

Whites generally have higher suicide rates than nonwhites in the same society. This is true both in the United States and in biracial countries such as South Africa. This fact is consistent with the earlier observation that the suicide rates of poorer countries are lower than in affluent countries. Indeed, it appears that racial differences in suicide rates have far less to do with race *per se* than with the relatively poor or powerless status of most nonwhites as compared with whites.

Before turning to the question of status, though, we should make note of a significant trend in the suicide rate among young black males. You can see in Figure 4.2 that black rates for the age categories up to 34 years old closely parallel the high rates for white males. One researcher (Hendin, 1969), on the basis of 25 interviews with young black suicide attempters, concludes that they had violent, murderous impulses—implying that the higher suicide rates may be a further manifestation of aggressive rage that some direct inwardly. Breed (1970) has suggested that "suicide among young, low–class single Negro males is frequently fatalistic suicide" (p. 162) growing out of feelings of inferiority, powerlessness, and subjugation to arbitrary authority.

Occupation, Marital Status, and Religion

The relationship between occupational or social status and suicide rate is not clearly established. Durkheim (1951) concluded, using data he examined at the end of the nineteenth century, that suicide rates were highest among high status people and lowest for those of low status. However, while some studies since Durkheim's time have agreed with his finding (Kalish, 1958; Stengel, 1964), at least one study (Powell, 1958) found higher suicide rates in upper– *and* lower–level occupational groups with the smallest suicide rate among those in the middle.

There are certain occupational characteristics aside from status that seem to increase the probability of suicide. Occupations found to have exceptionally high suicide rates include pharmacists, physicians, dentists, cab drivers, police, farmers, and fishermen (Powell, 1958; Maris, 1969). One can speculate that jobs that either require intense, involved interaction with others or, at the other extreme, are relatively solitary

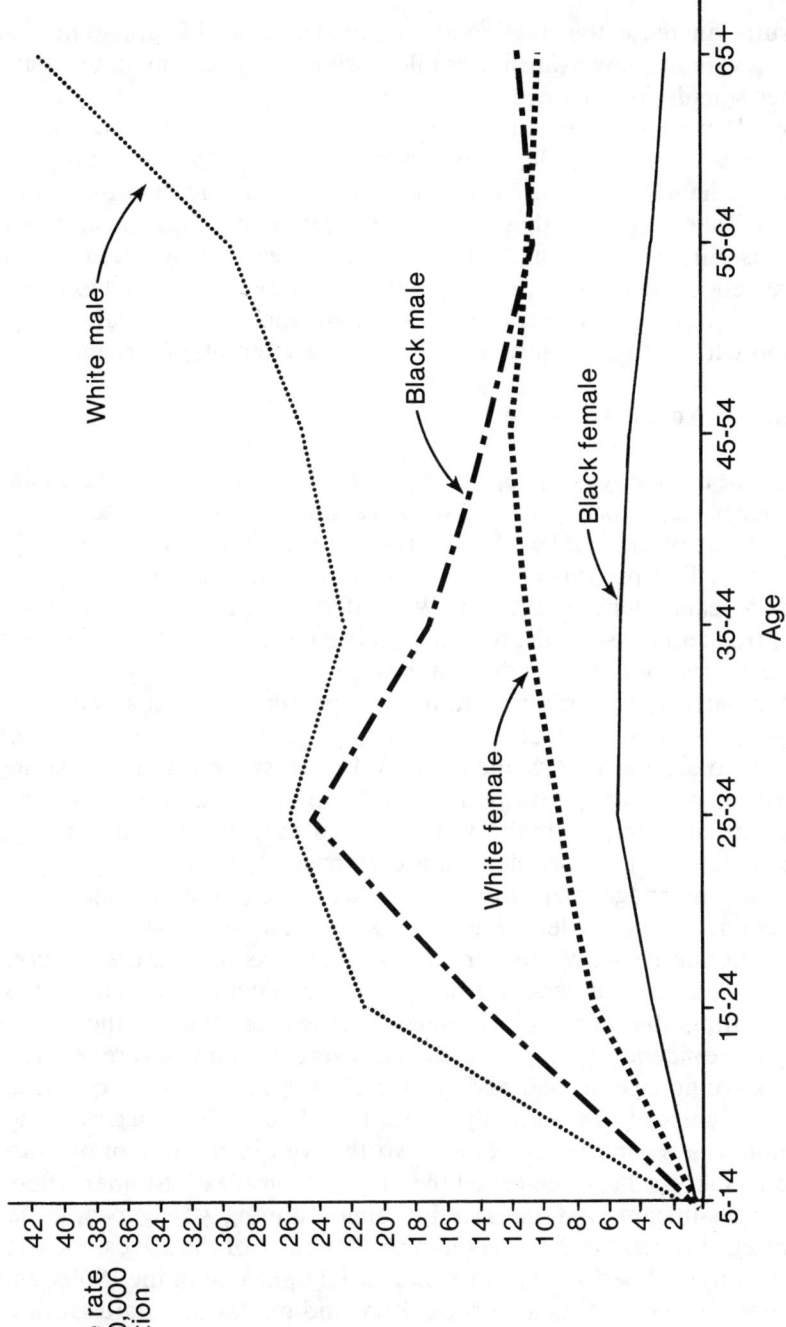

FIGURE 4.2. U.S. SUICIDE RATES BY SEX, RACE AND AGE GROUPS, 1978

Source: Statistical Abstract of the United States, 1981.

pursuits, increase the likelihood of suicide. It is also apparent that people who are downwardly mobile, losing occupational status, have higher suicide rates (Breed, 1963).

People who are married tend to kill themselves far less frequently than those who are single, divorced, or widowed. Moreover, the married who have children are less apt to commit suicide than those who do not. Taken together, these facts suggest that family relationships and responsibilities may act as a buffer protecting against suicidal impulses. More generally, it appears that people who have trouble establishing and maintaining warm, mutually interdependent social relationships are more likely to make serious, lethal suicide attempts (Worden, 1976).

Adolescent and Young Adult Suicide

Suicide among young people and college students has been increasing at a sharp, steady pace for the last 25 years. In the United States during 1981, 5,161 of the 27,596 officially recorded suicides were in the 15–24 age group. This proportion represents an increase of about 300% in the past 25 years (Hendin, 1982, p. 29). Self-destruction is now the third most frequent cause of death among those between the ages of 15 and 24, surpassed only by accidents and homicide.

Two particularly striking features are apparent in the characteristics of young suicides. First, unlike all other age groups, rates are *higher* for those who are married (Seiden, 1969). It is possible that many young marriages occur as an escape from unhappy parental homes that are frequently associated with the backgrounds of suicidal individuals. High divorce rates among people who are married very young also suggest that early marriage is apt to be particularly stressful and unstable.

Second, college students commit suicide at a higher rate than their nonacademic peers. Moreover, suicidal students have generally been found to be more successful, from outward indications such as grades, than comparable nonsuicidal students. However, even in the face of objective evidence of their success, many suicidal students are reported to lack confidence in their ability, to feel as though their success is an accident, and to fear eventually being "found out." This nagging anxiety about one's genuine ability and worth, even in the face of outward signs of success, has been called the "Fraud Complex" (Munter, 1966).

It is significant that the rise in suicide among young people has persisted through the relative quiet and stability of the 1950s, the outwardly directed period of protest and social upheaval in the 1960s, and the more inwardly directed drug culture and retreat into narcissism of the 1970s. Despite the fact that newspaper reports often imply that major tension-producing events such as campus unrest or increases in drug use account for higher suicide rates, researchers tend to disagree with this explanation. People familiar with youthful suicides suggest that the problem runs much deeper.

> Contrary to what might have been expected, the rise of student despair, alienation, experimentation with drugs for recreation, loss of confidence, and disillusionment with societal modes of regulation has not caused a wave of suicides. Private hopelessness or despair, rather than distress concerning public developments that is shared with one's peer group, is the paramount motive for suicide. (Farnsworth, 1972, pp. ix and x)

This is not to say that the rise in youthful suicide is unrelated to changes in our society. Hendin (1976) persuasively points to what he sees as an emotional atrophy in the family.

> Society is fomenting depression in the trend toward the devaluation of children and the family. The increasing emphasis on solitary gratification and immediate, tangible gain from all relationships encourages an unwillingness in parents to give of themselves or tolerate the demands of small children. It is not surprising that the family emerges through the eyes of many students as a jail in which everyone is in solitary confinement, trapped within their own particular suffering. The frequent absence of intimacy, affection, warmth, or shared concern, the prevalence of families in which no one had gotten what he needed or wanted has had a profound impact on this generation.
>
> Out of this disaffection has come a rising number of young people who are drawn to numbness because it has been their only security for a lifetime. Whenever the newness of coming to college, of graduating, of finding a person or a pursuit that interferes with that security and threatens to break the bond of deadness that held them to their parents, these students may be overwhelmed by suicidal desires. Certainly in their suicidal attempts these young people are moving toward becoming finally and forever what they felt they were meant to be. (pp. 332–333)

EXPLANATIONS OF SUICIDE

Social Integration and Regulation

Durkheim. One of the earliest and certainly most influential theories explaining suicide was proposed by the French sociologist Emile Durkheim in the late 1800s. He observed many of the same sorts of tendencies in official suicide rates that we can see now. Rates of poor countries are lower than affluent ones; the married have lower rates than other marital categories; and so on. Durkheim therefore reasoned that if suicide rates showed consistent patterns among social categories, there must be social characteristics to explain the consistencies.

Durkheim proposed four types of suicide—egoistic, altruistic, anomic, and fatalistic—with an explanation for each. Egoistic suicide occurs when a person has lost (or possibly never had) close social ties with others. The person is not well integrated into the society and life has become meaningless. Those most apt to commit egoistic suicide include the aged who are increasingly less integrated into the society as they retire and their family and friends either become more remote or die.

Altruistic suicide occurs when a person literally gives up his life for the benefit of the society or group. Examples would be Japanese kamikaze pilots during World War II who made suicidal crash attacks on enemy targets, or a soldier who jumps on a live grenade to save the rest of the unit. In the case of altruistic suicide, the person's integration into the group is extremely high—so high in fact that one's life is sacrificed for it.

Durkheim thought that *anomie* (normlessness) is an endemic condition of modern social life. However, it is most severe when there is especially rapid social change, especially economic upheaval in a society. He suggested that in periods of economic boom or bust, there is rapid upward and/or downward mobility in the society. People are moving from one social category to another at a much higher than normal rate. And as they move, people lose their social bearings in their new positions. They are less sure of the rules to guide their behavior and relationships with others. Norms lose their power to regulate peoples' expectations for themselves and for others. In this relatively insecure, normless, anomic social environment, Durkheim proposed that higher rates of *anomic* suicide would occur.

Finally, Durkheim briefly mentioned *fatalistic* suicide which happens when a person is overwhelmed by feelings of powerlessness in the face of "oppressive discipline." Durkheim thought that the suicides of slaves, who obviously suffer from excessive regulation of their lives, were fatalistic. In our earlier discussion of the rising suicide rate among young blacks, fatalism was proposed as a possible explanation (Breed, 1970).

At a more general level, Durkheim theorized that two sociological variables—the degree of a person's *integration* into social life and the amount of *regulation* over his behavior—were keys to understanding suicide rates. Low integration leads to high rates of egoistic suicide while altruistic suicide is characterized by extremely high integration.[1]

Persons who experience moderate levels of integration have low suicide rates. Likewise, high suicide rates are associated with the lack of social regulation in periods of anomie or normlessness; and high rates also occur among those who are so subject to arbitrary authority

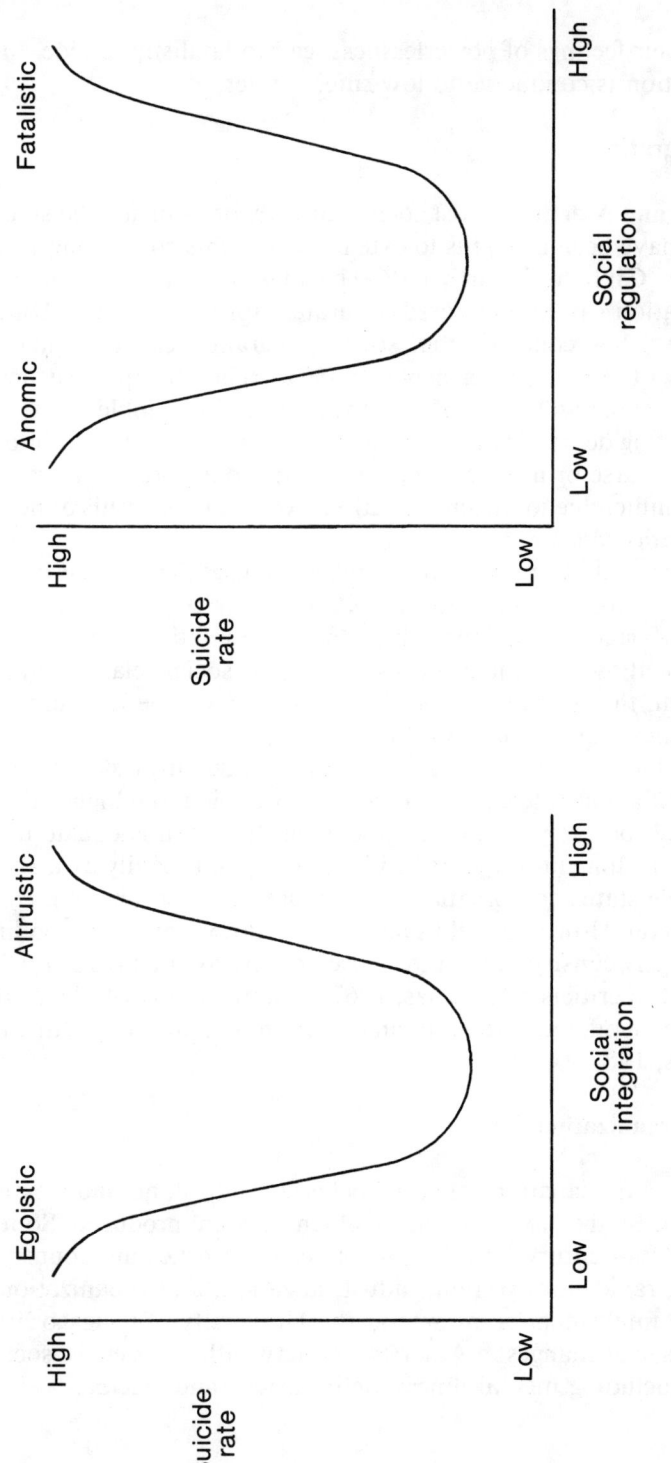

FIGURE 4.3. PREDICTIONS OF DURKHEIM'S THEORY OF SUICIDE

that their feelings of powerlessness lead to fatalistic suicide. Moderate regulation is conducive to low suicide rates.

Status Integration

Gibbs and Martin. Most sociological theories of suicide since Durkheim have been attempts to extend his insights concerning social integration. Gibbs and Martin (1964) begin with the question of how social integration can be measured accurately for a true test of Durkheim's theory. They conclude that social integration can be defined as the degree of stability in a person's social relationships. Further, social relationships will be stable to the degree that people are free of the conflicting demands of incompatible status expectations. For example, a male nurse or a female engineer is apt to experience a great deal of role conflict due to the incompatible expectations for his or her sex and occupational status.

Gibbs and Martin reason that when statuses conflict—as in the situation of a male nurse—people will avoid or get out of those socially uncomfortable situations. Thus, there are relatively few male nurses. But for those few male nurses who exist, social relationships will be difficult, their social integration with others will be less, and their suicide rates will be relatively high.

The theory predicts, then, that the less frequently a status or configuration of statuses (e.g., male nurses) is occupied, the higher the suicide rate will be. As you can imagine, collecting data adequate to test the theory is difficult because suicide rates are not readily available for all possible status combinations of sex, age, race, occupation, education, and so on. However, Gibbs and Martin do present some findings that are largely consistent with their predictions. While the theory has been subject to criticism (Douglas, 1967; Chambliss and Steele, 1966) since it was first offered, it remains an important stimulus for further research (Gibbs, 1982).

Social Disorganization

Cavan. Explanations of social behavior, like all human creations, are affected by the environment in which they are produced. So it is with early 20th-century American theorists who worked in a country experiencing rapid immigration, industrialization, and urbanization. Many whose intellectual home was at the University of Chicago linked the rapid social changes in American society with a variety of social problems including mental illness, delinquency, and suicide.

Numerous studies from this perspective concentrated on analyzing different areas of a city, frequently Chicago, to establish correlations between the amount of social disorganization in an area and the rates of deviance in it. The sequence of events was proposed to go something like this. Areas with high residential mobility and transient populations lack the traditions to create stable communities. Such areas, which are especially apt to arise in periods of rapid social change, suffer from social disorganization—they lack strong social values and traditions to control the behavior of the residents. As a result, people in them are especially prone to high rates of personal disorganization. Personal disorganization, in turn, leads to higher rates of deviance, including suicide.

Cavan's (1928) study of suicide relies heavily on this reasoning. And, like Faris and Dunham's (1939) ecological study of *Mental Illness in Urban Areas* discussed in Chapter 3, Cavan's findings could be interpreted using the "drift hypothesis" as an alternative to the social disorganization one. Indeed, Cavan actually seems to leave the drift hypothesis as a distinct possibility by saying:

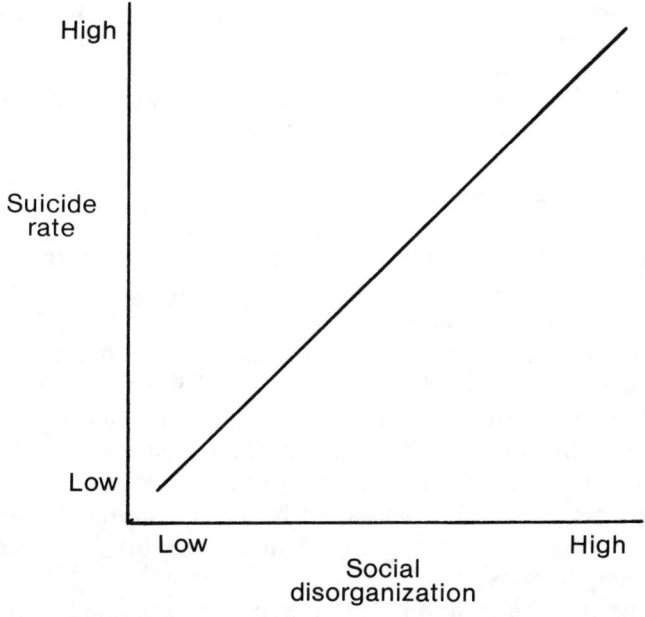

FIGURE 4.4. PREDICTED RELATIONSHIP BETWEEN SOCIAL DISORGANIZATION AND SUICIDE

> It is not to be thought that these institutions (dope peddlers, bars, houses of prostitution, rooming-houses and pawnshops) and types of conduct typical of the highly suicidal areas cause suicide. Rather they are symptoms of a general condition of personal and social disorganization which in the end may lead to suicide. There is in these areas a concentration of unsatisfied and disorganized persons, and therefore the probability of more suicide than in communities well organized as to community life and the characters of individuals (Cavan, 1928, pp. 104–105).

The concentration of unsatisfied and disorganized persons in these areas may, of course, occur because such people, unsuccessful in the mainstream life of the society, "drift" into the skid row areas of cities thereby contributing to the high suicide rates there.

At the same time, Cavan is careful not to suggest that social disorganization is the *only* cause of suicide. Rather, she argues that social disorganization increases its likelihood.

> In even the most stable social organization there is probably some personal disorganization, some people who cannot fit themselves wholly to the demands of customs and institutions. In times of social disorganization the difficulty is increased, and many people who would travel happily along under normal conditions find themselves unable to adjust to conflicting standards. It is these people, unable, under adverse social conditions, to work out a satisfying personal life organization, who contribute to the increased suicide rates in communities where social disorganization prevails. (Cavan, 1928, pp. 107–108)

Frustration and Aggression

Henry and Short. Some theorists have studied homicide and suicide as a pair of related phenomena. The source of the supposed relationship derives from the assumption that both homicide and suicide are forms of aggression that result from frustration. The fundamental difference is that homicide is a form of aggression directed outwardly, against another, while suicide is an aggressive act directed inwardly, against one's self. Beginning with this assumption, Henry and Short (1954) seek to answer the question: Why is there a tendency for people in some social categories (e.g., blacks) to have high homicide rates and low suicide rates while others (e.g., whites) have low homicide rates and high suicide rates?

Henry and Short first turn to the matter of blame for frustrations. If you have been ascribed a relatively low status in the society and feel relatively little power in controlling what happens to you, when you feel frustrated in reaching your goals, you are not likely to turn toward yourself as the source of your frustration or the target of your aggression. As a black person in a racially stratified society, the blame for your frustration obviously must lie elsewhere than in yourself. Therefore, aggression is more likely to be directed outwardly than inwardly. On the other hand, if you have a relatively high ascribed status with the advantages on your side as you try to reach your goals, who is there to blame other than yourself if you fail and are frustrated? According to this argument, whites in American society are more likely to direct aggression inwardly than outwardly.

The general principle proposed by Henry and Short to summarize these ideas begins with the concept of external restraint. Low-status people are subject to a high degree of external restraint or control by others. High-status people are less subject to the external restraint of others. Henry and Short reason that high external restraint of a population is associated with low suicide rates and high homicide rates. Likewise, low external restraint is associated with high suicide rates and low homicide rates.

Henry and Short next examine the role of child-rearing practices to explain inwardly-versus-outwardly directed aggression. Researchers

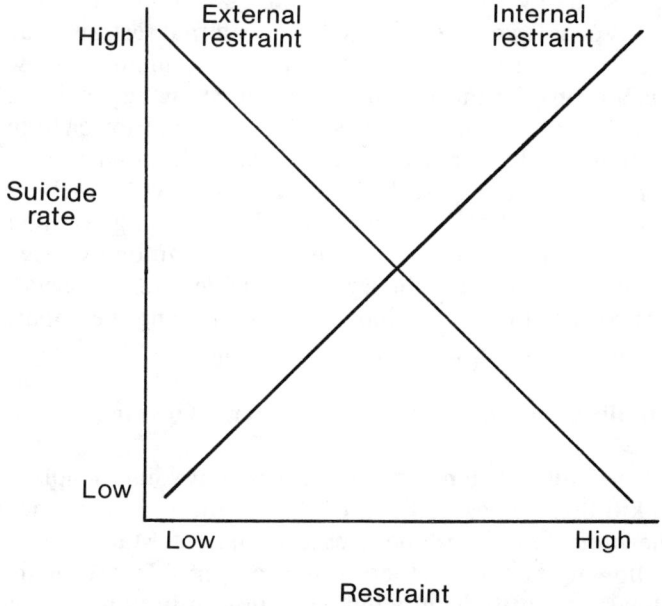

FIGURE 4.5. HENRY AND SHORT'S PREDICTED RELATIONSHIPS BETWEEN TYPE OF RESTRAINT AND SUICIDE

studying the different methods people use to raise children have found that working-class parents tend to use physical punishment while middle- and upper-class parents resort more to reasoning, threatened isolation, and "love-oriented" discipline. Further, it has been found that discipline by physical punishment is apt to hinder formation of strong internal controls and a heightened sense of guilt, while child-rearing techniques emphasizing loss of love rather than physical punishment lead to a strong internal control and superego formation. A person with the strong internal restraint of a well-developed superego (sense of guilt) is less likely to direct aggression against others. Weak internal restraint, in the form of a weak superego, means that there are lowered barriers against directing aggression outwardly against others. Henry and Short predict then that strong internal restraints will be associated with higher suicide rates and lower homicide rates and that weak internal restraints will be associated with low suicide rates and high homicide rates.

In sum, the theory is based on the concepts of external and internal restraint. Lower status people who are subject to both high external restraint and are socialized to have low internal restraint will be more likely to direct aggression against others (homicide) and, therefore, to be less likely to direct aggression against the self (suicide). Higher-status people who experience lower external restraint but are socialized with higher internal restraint will tend to blame themselves more for frustrations, be more inhibited in directing aggression against others, and, therefore, have higher suicide rates and lower homicide rates.

Henry and Short's explanation of differential rates of suicide and homicide is, like most theories, consistent with much of the data—but not all. Recall that whites generally have higher suicide rates than blacks. However, the high rate of suicide among young black males is not explained by the theory. The suicide rates by social class are even less consistent, one complicating factor being the apparently high suicide rates among both very high-status and very low-status people.

Suggestibility, Societal Reaction, and Social Meaning

Suggestion. The notion is not new that some people may be moved to kill themselves by the thought of imitating someone else. Probably the most famous modern case is that of Marilyn Monroe in 1962. Following her death there was a perceptible rise in the suicide rate. However, until recently evidence that imitation is a significant factor has been contradictory and inconclusive (Lester, 1972).

A study by Phillips (1974) seems to show quite clearly that the suicide rate increases immediately after a suicide has been publicized in newspapers. The greater the publicity devoted to the suicide, the larger the rise in suicides thereafter in the area which the publicity covers. While certainly not a major cause of suicide, it does appear that the highly publicized suicide of a prominent person may encourage others to imitate the self-destruction.

Societal Reaction. Suicide attempts have been appropriately described as a "cry for help" (Faberow and Shneidman, 1965). It makes sense, then, that how those around a person respond to him or her affects the decision to commit suicide. Attempted suicides far outnumber completed ones, and it appears that suicide attempts frequently are arranged in a way that there is a fairly high probability of being rescued. When people respond sympathetically to the cry for help, the suicidal person's life often changes sufficiently to inhibit further attempts.

Kobler and Stotland (1964) argue against a view of suicide in which the person is driven to self-destruction by a death instinct. Instead, they emphasize the reactions of others to a person who has demonstrated suicidal intent.

> Our conception views suicidal attempts and verbal or other communications of suicidal intent as efforts, however misdirected, to solve problems of living, as frantic pleas for help and hope from other people: help in solving the problems, and hope that they can be solved. Whether the individual then actually commits suicide—and this is our central concern—seems to depend in large part on the nature of the response by other people to his plea. If the response is hopeless and helpless, suicide is more likely to occur. It is our conviction that an implicit or explicit fear or expectation of suicide is most often communicated by a hopeless, helpless response, and that this communication is important in facilitating suicide. (p. 1)

As evidence for their position, Kobler and Stotland describe "an epidemic of suicide" in a psychiatric hospital whose staff was experiencing lowered morale and deteriorating self-confidence. In this situation, the staff was unable to respond favorably to the patients who came to the hospital with the expectation of being helped. Indeed, it appears that the hospital staff subtly communicated to the patients an expectation that the patients would kill themselves. Having their own feelings of hopelessness and helplessness reinforced and focused through the expectations of the staff, the patients apparently responded to the expectation by committing suicide.

Social Meaning. It is apparent from the theories discussed up to this point that most (with the exception of the societal-reaction perspective) examine and attempt to explain official suicide statistics. Recalling our earlier discussion in this chapter concerning the problematic definition of any particular death as a suicide and the barriers to consistent, complete reporting of suicidal deaths, one might be justified in questioning the validity of theories which take as their primary task the explanation of official suicide rates. One sociologist (Douglas, 1967) has taken this position and reasoned further that there is a need for careful observations and descriptions of actual individual suicide cases before we can explain why people commit suicide.

By applying this approach, Douglas has inferred some common patterns of meaning that people attach to their suicidal actions. They are:

- Suicide as a means of transforming the soul from this world to the other world. The person sees suicide as a vehicle of escape and a way of changing fundamentally one's relationships to others in the world after death.
- Transformation of the substantial self in this world or in the other world. By attempting or committing suicide, the suicidal person tries to reform others' images of him. The killing of oneself can be used as a general indication of how serious, sincere, and committed one is.
- Suicidal actions as a means of achieving fellow feeling. Suicide or its attempt is intended to elicit sympathy from others.
- A means of getting revenge. The suicidal act may be used to make others feel responsible or guilty.

Thus, Douglas claims that suicide cannot be explained without studying the concrete situations in which it takes place. We must understand the meanings the suicidal person attaches to his or her actions if we are to explain why they occur. This can only be done, he argues, through the comparative study of suicidal cases as opposed to the statistical study of suicidal rates.

Suicide Notes

On the face of it, the study of suicide notes would seem to be a highly effective way to explore the meaning of an individual's suicide. After all, at a person's self-chosen moment we might expect some profound statement of purpose and explanation. In fact, however, this is usually not the case. Reviewing the results of suicide note studies over the past 25 years, Shneidman (1976) observes:

> Suicidal notes are not like letters or diaries, which are written at leisure, often away from the scene of action. Suicide notes would seem to be comparable to battle communiqués, filled with the emotion of the cur-

rent scene and describing some special aspects of the contemporary dramatic event. And yet, as one reads hundreds of suicide notes, it becomes clear that many of them tell pretty much the same story. What is most disappointing is that most suicide notes, written at perhaps the most dramatic moment of a person's life, are surprisingly commonplace, banal, even sometimes poignantly pedestrian and dull. It is obviously difficult to write an original suicide note; it is almost impossible to write a note that is really informative or explanatory. (p. 258)

Approximately one-sixth to one-third of those who are officially labeled suicides leave suicide notes. However, studies comparing the characteristics of those who do leave notes with those who do not show no significant differences in age, sex, marital status, socioeconomic status, mental condition, and numerous other factors (Shneidman and Farberow, 1957; Tuckman et al., 1959). At the same time, it is impossible to say whether suicides who write notes have fundamentally different attitudes from those who do not.

In studies comparing genuine and simulated suicide notes, it has been shown that genuine notes are characterized by narrow reasoning, greater hostility and self-blame, more use of specific names and instructions to survivors, less introspection and more use of the various meanings of the word love (Shneidman, 1976:260). Indeed, the content of genuine suicide notes is generally sufficiently typical that after some practice, most people can learn to distinguish real from simulated suicide notes with a fairly high rate of success.

The repetitive themes in genuine suicide notes are also apparent from researchers' attempts to classify them. For example, Jacobs (1967) found that nearly all of 112 suicide notes he examined fell into one of six categories:

1. *first form notes*—begging forgiveness or indulgence on the part of survivors;
2. *sorry illness notes*—"... Before I get a stroke on top of my other troubles of my legs I decided that this would be easier for me ... Please forgive me. I cannot endure any more pains";
3. *not sorry illness notes*—"Dear Jane: You are ruining your health and your life just for me, and I cannot let you do it ...";
4. *direct accusation notes*—"You Bob and Jane caused this—this all";
5. *will and testament notes*—"I hereby bequeath all my worldly goods and holdings to Bill Smith ..."; and
6. *notes of instructions*—"I have gone down to the ocean. Pick out the cheapest coffin Jones Bros. has. I don't remember the cost. I'll put my purse in the trunk of the car."

Despite the early hopeful enthusiasm for what suicide notes might tell us about self-destruction, the promise has been largely unfulfilled. At the time one is about to commit suicide—at the end of hope—expression of the most deeply meaningful aspects of the act is probably impossible. "In other words, that special state of mind necessary to perform a suicidal act is one which is essentially incompatible with an insightful recitation of what was going on in one's mind that lead to the act itself" (Shneidman, 1976: 264).

A Basic Suicide Syndrome

There is no single theoretical formulation that will explain every suicide. As we have seen in this chapter, numerous types of suicide have been proposed—for example Durkheim's egoistic, altruistic, anomic, and fatalistic—with differing social conditions and personal motivations surrounding each. Still, Breed (1972) has made a worthwhile attempt to assemble a set of characteristics which appear to be present in at least half of American suicides. Further, these characteristics suggest possible modes of intervention to prevent an impending suicide.

First, many suicidal persons have a great deal of *commitment* to "making it" by the accumulation of things and being upwardly mobile; they have very high aspirations for themselves and have thoroughly internalized cultural norms of success. On the other hand, they have much lower commitment to people.

A second characteristic common among suicides is *rigidity*—an inability to bend or change either their roles or their goals. In the face of difficulties or failure, the person does not have the flexibility to try new paths, to adjust goals to fit a new situation.

Third is *failure*. For men, this frequently includes being fired from a job, passed over for promotion, demoted, or some other frustration in their work lives. Among women, analagous difficulties tend to occur in family-related activities including troubles in relationships with men or failures as mothers. Very often there is multiple failure—for example, the unemployed man whose wife leaves him.

The fourth element is *shame* as a response to failure. The person feels his shortcomings deeply, anticipates negative reactions from others, and experiences a disastrous blow to his or her self-esteem. "The self-image presented to others is felt to be shattered; the 'depression' often found among suiciders can easily follow" (Breed, 1972: 8). The person wishes to "run away and hide." The solution, of course, is to change one's commitments—to adjust one's goals. But this is impossible for the rigid person.

Fifth and finally, there is *social isolation*. As self-esteem declines, interactions with others become more difficult. The person withdraws. "Once a committed person feels shame over failure and cannot create a new life because of his rigidity, he feels worthless and, moreover, feels that other people also see him as worthless" (Breed, 1972: 8).

What can a potential rescuer do? The five components of the suicide syndrome do suggest tactics for altering a potential suicidal career. Breed (1972) admits that intervention on behalf of the most rigid of persons may be difficult. However, many who manifest this suicide syndrome can be helped to cope with the crisis. "In some cases the 'failure' is illusory, and the wise helper can point this out, thus reducing the shame and isolation. The helper can also counsel experimentation with *switching goals, roles,* and *social contacts,* and a reduction in commitment (placing the eggs in different baskets)" (Breed, 1972: 17).

SUICIDE PREVENTION AND SOCIAL POLICY

The main vehicles for implementing suicide prevention strategies in the United States have been programs that attempt to provide crisis intervention, usually by telephone. Generally, sympathetic volunteers who have received some training by professionals answer calls on the crisis hot-line and help the caller by referral to services. Some of the religiously affiliated services of this sort, like the Save-a-Life League in New York City, have been operating since the early 1900s. But a sharp increase in the prevention movement during the 1960s has resulted in the establishment of about 200 nonreligiously affiliated suicide prevention programs in the country today.

How effective are such programs in the prevention of suicide? Research results are not encouraging. The most carefully designed study (Lester, 1974) found no significant suicide rate changes according to whether cities had a suicide prevention center or not. Summarizing the situation, Hendin (1982) says that

> The evidence by 1980 is fairly conclusive that suicide prevention programs have had no demonstrable effect on the suicide rate of their communities. Few responsible suicide prevention centers in this country now make claims about the number of lives they have saved. (Hendin, 1982, p. 183)

This is not to say that such programs are useless and should be abolished. They unquestionably do fulfill useful functions by directing people in need to a variety of helpful services. Many prevention centers have served as excellent educational and training facilities or have stimulated important research. However, it is almost certain that they do not attract as callers the vast majority of suicide attempters or eventual completers. This shortcoming has led Hendin (1982) to the following analysis.

> Suicide is a problem of considerable magnitude. It is estimated that there are several hundred thousand suicide attempts in this country each year.... Follow-up studies have shown that about 10% of an attempted-suicide population go on to kill themselves within a ten-year period. Other retrospective studies in the United States have shown that between 20% and 65% of those who kill themselves have a history of prior attempts. These findings indicate that the attempted suicide population contains much of the eventual suicide population, plus an even larger number of people who will not go on to kill themselves. (Hendin, 1982, pp. 185–186)

By using our current knowledge about those most likely to eventually commit suicide, it is possible to identify high risk cases among attempted suicides. This strategy would better focus efforts on the people most likely to require intensive suicide intervention. Thus, Hendin concludes with this recommendation.

> The identification and treatment of the high-risk population might involve as many as ten thousand new cases a year throughout the country, but such a program would still be far more manageable—and probably more fruitful—than one attempting to identify and somehow treat the literally millions who call in to suicide prevention centers. Such treatment would have to include individual psychotherapy, the use of psychotropic medications when indicated, and in many cases the use of volunteers to work as befrienders in combination with a therapist. The efficacy of such an approach could first be tried and tested in a limited way in order to avoid the sequence of enthusiasm and disillusion that characterizes the history of the suicide prevention centers. (Hendin, 1982: 186)

SUMMARY

Suicide has been described as a distinctly human phenomenon that has pricked the curiosity of social theorists because of the remarkably stable patterns its rates exhibit among different social groups. Attitudes toward suicide have ranged from disdain to encouragement throughout history with the dominant reaction being some combination of fear and disapproval. Indeed, the contemporary stigma attached to the act contributes in part to the difficulties in amassing accurate official statistics about it. Still, it is possible to identify several persistent variations in suicide rates that are sufficiently great to ensure their validity despite shortcomings in the data. For example,

- Suicide rates are generally higher in developed, industrialized countries than in developing ones.
- In the United States and other multiracial countries, whites have higher suicide rates than nonwhites.
- Suicide rates are generally highest among the old, although rates among young people have been increasing dramatically over the past 25 years.
- Women *attempt* suicide more frequently, but men have the highest *completed* suicide rates.

At the sociological level of explanation, Durkheim proposed the importance of social integration and regulation. Extremes of either—integration or regulation—in his theory account for one of four types of suicide (egoistic, altruistic, anomic, or fatalistic). Thus old people, who by virtue of retirement and loss of friends and relatives through death become less well integrated into the society, are more apt to commit egoistic suicide (caused by low social integration). At the other extreme, the soldier who jumps on a live grenade to save his comrades demonstrates his intense integration into his group by sacrificing his life for it (altruistic suicide). Gibbs and Martin's status integration theory and Cavan's social disorganization approach are additional sociological explanations.

Social psychological theories include Henry and Short's analysis of the relationship between suicide and homicide. They conceptualize both as manifestations of aggression in the face of economic frustration. The poor and the powerless, when frustrated, are more apt to direct their aggression outwardly (homicide) while the well-to-do and powerful are more apt to blame themselves for whatever shortcomings they experience and direct aggression toward themselves (suicide). Henry and Short combine this idea with evidence about how different child-rearing practices permit or inhibit peoples' tendencies to lash out against others.

Also at the social–psychological level, we considered the role of imitation as a suicide motivator. Societal reaction or labeling theory has been used in one study (Kobler and Stotland) to account for a "suicide epidemic" in a small mental hospital. Apparently, when subtle cues from a demoralized hospital staff conveyed to patients the expectation that they would commit suicide, more of them did.

Although there are undeniable social regularities in suicide rates, a full understanding of the act requires trying to infer the meaning that people attach to their suicidal actions. Douglas' approach to the social meaning of suicide and the study of suicide notes were considered in this light. Consistent with the information in much of the chapter, we then presented Breed's set of characteristics often associated with suicidal individuals: commitment to upward mobility, rigidity, failure, shame, and social isolation. In conclusion, we described the limited effectiveness of current suicide prevention programs and offered Hendin's strategy for identifying high-risk cases as a viable alternative.

NOTE

1. In a more recent formulation, Straus and Straus (1953:469) suggest that suicide rates will be relatively high in closely integrated social structures with the addition that higher homicide rates will be associated with more loosely integrated social structures.

REFERENCES

Breed, W.
    1963   Occupational mobility and suicide among white males. *American Sociological Review, 28,* pp. 179–188.

Breed, W.
    1970   The Negro and fatalistic suicide. *Pacific Sociological Review, 13,* pp. 156–162.

Breed, W.
    1972   Five components of a basic suicide syndrome. *Life-Threatening Behavior, 2,* pp. 3–18.

Camus, A.
    1955   *The myth of Sisyphus and other essays.* New York: Vintage Books.

Cavan, R. S.
    1928   *Suicide.* Chicago: University of Chicago Press.

Chambliss, W. J., & Steele, M. F.
    1966   Status integration and suicide. *American Sociological Review, 31,* pp. 524–532.

Douglas, J. D.
    1967   *The social meaning of suicide.* Princeton, N.J.: Princeton University Press.

Durkheim, E.
    1951   *Suicide.* J. A. Spaulding & G. Simpson, Trans. New York: Free Press.

Farberow, N. L., & Shneidman, E.
    1965   *The cry for help.* New York: McGraw-Hill.

Farberow, N. L.
    1975   *Suicide in different cultures.* Baltimore: University Park Press.

Faris, R. E. L., & Dunham, H. W.
    1939   *Mental disorders in urban areas.* Chicago: University of Chicago Press.

Farnsworth, D. L.
    1972   Foreword to E. S. Shneidman (Ed.), *Death and the college student.* New York: Behavioral Publications.

Gibbs, J.
  1982   Status integration and suicide rates. *American Sociological Review 47,* pp. 227–237.
Gibbs, J. P., & Martin, W. T.
  1964   *Status integration and suicide.* Eugene, Oregon: University of Oregon Press.
Giddens, A.
  1971   *The sociology of suicide.* London: Frank Cass.
Hendin, H.
  1969   *Black suicide.* New York: Basic Books.
Hendin, H.
  1976   Growing up dead: Student suicide. In E. S. Shneidman (Ed.), *Suicidology: Contemporary developments.* New York: Grune and Stratton.
Hendin, H.
  1982   *Suicide in America.* New York: W. W. Norton.
Henry, A. F., & Short, J. F.
  1954   Suicide and homicide. Glencoe, Ill.: The Free Press.
Jacobs, J.
  1967   Phenomenological study of suicide notes. *Social Problems, 15,* pp. 60–72.
Kalish, R. A.
  1968   Suicide. *Bulletin of suicidology,* December 1968, pp. 37–43.
Kobler, A. L., & Stotland, E.
  1964   *The end of hope: A socio-clinical study of suicide.* New York: Free Press.
La Fontaine, J.
  1960   Homicide and suicide among the Gisu. In Paul Bohannon (Ed.), *African homicide and suicide.* Princeton, N.J.: Princeton University Press.
La Fontaine, J.
  1975   Anthropology. In S. Perlin (Ed.), *A handbook for the study of suicide.* New York: Oxford University Press.
Leighton, A., & Hughes, C. C.
  1955   Notes on Eskimo patterns of suicide. *Southwestern Journal of Anthropology, 11,* pp. 327–338.
Lester, D.
  1972   *Why people kill themselves: A summary of research findings on suicidal behavior.* Springfield, Ill.: Charles C Thomas.
Lester, D.
  1974   Effect of suicide prevention centers on suicide rates in the United States. *Health Services Reports, 89*:37–39.
Maris, R. W.
  1969   *Social forces in urban suicide.* Homewood, Ill.: Dorsey Press.
Munter, P. K.
  1966   Depression and suicide in college students. In L. McNeer (Ed.), *Proceedings of conference on depression and suicide in adolescents and young adults.* Fairlee, Vt.: Vermont Department of Mental Health.

Phillips, D. P.
   1974   The influence of suggestion on suicide: Substantive and theoretical implications of the Werther effect. *American Sociological Review, 39,* pp. 340–354.
Pokorny, A. D., Smith, J. P., & Finch, T. R.
   1972   Vehicular suicides. *Life-Threatening Behavior, 2,* pp. 105–119.
Powell, E. H.
   1958   Occupation, status and suicide: Toward a redefinition of anomie. *American Sociological Review, 23,* pp. 131–139.
Rosen, G.
   1975   History. J. S. Perlin (Ed.), *A handbook for the study of suicide.* New York: Oxford University Press.
Sciden, R. H.
   1969   *Suicide among youth.* Washington, D.C.: U.S. Government Printing Office.
Shneidman, E. S.
   1976   Suicide notes reconsidered. In Edwin S. Shneidman (Ed.), *Suicidology: Contemporary developments.* New York: Grune and Stratton.
Shneidman, E. S., & Farberow, N. L.
   1957   *Clues to suicide.* New York: McGraw-Hill.
Stengel, E.
   1964   *Suicide and attempted suicide.* London: Penguin.
Straus, J. H., & Straus, M. A.
   1953   Suicide, homicide and social structure in Ceylon. *American Journal of Sociology, 58,* pp. 461–469.
Tabachnick, N., & Gussen, J.
   1973   *Accident or suicide? Destruction by automobile.* Springfield, Ill.: Charles C Thomas.
Tuckman, J., Kleiner, R. J., & Lowell, M.
   1959   Emotional content of suicide notes. *American Journal of Psychiatry, 116,* pp. 59–63.
Tuckman, J., Youngman, W. F., & Kriezman, G.
   1964   Occupation and suicide. *Industrial Medicine and Surgery, 33,* pp. 818–820.
U.S. Bureau of the Census
   1980   *Statistical abstracts of the United States.* Washington, D.C.: U.S. Government Printing Office.
U.S. Department of Health and Human Services
   1978   *Vital statistics of the United States, 26,* 12 (Monthly). Washington, D.C.: U.S. National Office of Vital Statistics.
Worden, J. W.
   1976   Lethality factors and the suicide attempt. In E. S. Shneidman (Ed.), *Suicidology: Contemporary developments.* New York: Grune and Stratton.

Chapter 5
ALCOHOL AND OTHER DRUGS

AN OVERVIEW OF DRUG USE
  What Is a Drug?
  Alcohol as a Drug
  Drug Use as Deviance: Laws and Perceptions
MAJOR DRUGS AND THEIR EFFECTS
  Central Nervous System Stimulants
  Central Nervous System Depressants
  Hallucinogens
  Marijuana
  Trends and Prevalence of Drug Use
EXPLANATIONS OF DRUG ABUSE
  Alcoholism
  The Disease Model
  Sociocultural Models
  Marijuana Use
  The Political Economy of Drugs
SUMMARY

AN OVERVIEW OF DRUG USE

People have used mind–altering substances for ages, predating recorded history. The discovery that alcohol is produced from overripe fruits almost certainly dates back to the Stone Age and it appears from archeological evidence that cultivated grain may have found one of its earliest uses in beer making. Likewise, ancient peoples long before Christ used opium, mescal buttons (mescaline), hallucinogenic mushrooms, and numerous other substances ingested with the intention of altering moods or perceptions. During the more recent period of recorded human history, there have been very few societies in which the use of drugs has been totally absent. Indeed, the use of alcohol among the world's societies comes close to being universal. Drug use is neither exclusively modern nor a phenomenon restricted to complex urban societies.

What Is a Drug?

Of course, not all drugs alter moods or perceptions. Antibiotics, aspirin, penicillin, and numerous other drugs are prescribed and taken with only the most minor of mind–altering effects, if any at all. However, when most people consider drug use in the context of deviant behavior or abuse, they usually think of substances that are ingested or injected with the intention of changing moods or perceptions. It is possible to alter your state of mind without ingesting or injecting a substance into your body. Practitioners of transcendental meditation, hypnosis, or avid long distance runners who have experienced a "runner's high" are examples. However, for our purposes, the definition of drugs will be restricted to physical substances ingested or injected into the body with the intention of altering moods or perceptions. The intention may be linked either to a medical or therapeutic rationale (as with morphine to reduce pain or Valium to suppress anxiety), recreation (drinking alcohol or smoking marijuana at a party), or physical dependence (the alcoholic or heroin addict).

Having defined our use of the term drug, it is next important to remember that drugs will never have exactly the same effects upon all people in all places. We are all aware that some people are able to hold their liquor better than others. There are some who, when drunk, become mellow while others become aggressive. These and other differences depend upon factors such as physique, cultural beliefs about drinking and drunkenness, the setting in which the drinking takes place, and so forth. Put simply, drugs do not themselves alter states of consciousness in specific ways. Rather, drug effects result from an interaction of numerous conditions which can vary enormously from one drug-taking situation to the next. Understanding drug effects requires taking account of the social setting in which the drug taking occurs.

The importance of social context as related to drug use is nicely captured by Erich Goode's (1978, pp. 190–194) list of factors that influence drug effects.

1. *Identity.* What does the user believe he or she has ingested? Frequently people think they have ingested one thing (e.g., marijuana, mescaline, LDS) when a bogus alternative has been substituted by a dealer. As numerous experiments have shown, the *placebo* effect of expecting a certain feeling or mood change can often stimulate that change in the absence of any active physical substance.
2. *Dose.* Generally, the more of a drug ingested, the more extreme the effect. However, in some cases, low doses may have the opposite effects of high doses. Very low doses of alcohol, in many people, increase the capacity to do certain intellectual tasks—possibly by lowering anxiety levels. However, larger doses of alcohol may dull the senses to the point of making the same task impossible.
3. *Potency and purity.* Some drugs, for example LSD, require taking only a tiny amount to produce extreme psychoactive effects. Other far less potent drugs, like alcohol, require far greater amounts to have marked effects. Well known also is the fact that many drugs available illegally on the street have been cut with inert substances by as much as 95%. In combination, potency and purity can account for part of the variation in the amount of a substance needed to produce a certain level of effect.
4. *Mixing.* Numerous drugs, when taken at the same time, have stronger effects than either taken separately. Probably the best known example is alcohol and barbiturates which have an increased likelihood of deadly depressant effects when taken together.

5. *Route of Administration.* Some drugs may be ingested a variety of ways. Marijuana may be smoked, eaten (mixed in food or sprinkled on it), drunk (as a tea), or swallowed as a tablet (in THC, or tetrahydrocannabinal, experiments). Different methods of administering the same substance may produce different effects. Other alternatives are sniffing (glue), snorting (cocaine), or injection (heroin). Often the mode chosen is more dependent upon cultural custom than differences in potency or effect.
6. *Habituation.* Continuous use of many, but not all, drugs produces increased tolerance; as the user becomes tolerant, more of the drug is needed to produce the desired effect. In addition, increased experience with a drug brings with it a greater assurance of how to handle and even enjoy strange sensations.
7. *Set and Setting.* "Set" includes the various subjective factors—expectations, mood, anxiety level, tiredness, and so on—that characterize the person taking a drug. To these variables, we can add the setting: alone in one's room, a party, a bar, an airplane, a formal dinner, a football game. Drinking the same quantity of the same alcoholic beverage by the same person may result in vastly different alterations of mood and behavior in different settings.

To sum up, then, drugs alone do not have specific effects. Drug effects result from a combination of the substance's chemical properties, the physical and mental condition of the drug user, and the setting in which the drug is taken.

Alcohol as a Drug

You will note that in a number of examples used so far in this chapter, alcohol has been treated as a drug. Most doctors and researchers who specialize in alcohol abuse would argue strenuously that alcohol is as much a drug as marijuana or even heroin. This is true despite the more popular image of alcohol as a substance quite apart from these more "dangerous" drugs. In contrast to the popular nondrug image of alcohol, official agencies like the National Institute on Alcohol Abuse and Alcoholism and private ones like Alcoholics Anonymous take the position that alcohol is a mind-altering chemical substance which fulfills every reasonable criterion to be labeled a drug.

Alcohol is a central nervous system depressant. It can produce several conditions that are usually regarded as measures of a drug's potential harmfulness. Alcohol can lead to *psychological dependence*. This is to say that a person may develop a powerful desire to drink—especially in particular social situations—even though he or she is not physically addicted. Alcohol shares with virtually all other mind-altering substances the capacity to produce psychological dependence. However, alcohol can also lead to *physical dependence* in some people. Alcohol is a potentially addictive drug. Heavy users, people who drink large amounts every few days, acquire a tolerance for it. In order to create the same effects, greater amounts of alcohol must be ingested. Finally, people addicted to alcohol suffer from severe withdrawal symptoms (tremors, delirium, and convulsions) when they attempt to stop drinking. The experience of immediate cessation, going "cold turkey," is a harrowing one that dramatizes the toxic effects of alcohol on the body.

Alcohol, then, has the potential to produce effects as serious and diverse as any other drug. Psychological dependence and physical dependence characterized by the tolerance-withdrawal syndrome are possible outcomes for excessive users. Moreover, the extent of excessive use in the United States far exceeds that for any other mind-altering substance. The most typical addict in America is not a heroin junkie, but an alcoholic.

Drug Use as Deviance: Laws and Perceptions

Obviously, not all drug taking is considered deviant. Medications that alter states of consciousness may be legally taken under the direction of a physician with no deviant stigma attached to the taker. Indeed, some mind-altering substances like caffeine, nicotine, and alcohol in moderation may be taken freely in the United States, within certain age restrictions, without legal threat or severe negative reactions from others. Even an illegal drug, like marijuana, may be used among some groups with no negative stigma or sense of impropriety. These observations suggest that two dimensions of drugs are particularly important when considering them from a sociological viewpoint. First is the drug's legal status: legal or illegal. Second is how the drug's use is perceived by others: Is it considered proper, normal use or is it improper, deviant abuse?

These two dimensions should be examined together, as in Figure 5.1, when considering drug use as deviant. By combining a drug's legal status and perceptions of use, we can see that: (1) Many drugs may be taken legally without deviant stigma; (2) Taking legal drugs may result in negative reactions from others if the dosage is extreme and/or it inhibits carrying out normal social roles; (3) A drug may be illegal, but its use may be so widespread in a group that its use is regarded as

ALCOHOL AND OTHER DRUGS

	Legal status	
Perceptions of use	Legal	Illegal
Proper use	Drugs prescribed by a physician in the prescribed dose. Coffee, nicotine Alcohol (in moderation) Methadone (prescribed)	Marijuana (particularly among some young people)
Improper use	Overdose or extended unprescribed use of prescription drugs. (e.g. Valium) Alcohol (regular drunkenness or alcoholism)	Heroin LSD STP

FIGURE 5.1. THE LEGAL STATUS AND PERCEPTIONS OF DRUG USE

normal and acceptable. Marijuana is an example, particularly in regard to its use and perceptions of its use by many younger people; (4) Some drugs are both illegal and widely considered improper and even dangerous to use. We should also be aware that any drug can change its legal status (e.g., the manufacture, sale, or transportation of alcohol was illegal in the United States between 1919 and 1933) and its image among large segments of the population (e.g., marijuana has been gaining steadily in rate of use and popular acceptance over the past 20 years).

Drug use or abuse is not merely a narrow physiological issue. The normal or deviant use of drugs must include consideration of a drug's legal status and how it is commonly perceived. In turn, laws and popular perceptions are very much matters of concern for the student of norms and deviance.

MAJOR DRUGS AND THEIR EFFECTS

The number of chemical substances known to have the potential to alter states of consciousness certainly runs into the thousands. However, only a relative few are regularly used nontherapeutically in the general population. Recognizing that the examples provided are far from exhaustive, we will be concentrating upon the most readily available and commonly used drugs—especially those that are illegal and/or frequently abused. Drugs may be classified by their usual mind-altering effects—their psychoactive properties, The major categories are:

1. Central nervous system stimulants
2. Central nervous system depressants
   a) analgesics
   b) sedative–hypnotics
3. Hallucinogens
4. Others (marijuana, hashish)

Central Nervous System Stimulants

These substances produce wakefulness and alertness. Caffeine, found in coffee, tea and some soft drinks, and nicotine in cigarettes are two widely used, largely unrestricted, legal stimulants. Amphetamines are frequently prescribed by physicians to treat depression, fatigue, appetite control in obesity, and hyperactivity in children. The most frequently illegally-used amphetamines in the United States include Desoxyn, Methedrine, Dexedrine, and Benzedrine. Because they increase alertness, nonmedical amphetamine use tends to be concentrated in certain occupational categories, such as truck drivers or assembly line workers and among college students. A recent survey (New York State Division of Substance Abuse, 1981b) found that in six months prior to the questioning, 3% of household residents had used stimulants nonmedically compared to 21% of college students.

Extended amphetamine use can lead to malnutrition and dehydration due to appetite suppression. The drugs are usually ingested orally as pills, but can be injected intravenously. Large dose, intravenous users, called "speed freaks," have a tendency to be highly irritable and even violently dangerous when "crashing" from several hours or days of "speeding." While amphetamines do not cause physical dependence, repeated use does lead to tolerance and the potential for psychological dependence.

Cocaine, also a central nervous system stimulant, is the illegal drug presently undergoing the most rapidly increasing use in the United States. Medically, it is prescribed as a local anesthetic. However, its expanding recreational use stems from its effects when "snorted" through the nose. In moderate doses, cocaine usually makes the user more active, talkative, and happy. Its effects are short-lived—a half hour or so; it produces no physical dependence and, rather than tolerance, sensitization is more likely so smaller doses achieve the same effect over time. Add to this a relatively high price tag and it is easy to see why cocaine has acquired an upper-status, *chic* image among illicit drugs.

The dimensions of cocaine's growth in popularity are indicated from a 1979 White House report. During that 12 month period, some

Drug type	Subtype	Examples	Perceptual effects	Psychological dependence possible	Physical dependence possible	Tolerance possible
Central nervous system stimulants		amphetamines, cocaine, caffeine, nicotine	Produce arousal, alertness, inhibit fatigue and lethargy	Yes	No	Yes (sensitization with cocaine)
Central nervous system depressants	analgesics	narcotics: opium, morphine, heroin, codeine. Also, Percodan, Methadone, Demerol	Reduce perception of pain	Yes	Yes	Yes
	sedative–hypnotics	alcohol, barbiturates, Valium, Librium, Miltown, Quaalude, Sopor, Parest	Produce drowsiness, relaxation, sleep	Yes	Yes	Yes
Hallucinogens (psychodelics)		LSD, mescaline, psilocybin, STP, DMT, peyote	Variable central nervous system effects	Yes	No	Yes
Others		Marijuana, hashish	Variable effects	Yes	No	No

FIGURE 5.2. A TYPOLOGY OF DRUGS AND THEIR EFFECTS

Sources: Goode, E., 1978, pp. 197–198; Bales, R. F., and Crowther, 1977, pp. 272–281; Clinard, M. B., and Meier, R. F., 1979, pp. 291–299.

10,000,000 Americans had taken cocaine compared with only 10,000 people 20 years before. During 1980, U.S. cocaine imports were estimated to be around 100,000 pounds. An illicit retail dealer today can sell the drug, cut with various other substances, for between $100 to $140 per gram. The National Narcotics Intelligence Consumer's Committee, from its estimate of 1980 cocaine imports,

> puts the retail value of the industry at between $27 and $32 billion. If the cocaine trade were included by *Fortune* in its list of the 500 largest industrial corporations, cocaine would rank seventh in volume of domestic sales, between the Ford Motor Company and the Gulf Oil Corporation. Based on U.S. estimates, the monetary value of Bolivia's cocaine exports may now surpass the value of the country's largest legal industry, tin. Colombia's more highly refined cocaine exports total about $1 billion annually, half the value of the coffee crop. (Van Dyke, C., & Byck, R., 1982, p. 128)

Central Nervous System Depressants

Analgesics. Opiates, derived from the opium poppy, have long been used to reduce physical pain and mental suffering. While the popular image of drug addiction in the United States portrays it as a unique, recent urban problem of the past couple of decades, narcotics use and widespread addiction in this country date back to the Civil War. Morphine, a very effective pain-killer, was used liberally during the Civil War creating addiction sufficiently extensive to be called "the soldier's disease." Later, with no legal restraints, opium and morphine were often the primary active ingredients, along with alcohol, in the patent, "snake oil" medicines claimed by the itinerant medicine man to cure everything from warts to insomnia. Indeed, prior to passage of the Harrison Narcotic Act in 1914 which restricted narcotic purchases to prescription by a registered physician, narcotics were readily available, and addicts, having no particular trouble obtaining drugs to support their habits, did not form a distinct social group or subculture.

Narcotics include opium, morphine, heroin, codeine, and numerous synthetics such as Percodan, Methadone, or Demerol. They may be smoked, eaten, or injected and, rather quickly, the user becomes more tolerant and physically dependent. Withdrawal from narcotics is accompanied by restlessness, nausea, cramps, vomiting, and anxiety. Contrary to popular opinion, withdrawal from narcotics is not nearly as uncomfortable or dangerous as from alcohol or barbiturates. Likewise, although a racial–ethnic minority, urban, streetwise heroin junkie serves as the public focal point of the drug problem in America, even narcotics addiction does not fit neatly into categories of race, ethnicity, or social

class. For example, doctors and nurses have sufficiently high rates of narcotics addiction to regard it as an occupational hazard for them.
Sedative-hypnotics. This class of drugs is the most commonly used in the United States. Taken recreationally, as in the case of alcohol, the intent is usually relaxation. Medically, barbiturates are usually prescribed to relieve anxiety and produce sleep. Several characteristics, it seems, argue convincingly that sedative-hypnotics can be considered the most dangerous of drugs. First, they tend to disorient the user's perception of time. As a result, one may easily ingest a lethal overdose being unaware of how frequently the drug is being taken. Second, sedative-hypnotics dull physical reactions. The tragic effects of this characteristic are apparent from the statistics on alcohol-related automobile accidents and fatalities. Berry and Boland (1977, p. 118) estimate that alcohol abuse is present in *at least* 50% of all fatal auto accidents and the economic cost of motor vehicle accidents attributable to alcohol abuse approaches $5 billion annually. Third, both alcohol and barbiturates are addictive and habitual users increase their tolerance rapidly. The withdrawal symptoms are severe, painful, longer lasting, and more life threatening than for any other class of drugs. Fourth, particularly in the case of barbiturates, the difference is small between the dosage that is necessary for a high and the dosage that is potentially lethal. This fact, added to the increased likelihood of miscalculation brought on by a disoriented time perspective, increases the chances of death due to overdose. Fifth, when taken together, the effects of two or more sedative-hypnotics can be more intense than simply the sum of separate doses. This multiplier effect or interaction effect of drug mixing is best known in regard to barbiturates taken with alcohol.

Sedative-hypnotics, particularly tranquilizers prescribed to treat anxiety, are also major contributors to what one observer has called "an epidemic of *legal* drug use" in the United States (Rogers, 1971). Through advertising in medical journals, pharmaceutical companies urge doctors to prescribe an array of drugs such as Quaalude, Parest, Sopor, Ribrium, Valium, Miltown, Equanil, and Placidge to quiet people's nerves. Valium, the largest selling prescription drug in America, was prescribed by doctors over 61 million times in 1975. It is estimated that 15% of the American population take Valium and at least one-third of all adults have used minor tranquilizers. Increasingly, experts like Peter Schrag (1978), argue that Americans are taught to believe in a "pill for every problem" approach to their personal troubles. Rather than searching for the causes and solutions for their anxieties in the demanding, demeaning, impersonal social arrangements of an advanced industrial society, they learn to blot out the symptoms with a small tablet, effortlessly swallowed.

Hallucinogens

Natural hallucinogens, or psychedelics, such as peyote from cactus plants or psilocybin from mushrooms, have been used since ancient times. Their use, as with peyote in the Native American Church, has usually been in conjunction with religious rituals. However, LSD (lysergic acid diethylamide) is today the most widely used drug in this class both because it is relatively easy to produce synthetically and is relatively low in cost. LSD is the most potent of known psychoactive substances requiring only 50 to 200 micrograms—a quantity barely visible to the naked eye—for an average trip.

LSD has extreme effects upon mood and perception which users describe as ranging from beautiful and revealing to terrifying. In addition to spectacular visual images of brilliant colors and shimmering surroundings, one may lose a sense of time, feel indistinguishable from one's setting (ego loss), and experience sharp disorientation in relation to the physical and social worlds. Despite its unquestioned potent psychoactive properties, the dangers of psychedelic use are unclear and controversial. First, there is no physical dependence or addiction possible on hallucinogens. People do not get physically hooked as with the depressants. Tolerance does occur; regular users require large doses to maintain the same level of effects. Second, there have been reports of psychotic or panic reactions to hallucinogens—bad trips—that may have contributed to accidental deaths or suicides. However, popular opinion notwithstanding, such incidents are quite rare. Fort (1969) estimates that damaging behavior connected with psychedelics may happen between 1 in 10,000 and 1 in 100,000 experiences with the drugs. Third, the long-term physical effects of LSD, for example, have not been unequivocally determined. There is evidence that the substance can cause genetic damage in laboratory animals, but similar effects in humans, especially given the small doses usually ingested, are unconfirmed.

Despite the rather sensational attention accorded psychedelic drug use in the news media during the 1960s and early 1970s, they have never been widely used in the general population. Almost certainly at no time have as many as 10% of Americans ever used a hallucinogen. Still, there is some evidence that the incidence of use was rising slightly through the mid-1970s.

Marijuana

Marijuana, or cannabis, is certainly the illegal drug used most widely for recreational purposes in the United States. Most often smoked, but occasionally eaten, it comes from a plant that grows wild in many parts of the world. The flowering part and upper leaves of the female plant are dried, and crushed into a tobacco–like consistency or sometimes a powder. The psychoactive ingredient in marijuana is THC (tetrahydrocannabinal) which can vary from a trace in the case of cannabis grown in the United States to 5% in varieties grown in Jamaica or Southeast Asia. Hashish is a still more potent form usually imported from the Middle East.

The subjective effects of marijuana vary. Americans sometimes report one or more of the following: euphoria, disoriented time perspective, heightened appetite, relaxation, inability to concentrate, a tendency to think that many things are funny, giggling, increased appreciation of art or music, and rambling and unfocused thoughts. However, many of these feelings or perceptions are apparently conditioned by cultural expectations, because in other societies marijuana may produce quite different sensations. For example, in Jamaica rural laborers smoke the drug while they work (as opposed to during relaxation) and they report almost none of the same effects North American users do (Rubin, V., & Comitas, L., 1975). When very large doses of synthetic THC are taken, the effects can be more intense, including hallucinations and transient psychotic episodes.

Marijuana does not produce either tolerance or physical dependence— it is a nonaddictive substance. There have been claims that marijuana use, especially frequent long–term use, causes a number of pathological conditions including brain damage, genetic abnormalities, lowered levels of testosterone, cancer, paranoia, and sharp reductions in motivation. The evidence in respect to all of these claims is contradictory; the conclusions remain ambiguous. There is no indication that marijuana use inevitably leads to use of other drugs such as heroin. Probably the only definite evidence of physical damage from smoking marijuana is the finding that chronic use appears to irritate and reduce the efficiency of the lungs in the way that cigarette smoking does.

Trends and Prevalence of Drug Use

The late 1960s to the early 1970s is a watershed period for American drug use patterns. Prior to 1962 an average of only 2% of the population had ever had experience with an illicit drug. Between 1962 and 1967, greater numbers of youth and young adults began marijuana use, although throughout this period use of stronger illicit drugs like heroin, cocaine, or hallucinogens remained at very low levels.

> Between 1967 and 1972 dramatic changes occurred in the use of both marijuana and stronger drugs. Lifetime experience with drugs among young adults and youth, males and females in all regions of the country doubled and, among some groups, more than doubled. Exceptions to this pattern were certain groups in which social change is traditionally slower; adults over 26 years old and people living in southern nonmetropolitan or rural areas. Use of marijuana grew at a greater rate among whites than any other races, eradicating the racial differences from earlier years. . . . Despite the recent decline in student protest and campus unrest with which the drug culture of the late sixties was popularly associated, drug use has continued to climb. . . . By 1977 more than half of the young adults (i.e., adults between 18 and 25 years old) reported having used marijuana at least once, as did more than one-fourth of all youths 12 to 17 years old. (Cisin et al., 1977, pp. 15-16)

Recent findings, presented in Table 5.1, show that alcohol is the drug which most people have ever used, followed by marijuana. Ninety-five percent of young adults (18-25 years old) have used alcohol, 68% have used marijuana, and this age group has the highest use rates for every other category of drugs listed as well. Note that cocaine has been used by over one-fourth of the young adult population, a fact that reflects the recent sharp rise in experience with this drug among all age groups. The percentages in Table 5.1 also make it apparent that age is a key to understanding American patterns of drug use.

> . . . Among young persons (youth and young adults) drug use does not, at the present time, appear to be strongly influenced by demographic factors, such as area of residence, race or even socioeconomic status. To the extent that such differences exist today, those more likely to use or experiment with drugs are white, middle- to upper-middle-class young persons and/or young adults who live in metropolitan areas (regardless of whether the particular neighborhood may be classified as urban or suburban or even rural) and in the West and Northwest regions of the country. However, age so overshadows such demographic factors that it is tempting to conclude that some degree of illicit substance use (e.g., marijuana experimentation) may be a typical maturational experience for many of today's youth and young adults—a part of 'growing up.' (Cisin et al., 1977, pp. 9-10.)

EXPLANATIONS OF DRUG ABUSE

Alcoholism

No one knows how many alcoholics there are in the United States. Nine million is the figure often cited, but between the problems of

TABLE 5.1. PERCENT OF PEOPLE REPORTING HAVING EVER USED DRUGS: YOUTH, YOUNG ADULTS, OLDER ADULTS, AND COLLEGE STUDENTS

Substance	Population			
	Youth (12-17)[a]	Young adults (18-25)[a]	Older adults (26 and older)[a]	College students NY state[b]
Stimulants				
Cocaine	5	28	4	26
Nonmedical prescription	3	18	6	28
Depressants				
Alcohol	70	95	92	—[c]
Nonmedical prescription	3	17	4	20
Tranquilizers	4	16	3	17
Heroin	1	4	1	3
Other narcotics	3	12	3	10
Hallucinogens				
All types	7	25	5	18
Others				
Marijuana/hashish	31	68	20	45
Inhalants	10	17	4	16

Sources: Fishburne et al., 1979 and New York State Division of Substance Abuse, 1981[b]
[a]Based on interviews with a national sample.
[b]State-wide questionnaire sample of full-time undergraduates at public and private colleges.
[c]Not asked.

defining precisely who is or is not an alcoholic and then accurately counting the cases, this figure is only a very gross estimate. Studies of various business and government agencies indicate that at least 6 to 10% of an employee population suffers from alcoholism in its early, middle, or late stages (U.S. Senate Hearings, 1977). The economic costs of alcohol misuse and alcoholism were conservatively estimated at approximately $43 billion in 1975. Lost production was the most costly type of loss followed by health and medical expenses. Additionally, alcohol contributes to violent deaths including auto accidents, suicide, and murder. Alcohol misuse is present in about 40% of nonpedestrian and pedestrian traffic fatalities (Alcohol Health and Research World, 1974, p. 20). In a New York City study, researchers found that 58% of cases of unnatural deaths "had an identified problem with alcohol, narcotics, or both; 41% were classified as alcoholics and 28% as narcotic abusers" (Haberman and Baden, 1978, pp. 2-3).

Well over half of all homicides of adults in New York City may involve substance abusers as victims, perpetrators, or both. About one-half of all violent deaths are associated with alcohol use, and about the same amount of alcohol use may occur among the offenders in cases of homicide or other fatal violence. Adding to this the medical examiner cases involving narcotics users, at present more than two-thirds of the violent deaths in New York City are associated with the use or abuse of these substances (p. 8).

Finally, the amounts of resources devoted to the social control of alcohol-related problems are reflected in arrest data. In 1980, the almost 3 million abuse violations accounted for 29% of *all* arrests in the U.S. Despite a downward trend in arrests for public drunkenness due to some states having reclassified alcohol abuse as a disease rather than a crime, driving under the influence, drunkenness, and liquor law violations contribute heavily to the national arrest rate.

TABLE 5.2. ECONOMIC COSTS OF ALCOHOL MISUSE AND ALCOHOLISM IN THE UNITED STATES, 1975

Item	Cost (in billions)
Lost production	19.64
Health and medical	12.74
Motor vehicle accidents	5.14
Violent crime	2.86
Social responses	1.94
Fire losses	.43
Total	42.75

Source: Berry, R. E., Jr., and Boland, J. P., 1977.

The Disease Model

Heredity. For years, studies have indicated that alcoholism has some tendency to "run in families." However, it is not necessarily true that if some behavioral characteristic, like excessive drinking, appears to be passed down in families that the mode of transmission is genetic. For example, alcoholism might run in families because alcoholic parents, by their behavior, inadvertently teach their children to drink excessively. Thus, evidence that alcoholism is familial is not automatically evidence that it is genetic.

One way to sort out this problem is to see whether the children of alcoholic parents who are raised away from those parents by nonalcoholic stepparents, still have a higher risk of becoming alcoholics than children of nonalcoholic parents. Such a study by Goodwin (1976) "indicated that children of alcoholics are more likely to have alcohol problems than children of nonalcoholics, despite being separated from their parents in early life" (p. 72). However, we should be very cautious not to draw inappropriate conclusions from this evidence. It does not mean that all children of alcoholic parents will become alcoholic; nor does it say that not having alcoholic parents is a guarantee against becoming alcoholic. Goodwin goes on to say that "severe forms of alcohol abuse may have a genetic predisposition but heavy drinking itself, even when responsible for occasional problems, reflects predominantly nongenetic factors (p. 74)." While some people may run a greater risk of becoming alcoholics due to their genetic backgrounds, genetic predisposition, at best, provides only a tiny portion of the total explanation for alcoholism or alcohol-related problems.

The Jellinek Classification and Alcoholics Anonymous. The traditional model of alcoholism has been heavily influenced by the writing of E. M. Jellinek (1952 and 1960) in which he proposed a classification of alcoholics and a series of stages from prealcoholism to alcoholism. His four main types of alcoholism, designated by Greek letters, were divided into two disease and two nondisease categories. Gamma alcoholism is characterized by increased tissue tolerance to alcohol, adaptive cell metabolism, withdrawal symptoms, and loss of control. Delta alcoholism is very closely related to gamma with "inability to abstain" being substituted for "loss of control." Both of these were considered a disease. In contrast, Alpha alcoholism consists of habitual drinking due to psychological dependence with no serious physical complications. Beta alcoholism is characterized by physical complications from use of alcohol but with neither physical nor psychological dependence. Alpha and Beta alcoholisms are not diseases in the Jellinek formulation. He believed that Gamma alcoholism was most typical in the United States and it has become the type targeted by Alcoholics Anonymous.

The stages Jellinek proposed were divided into one prealcoholic phase that might last a few months to several years, and three alcoholic phases terminating in severe medical complications.

> Phase I, Prealcoholic: Alcohol is used as a drug to "treat one's nerves." Larger amounts are continually needed to produce the desired effect.
>
> Phase II, Early Alcoholic: Blackouts during heavy drinking begin. Other symptoms include a preoccupation with alcohol, sneaking drinks accompanied by feelings of guilt, and defense mechanisms such as denial or rationalizations for drinking.

Phase III, The Crucial Phase: The drinker experiences *loss of control* and a physical demand for alcohol.

Phase IV, The Chronic or Final Phase: This is characterized by uncontrolled "benders," uncontrollable craving, delirium tremens (D.T.'s) and other severe medical problems such as cirrhosis of the liver, malnutrition, and brain damage.

Although Jellinek took great care to treat his disease model and its proposed stages as tentative working hypotheses, they quickly became a part of official Alcoholics Anonymous ideology and central to the popular image of alcoholism. Presently, this traditional model is under attack from various perspectives. Schneider (1978) argues that "the disease concept owes its life to variously interested parties (e.g., the Temperance movement, the AA, and the Yale Research Center), rather than to substantive scientific findings" (Schneider, 1978, p. 371). Moreover, public acceptance of the disease image is enhanced by its connection, in the AA, to a repentant role (Trice & Roman, 1970). Fundamental middle-class values are invoked in the call for strict self-control and total abstinence. Thus the disease model is used to foster a moralistic stance. Still others (Orcutt, 1976 and Hills, 1980) emphasize the negative consequences of the AA's permanent assignment into an alcoholic role. (There is no such thing as a *former* alcoholic—only a *sober* alcoholic.) Also, "the increasing influence of the medical ideology on alcoholism may have the undesirable consequence of locking the alcoholic into a nonresponsible, but stigmatized role" (Orcutt, 1976, p. 419). Finally, the traditional view of alcohol dependence is being challenged by evidence from a broad range of studies that have provided the foundation for a new model which challenges the old (Pattison, et al., 1977). The two models of alcohol dependence are summarized for comparison in Figure 5.3. It remains to be seen whether the traditional view, inspired by Jellinek's work as incorporated by the Alcoholics Anonymous ideology, can be dislodged from the central place it has had in popular images of alcohol dependence over the past 30 years.

Sociocultural Models

Norms, Ambivalence, and Integration. Ogden Nash once captured the most common popular belief about the effects of alcohol by saying: "Candy is dandy/But liquor is quicker." He was, of course, referring to the strategy a man might use to assure the amorous response he was seeking from a woman. And the implication is that alcohol leads people to let down their guard, let loose—in short, alcohol is presumed to cause people to lose their inhibitions. To be sure, there can be no

FIGURE 5.3. TWO MODELS OF ALCOHOL DEPENDENCE

The Traditional Model	The New Emerging Model
1. There is a unitary phenomenon which can be identified as alcoholism.	1. Alcohol dependence summarizes a variety of syndromes defined by drinking patterns and the adverse physical, psychological, and/or social consequences of such drinking. These syndromes, jointly denoted as "alcohol dependence," are best considered as a serious health problem.
2. Alcoholics and prealcoholics are essentially different from nonalcoholics.	2. An individual's pattern of alcohol use can be considered as lying on a continuum, ranging from pathological to severely pathological. Any person who uses alcohol can develop a syndrome of alcohol dependence. Continued drinking of large doses of alcohol over an extended period of time is likely to initiate a process of physical dependence which will eventually be manifested as an alcohol withdrawal syndrome.
3. Alcoholics may sometimes experience a seemingly irresistible physical craving for alcohol, or a strong psychological compulsion to drink.	3. Recovery from alcohol dependence bears no necessary relation to abstinence, although such a concurrence is frequently the case. The consumption of a small amount of alcohol by a person once labeled as "alcoholic" does not initiate either physical dependence or a physiological need for more alcohol by that individual.
4. Alcoholics gradually develop a process called "loss of control" over drinking and possibly even an inability to stop drinking.	4. The development of alcohol problems follows variable patterns over time and does not necessarily proceed inexorably to severe fatal stages.
5. Alcoholism is a permanent and irreversible condition.	5. Alcohol problems are typically interrelated with other life problems, especially when alcohol dependence is long established.
6. Alcoholism is a progressive disease which follows an inexorable development through a distinct series of phases.	

Source: Adapted from Pattison, E. M., Sobell, M. B., and Sobell, L. C., 1977, pp. 1–6.

denying that physiological consequences of drinking alcohol in large quantities include dulled senses and lowered reaction time characteristic of depressants generally. However, it does not follow that alcohol necessarily leads to any particular social behavior. Indeed, among the world's various cultures examples can be found in which alcohol appears to be associated with virtually opposite responses. For example, MacAndrew and Edgerton (1969), in their comparison of drunken comportment in a large number of societies, found that drinking might characteristically lead to violence in one culture (the Abipone Indians of Paraguay) but passiveness in others (the Yuruna Indians of South America); increased sexual activity in one (the Tarahumara of Mexico) but no change in sexual activity in others (the Camba of Bolivia); gregarious sociable interaction in one (Mixtecs of Mexico) or solitary withdrawal in another (Aritama of northern Columbia).

The differences in social behavior while "under the influence" do not suggest that alcohol directly causes certain attitudes or activities. Instead, being "drunk" may be better conceived as a learned social role. As MacAndrew and Edgerton (1969) put it:

> Rather than viewing drunken comportment as a function of toxically disinhibited brains operating on impulse-driven bodies, we have recommended that what is fundamentally at issue are the *learned* relations that exist among men living together in a society. More specifically, we have contended that the way people comport themselves when they are drunk is determined *not* by alcohol's toxic assault upon the seat of moral judgment, conscience, or the like, but by what their society makes of and imparts to them concerning the state of drunkenness (p. 165). (Italics added.)

Just as there are vast cultural differences in people's responses to drunkenness, there are variations in rates of alcoholism among ethnic groups. It is *not* true that groups in which drinking occurs frequently will inevitably have high rates of alcoholism. For example, both Orthodox American Jews and Italian–Americans drink with relatively great frequency but their rates of alcoholism are low. Actually, more important than the average frequency of drinking as a correlate with rates of alcoholism are the norms that guide drinking when it occurs. Generally, rates of alcoholism are relatively low in groups whose customs integrate drinking with social and religious practices. This provides clear guidelines for when, how much, and in what situations one should drink (Mizruchi and Perrucci, 1970). Thus,

> ... Apparently, in cultures which use alcohol but have a low incidence of alcoholism, people drink in a definite pattern. The beverage is sipped

slowly, consumed with food, taken in the company of others—all in relaxing, comfortable circumstances. Drinking is taken for granted. No emotional rewards are reaped by the man who shows prowess of consumption. Intoxication is abhorred. Other cultures with a high incidence of alcohol-related problems usually assign a special significance to drinking. Alcohol use is surrounded with attitudes of ambivalence and guilt. Maladaptive drinking, drinking without food, and intoxication are common.... (Chafetz, 1971, pp. 3-4)

Orthodox Jews have been taken as a particularly striking example of the apparent effectiveness of the cultural integration of drinking as a mechanism for preventing alcohol problems. In a classic study, Snyder (1958) observed that "the noteworthy sobriety of the Jews appears to be primarily associated with the culture with a ritualistic emphasis, prescribing frequent drinking which is integrated with familial religious practices" (p. 56). Even as Jewish Orthodoxy has declined in the intervening period, the rate of alcohol problems remains low among Jews—a fact that Glassner and Berg (1980) attribute to four "protective processes": (1) association of alcohol abuse with non-Jews; (2) integration of moderate drinking norms, practices, and symbolism during childhood by means of religious and secular ritual; (3) restriction of most adult primary relationships to other moderate drinkers; and (4) a repertoire of techniques (such as joking about their moderation) to avoid excess drinking under social pressure.

In contrast, cultural groups like the Irish which have high rates of alcoholism, are said to emphasize drinking as an activity in itself, often done at special locations (bars or pubs), separate from other aspects of daily life and ritual (Bales, 1946). Moreover, heavy drinking is apt to be taken as a symbol of manliness. This reinforces heavy alcohol use as an activity that actually differentiates men and women. In this sense, drinking—especially heavy drinking—becomes a disintegrating ritual that sets the stage for mixed cultural messages and guilt about alcohol consumption. Attempts to wash away the guilt by overindulgence may contribute to alcohol-related problems in these cultures.

If it is correct that ambivalent, inconsistent, mixed cultural messages about drinking behavior can be said to account for some measure of alcoholism, then some of the alcohol problems in American society can be attributed to a general cultural ambivalence toward alcohol use. Side by side—and frequently in sharp conflict throughout our history—have been temperance groups calling for total abstinence and the banning of alcohol consumption while other forces, including the movies, television, and the liquor industry, entice us to drink by portraying alcohol as the beverage of the sophisticated and the successful. Certainly American culture as a whole does not provide its members with a clear, verified set of guidelines in regard to drinking. This is readily understandable given the widely varying cultural origins of the American people. And, as we shall see momentarily, this divergence of subcultural norms has not only contributed to ambivalent attitudes and behaviors involving drinking on the part of individuals, but has, at times, been at the core of national-level political conflict.

The Social Functions of Drinking. People in our society are usually quite frank about the intent or even the need to serve alcoholic beverages at social gatherings. Many of us have had occasion to remind ourselves and others that the party will get going after people have a few drinks and loosen up. This imagery, of course, fits with the popular belief of alcohol as disinhibitor. It suggests that one manifest function of drinking is to provide social lubrication—to encourage people to unwind and interact more easily, freely, and naturally. However, as we have just noted a few paragraphs earlier, drunken comportment varies widely across different cultures and disinhibited behavior is only one of numerous possible reactions to drinking depending upon the expectations conveyed by one's culture. In American culture, alcohol is widely believed to be a social lubricant and people normally react to drinking it in that way.

Drinking serves a related social function, latent or less openly acknowledged, that in our society (among others) amounts to suspending temporarily a person's responsibility for his or her behavior. Our beliefs about the disinhibiting effects of alcohol allow us to excuse what would otherwise be considered impolite, outrageous, or even dangerous behavior with the simple phrase "I guess I was drunk." As MacAndrew and Edgerton put it, in some societies like ours:

> ... the state of drunkenness is a state of societally sanctioned freedom from the otherwise enforceable demands that persons comply with the conventional proprieties. For a while—but just for a while—the rules (or, more accurately, *some* of the rules) are set aside, and the drunkard finds himself, if not beyond good and evil, at least partially removed from the accountability nexus in which he normally operates. In a word, drunkenness in these societies takes on the flavor of *"time out"* from many of the otherwise imperative demands of everyday life. (1969, pp. 89-90)

In this sense, drinking is the functional equivalent of ritualized occasions found in societies the world over in which people are briefly permitted to ignore some of the norms that apply to their age, sex, or social status. Mardi Gras, a period of merrymaking revelry prior to Lent, appears to fit this cultural pattern. Possibly, by punctuating the routine rhythm of social life with ritually contained periods of rule violation, the norms of everyday life are made both more tolerable for those who are oppressed and more evident to all. However, in its power to excuse, drinking in our culture may even go beyond suspending judgment and responsibility for relatively harmless transgressions like loud, discourteous, disruptive behavior. It may, in the minds of some, provide very subtle license for harmful activities including reckless driving, sexual harassment, rape, or child molesting (McCaghy, 1968). Thus, calling "time out" by resorting to the widely accepted excuses "I'm going to get drunk," "I am drunk," or "I was only drunk," serves an important social function in our society. It provides us a ready means to cut loose and disavow our transgressions. At the same time, this opportunity to deny responsibility may subtly provide some with the license to avoid a measure of the psychic costs (guilt and shame) usually attached to particularly harmful or odious behavior. Taken to this latter extreme, drinking may be said to be *dysfunctional* in our society. This is most certainly the case for indirect victims of alcohol abuse such as those killed or injured in drunk driving accidents or those who suffer the daily tribulations of living with an alcoholic family member.

The Politics of Definition. To drink or not to drink has been a political issue in the United States since its founding. In fact, there may be no better example of how deviance is a product of political struggle among various interest groups than Gusfield's (1963) interpretation of the American Temperance Movement. Drinking (or abstinence) has been one of the significant ways of distinguishing one subculture from another in American society. As we have just noted in this chapter, different religious or ethnic groups have different norms in regard to whether or not, what, when, where, how much, and with whom to drink alcoholic beverages. This makes drinking similar to numerous other consumption habits that distinguish various groups and provide people the means to establish their group identity. Thus, consumption taboos (e.g., no smoking or alcohol use among devout Moslems) or patterns of consumption (e.g., smoking grass among some segments of the American youth culture) provide a means for group members to say to each other, as well as to outsiders, "This is our custom—our way of showing who we are." Of course, to the things people characteristically consume as food or drink we could add other cultural identifiers such as their usual clothing (blue jeans or jacket and tie), music preferences (soul, country and western, or classical), or style of speaking (dialect or accent) among others.

In mid–19th century America, abstinence from drinking was becoming one symbol of middle–class membership. Moreover, the waves of immigrants entering this country from Ireland, Eastern Europe, and Italy tended to have drinking as one of the cultural customs they shared in common. Thus, in the latter part of the 1800s, Temperance emerged as a means of distinguishing the "native" American from the immigrant; the Protestant from the Catholic. The political struggle to make Temperance the law of the land through an amendment to the Constitution occurred because Temperance had become a *symbol* of social status. Establishing the dominance of that symbol in law became important because "public support of one conception of morality at the expense of another enhances the prestige and self esteem of the victors and degrades the cultures of the losers (Gusfield, 1963, p. 5). The Prohibition Amendment, passed in 1919, signaled the dominance of nativist, American Protestantism just as its repeal in 1933 symbolized the fall of this group from its exclusive privileged position. In Gusfield's words,

> ... The Eighteenth Amendment was the high point of the struggle to assert the public dominance of old middle–class values. It established the victory of Protestant over Catholic, rural over urban, tradition over modernity, the middle class over both the lower and the upper strata.
> The significance of Prohibition is in the fact that it happened. The establishment of Prohibition laws was a battle in the struggle for status between two divergent styles of life. It marked the public affirmation of the abstemious, ascetic qualities of American Protestantism. In this sense it was an act of ceremonial deference toward old middle–class culture. If the law was often disobeyed and not enforced, the respectability of its adherents was honored in the breach. After all, it was *their* law that the drinkers had to avoid.
> If Prohibition was the high point of old middle–class defense, Repeal was the nadir.... In the Great Depression both the old order of nineteenth-century economics and the culture of the Temperance ethic were cruelly discredited.
> The repeal of the Eighteenth Amendment gave the final push to the decline of old middle–class values in American culture.... (Gusfield, 1963, p. 7)

Thus, we can see that the drive to establish officially a particular behavior as deviant may have behind it large scale conflicts of interest and the struggle of status–group politics.

Public Attitudes and Public Policy. Commonly held theories used to explain deviant behavior exert a powerful influence upon public policy designed to control it. For example, if people generally believe that alcoholism is the result of some moral failing deep within the alcoholic, they are apt to advocate public responses to drunkenness that emphasize either criminal punishment or repentance. If, instead, the common wisdom attributes alcoholism to psychological or biological illness, public policy is apt to emphasize decriminalization of drunkenness and institution of medical intervention.

In fact, several researchers have identified changes of this sort. Gusfield (1967) argues that since the early 1800s in America drinking has undergone two "moral passages" or changes in the public image of the heavy drinker. The first is from the "repentant drinker" to the "enemy drinker" which transformed the alcoholic from an object of pity to an evil to be stamped out. Of course, central to the effort to stamp out alcoholism was the Prohibition Movement which, as we have just noted, was also motivated by issues of status politics. The second major transition of public attitudes was from the "enemy drinker" to the "sick drinker." Linsky (1971) has found that a similar movement in public images of alcoholism and alcohol problems is evident in the explanations of alcoholism projected in articles from popular magazines since 1900. Generally, since 1900 there has been a distinct decline in moralistic "free will" and "social criticism" explanations that place blame for alcoholism on the corruption of individuals, groups, or institutions. At the same time, naturalistic (nonmoralistic) psychological, biological, and sociological explanations have become increasingly prevalent and now dominate the popular imagery.

The American history of changing public attitudes and laws in regard to alcohol stands as testament to Durkheim's (1966) observation that no act or individual is intrinsically deviant; rather, deviance is a product of collective definition dominant among members of a group at any given moment. Above all, the collective definition that confers the label "deviant" upon any particular behavior or individual can be, and often is, altered over time.

With such alterations come changes in public policy. Nationally, public drunkenness accounts for over 630,000 arrests annually in the United States which made this crime second only to driving under the influence of alcohol and larceny–theft in the number of arrests in 1983. (The drunkenness arrests do not include arrests for driving under the influence, disorderly conduct, or vagrancy, all of which are likely to involve alcohol abuse.) Despite this high proportion of law enforcement effort directed at public drunkenness, there has been a trend toward relative decrease in criminal processing for drunkenness since the late 1970s. In part, this is because some jurisdictions, such as New York State, have effectively decriminalized public drunkenness making it instead a problem to be handled through medical intervention (detoxification or drying–out centers and related rehabilitation programs).

The ultimate consequences of this trend in policy are at the moment unclear. Certainly it is futile and unjust endlessly to cycle skid row alcoholics in and out of drunk tanks to serve life imprisonment sentences "on the installment plan." Spradley (1970) argues "that incarceration in jail, intended as a *punishment* for public drunkenness, is a *cause* of public drunkenness" (Spradley, 1970, p. 5) because the indignities of being processed and serving time provide an alibi for hitting the bottle upon release. In the words of the title of his book, after 30 days in jail, *You Owe Yourself a Drunk*. However, decriminalization and subsequent medicalization of the problem has yet to demonstrate its effectiveness although it does appear than when assigned the task, medical units formally process drunks they encounter at a much higher rate than comparable police units (Pastor, 1978). From one viewpoint it can be argued that reconceptualizing the problem of public drunkenness has merely substituted a system of medical control (consistent with the public image of the alcoholic as sick) for a system of legal control (outmoded as the public image of alcoholic as enemy fades into the past). A firm assessment of the newer approach must await the evidence.

Marijuana Use

Despite its illegality, marijuana is the drug people most frequently report ever having used with the exception of alcohol. Correspondingly, it has been the object of considerable sociological theorizing about why people use it, why they discontinue its use, and how the law should treat the drug and its users.

Social Learning. In a manner no different than with other types of deviant behavior, much of the research on marijuana use has focused upon the question of "Why do they do it?" The answer has frequently been assumed to reside in some psychological motive or need for the individual to escape, to avoid facing the realities and responsibilities of daily living. The approach of Howard S. Becker (1963) challenges the assumption that some pathological motive must lie behind a behavior like regular marijuana smoking. Rather, according to Becker, people frequently have their first experience with marijuana quite by chance when they find themselves in the presence of another who has some of the drug and can show them how to use it. Thus, they are probably not motivated to try marijuana by some deep need to escape. Instead, most marijuana users are first motivated to try it out of some vague mixture of curiosity, opportunity, and momentary peer pressure to join in the experience with the group.

Becker's point is so important, it is worth quoting him for emphasis.

> ... Attempts to account for the use of marijuana lean heavily on the premise that the presence of any particular kind of behavior in an indi-

> vidual can best be explained as the result of some trait which predisposes or motivates him to engage in that behavior. In the case of marijuana use, this trait is usually identified as psychological, as a need for fantasy and escape from psychological problems the individual cannot face.
>
> I do not think such theories can adequately account for marijuana use. In fact, marijuana use is an interesting case for theories of deviance, because it illustrates the way deviant motives actually develop in the course of experience with deviant activity. To put a complex argument in a few words: instead of the deviant motives leading to the deviant behavior, it is the other way around; the deviant behavior in time produces the deviant motivation. Vague impulses and desires—in this case, probably most frequently a curiosity about the kind of experience the drug will produce—are transformed into definite patterns of action through the social interpretation of a physical experience which is itself ambiguous. (pp. 41–42)

Of course, simply trying marijuana does not, in the least, guarantee that a person will become a regular user. Becker extends his argument to show how a novice may go through three steps which "leave him willing and able to use the drug for pleasure when the opportunity presents itself" (p. 46). First, a person must *learn the technique* of smoking marijuana (since this is the way it is most often ingested in our society). This includes such particulars as learning how to roll a joint, how to inhale the smoke, how to hold it in the lungs, and how often to do so. Only by learning the proper technique will the drug produce its effects. And those who fail to learn how will not become regular marijuana users.

Second, one must *learn to perceive the effects.* The effects of marijuana can be quite subtle. To perceive them, the first-time user is often coached by her tutors. "How do you feel?" "A little bit dizzy?" "Kind of silly?" "Are you hungry?" These cues tell the novice what to look for, what to attribute to the substance being smoked.

Finally, the user must *learn to enjoy the effects.* To feel dizzy, thirsty, hungry, or to misjudge time or distances are not intrinsically pleasurable experiences. Indeed, some people find the effects of marijuana smoking uncomfortable or even frightening. They will not become regular users. Moreover, learning to define the effects of marijuana favorably is facilitated by the encouragement of the others with whom one smokes. Only by learning from others what to expect and to perceive those sensations as pleasant, desired, and sought often will one become a regular user.

Becker's theory implies, above all, that drug use can be learned, just like any other behavior. Furthermore, peer-group influences are highly important to the learning. Social learning theory proposes, specifically, that differential association—interaction and identity with peer groups, family, and others—sets the stage for the experience, reinforcement, definitions, and imitation of substance use including alcohol and marijuana (Akers, et al., 1979). Recent studies have shown that the greater the number of one's adolescent friends who use marijuana, the lower the likelihood that a person will expect negative outcomes from use and the greater the expectations of positive experiences (Orcutt, 1975). Kandel et al. (1976) found that drug use by one's peers is most important with respect to marijuana use. If their friends use marijuana, most adolescents will also do so, irrespective of social, psychological, or familial characteristics. Another comprehensive test of social learning theory used survey data on adolescent drinking and marijuana use. The major social learning variables: differential association, differential reinforcement, definitions, and imitation combined to account for 68% of the explanation of marijuana use and 55% of alcohol use (Akers et al., 1979). The most powerful explanatory variable was differential association.

The importance of peer influences in marijuana use is further demonstrated by the similarity of social characteristics that separate smokers from nonsmokers. In a sample of students from 20 New York City colleges, Johnson (1973) found a remarkable sociopolitical homogeneity among users strongly suggesting that marijuana smoking has evolved into an integral part of one segment of the youth subculture. Among all nonreligious, politically liberal, daily cigarette-smoking men, 97% had tried marijuana and 62% smoked it at least weekly. This contrasts to religious, politically conservative, noncigarette-smoking women of whom only 4% had tried marijuana and not one smoked marijuana weekly.

The evidence we presently have points consistently to the role of social learning in differential association with peers as a key to explaining marijuana use among young people. Indeed, some social learning theorists (Akers, 1973) argue that the principles of this approach apply to other substances, both legal and illegal, ranging from alcohol to hallucinogens. We next turn to why people cease using marijuana.

"Turning Off." While some marijuana users continue to use the drug regularly beyond adolescence into their 30s and 40s, a typically large proportion of youthful users cease smoking as they get older. Studies of former college marijuana users indicate strongly that it is not aging *per se* or a rejection of values common to the marijuana smoking youth culture that accounts for cessation, but instead significant status changes of marriage, entry into parenthood, and change of associates after graduation that lead to nonuse (Henley & Adams, 1973, and Brown, et al., 1974). Tom, a 24 year-old, married business major who now works as a bank executive, is a typical case.

Tom first tried marijuana when a freshman in college because he says, "Everyone was trying it." He reports that he did not get much from the drug at first, but later would become very high, more extroverted and happier than usual, similar to getting drunk. He smoked about once a week for five years, except during his sophomore year, when he "smoked pot every day for six to nine months." He never smoked alone, only with friends.

In his junior year, Tom began limiting his marijuana smoking to weekends because he started going with the girl he later married. She did not smoke, and though he found it no fun to smoke alone, after graduation he stopped completely when he procured a bank position saying, "I was afraid a bust would ruin my career." He says it was not difficult to give up marijuana, although he missed it somewhat at first and might use it again "sometime" in the future. (Brown et al., 1974, pp. 533–535)

Tom's case, consistent with the survey findings from large numbers of people, underscores the importance of one's social position and associations both for the use of marijuana and cessation of its use. Smoking pot is an activity that invariably begins and continues in the context of strong social group supports. When a person moves away from these supports into a new social context, he or she is apt to stop using marijuana. Thus to Becker's three requirements for regular marijuana use—learning the smoking technique, learning to perceive, and learning to enjoy the effects—we should add an additional condition. One must continue association in groups with norms and values favorable to recreational pot smoking. The upshot is that from initiation, through regular use to cessation, marijuana smoking is a highly social activity that can be better explained by factors of one's social situation than by searching for pathological traits in individuals.

Medicine and Morals: Marijuana as a Public Issue. Concern for legal control over marijuana use is largely a 20th century phenomenon. State legislation to outlaw its possession, sale, or use dates back to the 1920s, and by 1930 16 states prohibited use of the drug. The Marijuana Tax Act of 1937 was the key piece of federal legislation aimed at controlling marijuana on a national level. The tendency, until the 1970s, was for state penalties for use, possession, or sale to be, in many cases, very severe including lengthy jail sentences for possession and even capital punishment for second sale offenses to minors. Recently, most states have reduced penalties for simple possession and in 11 jurisdictions some form of decriminalization has occurred (Inciardi, 1981, p. 146). Still, it would be incorrect to say that the nascent decriminalization movement of the 1960s and 70s is likely to meet with widespread success in the 1980s. The legalization debate is likely to continue, if in somewhat less shrill tones, into the foreseeable future, without a clear-cut resolution.

Should marijuana use be legalized? One rational way to approach this social policy question is to conduct a cost/benefit analysis of continued criminalization versus decriminalization. Inciardi has proposed a sensible framework for such an accounting.

> On the one hand, there are the physiological and psychosocial costs of marijuana use—undesirable personality changes, antisocial behavior patterns, alterations in properly coordinated motor activity, psychological dependence liabilities, and the undetermined spectrum of health consequences from the drug's long term chronic use. Viewing these as physical, psychic, and social costs of marijuana use, their prevention could be considered as the *benefits* of criminalization policies *if* existing marijuana statutes were indeed effective in deterring those who might otherwise use the drug.
>
> By contrast, there is a perplexing series of personal, social and economic costs which can be attributed to the very bearing of current antimarijuana laws. The *personal costs* include the temporary, long-term, or even permanent disruptions in users' lives which result from arrest, conviction, sentencing, and incarceration. The *social costs* involve society's loss of productive (or potentially productive) citizens when official adjudication interrupts, prevents, or otherwise limits the pursuit of occupational careers, places users into nonproductive treatment or correctional settings, or when the prisonization and criminalization processes associated with incarceration introduce users to more serious and predatory criminal vocations. The *economic costs* can be defined by the total budgetary allocations to the three segments of the criminal justice system—police, courts, and corrections—for the enforcement of the marijuana laws and the processing and management of offenders. (Inciardi, 1981, pp. 146–147)

But is it likely, even if such evidence is carefully researched and assembled, that it would convince a substantial number of people to change their minds—either for or against decriminalization? The answer, probably, is a resounding "no" and the reason is that the political question of marijuana legalization is more than a simple matter of personal harm or social costs. Marijuana is a symbol. As a consumption habit, it bears significance not at all unlike the importance drinking alcohol had as identifier of the immigrant, urban, Catholic in the late 19th and early 20th centuries. Marijuana is symbolically linked in the popular mind to a segment of the youth culture identified as liberal (even radical), sexually promiscuous, and socially irreverent (Goode, 1969). This fact, not objective evidence of costs or benefits, is the "bottom line" of the decriminalization debate. To the extent that marijuana remains symbolically attached to this portion of the youth culture, and this collectivity remains politically impotent, marijuana legalization remains unlikely. Again, in a manner closely akin to our earlier consideration of the Temperance Movement, Prohibition, and its repeal, we are drawn to realize the inherently political aspects of deviance and the politics of strategies to control it.

The Political Economy of Drugs

The Control of Drugs: The Case of Opiates. When considering the control of drugs, we usually today think in terms either of restricting access to certain legal drugs by placing their distribution under the control of a physician or attempting to deter their use by making them illegal to use, possess, or sell. Of course, as we have already noted, attempts to limit drug use in either manner are relatively recent phenomena. Up until the end of the 19th century, virtually any substance, including opiates, was available to anyone who could pay the going market price. Particularly during the 1800s, America was populated with thousands of addicts, in all social classes, who fed their habits quietly and unobtrusively from the endless, unrestricted supply of legal drugs.

Perhaps even more astonishing in historical perspective, however, is the fact that Western European nations, including the United States, were actively and openly engaged in the promotion of drug traffic until recently. William J. Chambliss (1978) has pieced together the story of how opiates (opium and heroin) became an important commodity linked to the colonial domination of the world capitalist system between the 15th and 19th centuries. His account, moreover, provides an excellent example of how historical experience (promotion of the opiate trade) has laid foundations of habits, institutions, and economic relationships that help to make reversal of our policy toward drugs a difficult task, at best.

Opium has been used since antiquity. It comes from the juice of a poppy that grows chiefly in a warm, mountainous region stretching from Turkey to Southeast Asia. The Turks, who grew most of the ancient world's supply, carried small quantities of the substance to the East over trade routes. However, widespread use throughout the world—especially in the Far East—came with expansion of the capitalist world economy outward from Europe. Beginning in the 1500s, the Portuguese, the Dutch, and the English colonized much of Asia as they searched for products, raw materials, new markets, and labor. The Portuguese were the first to recognize the potential of the opium trade in Asia.

> The Portuguese traders . . . were quick to realize that for at least a small part of their trade they could use opium instead of gold and silver. They first crushed the Asian traders and ran their vessels out of the seas. Then they began purchasing opium from Turkish and Indian traders, trading opium in turn for spices and tea and so forth which they could sell profitably in Europe.
>
> For the next three hundred years, European powers fought over Asian colonies, with the Dutch gaining the upper hand in Indonesia and much of the Southeast Asia. During this period the colonial powers expanded into the interior of Asia, colonizing territories to varying degrees. Increasingly the European colonizers turned to the opium trade as a source of income to pay for the spices, tea, silk, and pottery they sought (Koh, 1974, pp. 51–52; Scott, 1969; Alexander, 1930; and Lubbock, 1933).
>
> Opium dens began appearing in the major cities of Asia (Koh, 1974: 20). India gradually replaced Turkey as the main opium-growing area. India's opium was produced mainly by the British East India Company, a private company which had been given almost total political and economic control over the Indian colony by the British government. The British East India Company, through its representatives in Asia and local colonial governments, encouraged and expanded opium addiction throughout Asia and especially among the huge Chinese population. (Chambliss, 1978, pp. 112–118)

Recognizing the economic and human price of having their country infested by opium, the Chinese government attempted to resist by restricting importation of the substance. The British pressure to expand the opium trade persisted and war ensued. The Opium War between England and China (1839–1842) and a subsequent conflict in 1856 eventually forced Chinese legalization of opium smoking and trading.

> The immediate consequence of China's legalization of opium was to vastly increase the potential and actual market. Now British traders could bring to bear all their skills and imagination to spread the opium habit to the interior of China. The market was truly overwhelming and couched in the nicest of terms when the head of one of the major opium-trading companies noted that opium was a "comfort to the hard-working Chinese." (Owen, 1934, p. 243). (Chambliss, 1978, pp. 119–120)

Legalization eventually diminished the British profits in the opium trade, because Chinese growers began to compete with British traders. "From 1850 onward, however, British capitalism in China flourished in large part on the profits and labor advantages from opium traffic. By the end of the 19th century it was often said that China had become a nation of opium smokers" (Chambliss, 1978, p. 120).

Throughout the 19th century European colonial powers tightened their hold on Asia. A combination of famine, war, and a poor economic situation in the latter 19th century caused a large number of the opium–smoking Chinese of South China to emigrate to cities of Southeast Asia like Saigon or Bangkok.

> In every major city of Southeast Asia from Rangoon to Saigon, colonial and local governments developed opium dens. The opium trade was carefully, albeit corruptly, organized by an unholy alliance between colonial officials, local governments, and a new class of entrepreneurs who were given government franchises to import and sell opium. Opium sales provided 40–50% of the income of colonial governments (McCoy, 1972: 63 and Wen, 1961: 52–75). Opium profits helped finance the railways, canals, roads, and government buildings as well as the comfortable living conditions of colonial bureaucrats.... Opium became the mainstay of the government revenues. It was simultaneously the main thread on which the working class hung and was ensnared into providing labor for the European trade with these nations. It was opium, not religion, that was the opiate of the masses in Southeast Asia. By the 1940s there were in Indochina (Cambodia, Laos, and Vietnam) over 2,500 opium dens providing 45% of all tax revenues and an immeasurable percentage of the unclaimed salaries to both local and colonial government officials. (McCoy, 1972, p. 76; Chambliss, 1978, pp. 121–122)

Although not quite as extensive as that of the British, the American opium trade was large, profitable, and contributed to our industrial development by providing significant capital. "The profits from opium trading were invested in the textile mills in Massachusetts and other New England states following the introduction of the power loom in 1814. Thus the neat paradox that opium helped create a labor force for capitalist expansion in Asia and America and the profits from the opium trade provided the capital for the development of the factory system in New England" (Chambliss, p. 122). Moreover, the introduction of opium and heroin in the United States came with the importation of Chinese coolies to work the gold and silver mines of the West and build the railroads across the continent. At this time, opium smoking was an ideal medium for dulling the pain of workers laboring without families under the most horrible of conditions. "From the point of view of the employers, the laborer's opium smoking was a blessing. The employers, by controlling the importation and distribution of opium, made a profit from selling it to workers. Furthermore, the threat of withdrawing the supply of opium kept many potential labor complaints from becoming a serious threat to the employer" (p. 128).

By the late 1800s, Western mining and railroad construction declined, massive European immigration was supplying a large body of cheap labor reducing the need for a drugged, suppliant army of laborers, and the British controlled the bulk of the opium market. In 1886, the United States passed the first antiopium legislation ever, making it illegal to trade in the substance. This is not to say, however, that the opium and heroin business disappeared from the United States. Indeed, except for the interruptions of the two World Wars, the heroin industry has been growing. Today, it is estimated that the annual gross sales of heroin in the United States exceed $30 billion (DuPont & Greene, 1973). "Some sense of the importance of this industry to the national economy is gleaned from the fact that this would make the heroin industry comparable in gross volume of business to the largest corporations in the United States: in 1970 General Motors, Exxon, IBM, ITT, and a half dozen other of the largest multinational corporations in the world had a gross volume of business of *less than* $30 billion a year" (Chambliss, p. 132).

Analogous to the tendency toward corporate takeovers and the ruthless trend toward the concentration of economic power in the "legitimate" sector of American business, the illicit heroin industry is presently undergoing a transitional period of instability. Chambliss surveys the present shaky state of affairs and reminds us that the heroin industry remains a major force in the capitalist world economy.

> There is warfare among competing groups of middlemen in Latin America and Europe (Amsterdam has emerged as a major transfer point for heroin from Europe to the United States, and Chinese merchants involved in trade are killing each other—literally). And in the United States the battle for control is taking the form of marshaling political assistance from friendly government politicians as well as eliminating competition wherever and whenever possible. The end is not in sight, but the tendency to monopoly is strong. No one, least of all the police and cooperating politicians, want the war to continue. They, as well as the most powerful executives in the industry are doing everything possible to bring order into the industry and re-establish a smooth-working monopoly. Exactly who will control the business when the present crisis ends is at the moment problematic. What is not problematic, however, is the state of this industry: it will continue to thrive, to expand, to reap large profits and to support large numbers of law enforcement people, politicans and specialists in illegal business.
>
> The heroin industry is a mainstay of the political economy of much of the capitalist world and it shall not be eliminated any more readily than the automobile, banking or construction industries. (pp. 138–139)

Two things must be emphasized from this account of the rise of the opiate industry. First, the history of political and economic policy toward any particular behavior, no matter how severely condemned and sanctioned today, may reveal that it was at one time legal, exploited, and even encouraged. To understand today's social problems requires historical perspective. Second, and related to the first, we should be reminded that actions of each generation establish modes of exploitation that may come back to haunt the progeny of their originators. The early colonial capitalists promoted and profited from the opiate trade with no concern for the addicted. Today governmental attempts to stem the opiate trade are faced with a massive international network whose roots took hold with those same governments' legitimation 200 years ago. "For whatsoever a man soweth, that shall he also reap." (Galatians 6:7)

Drugs as Control: The Legal Drug Epidemic. Most legal, medical, and sociological attention on drugs (excluding alcohol) as a social problem has been directed at the illegal ones like marijuana, hallucinogens, cocaine, or heroin. There is, however, in the United States a huge pharmacological industry that specializes in the promotion, production, and distribution of legally available drugs. To be clear at the outset, many of the drugs produced by this industry definitely benefit those who take them. At the same time, numerous critics have pointed out that the way the pharmacology business is organized and operates contributes to the overuse of legal drugs and may even instill attitudes and habits among people that provide a more receptive environment for the pushing of illegal substances.

Legal drugs can be readily obtained through two sources: (1) unrestricted substances that can be bought over the counter and (2) restricted substances requiring a prescription by a physician. Both avenues stem from a very large, growing, and profitable industry.

> In the United States, the volume of the drug business has grown by a factor of 100 during the current century: 20,000 tons of aspirin are consumed per year, almost 225 tablets per person. In England, every tenth night of sleep is induced by a hypnotic drug and 19% of women and 9% of men take a prescribed tranquilizer during any one year. In the United States, central-nervous-system agents are the fastest-growing sector of the pharmaceutical market, now making up 31% of total sales. (Illich, 1976, pp. 63-64)

Overall, the pharmaceutical industry outperforms all other major American industries in net profit after taxes with drug companies regularly being among the very highest (Goddard, 1981, p. 248). To maintain this profit margin requires huge expenditures on advertising. The legal pushing of over-the-counter medications is obvious to us all. And we learn new ways to spell in the bargain: "How do you spell relief? . . . ROLAIDS." Or we learn that the solutions to our personal and social problems are to be found in a bottle of pills: "Life got *tougher,* we got *stronger* . . . Try extra-strength Excedrin." The underlying message is nearly always the same: some pill or potion is readily available to help one cope with or escape from the troubles of everyday life.

For stronger stuff, the consumer must go to a physician followed by a visit to a pharmacist. Thus, the advertising for prescription drugs is directed at doctors. The expense is considerable.

> It is estimated that the ethical-drug houses currently spend $1.2 billion per year on advertising and promotion. This represents about $1 in every $4 they receive for their products at wholesale and is nearly four times what they spend annually on research and development. Virtually none of the marketing expenditures are directed at the consumer who buys the product. They are directed at the physician who writes the prescription and at the pharmacist who, with increasing frequency, is in a position to select the brand when the prescription is written generically or when it allows him to substitute one brand for another.
>
> Since the marketing costs came to about $4,000 per physician per year they are deemed excessive by many critics of the industry. The $1.2 billion figure includes the salaries of more than 21,000 "detail men," each of whom costs the industry an estimated $35,000 per year; their sole job is to make periodic calls on physicians, pharmacists and hospital purchasing agents to push their firm's products. Also included in the $1.2 billion are such costs as advertising in medical journals, exhibits at medical conventions, direct-mail pieces (including physicians' samples), seminars, educational films, brochures and the practice of allowing wholesalers, retailers, and hospitals to return unsold merchandise for credit. (Goddard, 1981, p. 249)

Over one half of the American Medical Association's funds come from the drug industry and over three-quarters of the advertising in the Association's journal is bought by pharmaceutical companies. A large proportion of this advertising is devoted to tranquilizers such as Valium, Librium, or Pertofane that are said to relieve symptoms of anxiety, upset, or depression. Estimates suggest that as many as 60 percent of visits to physicians are for patient complaints for which there is no organically treatable cause. Apparently, a significant number of these organically untreatable patients, most of whom are women, leave the doctor's office with a prescription for a mood-altering drug. Doctors wrote 160 million prescriptions for tranquilizers, sedatives, and stimulants in 1979. "A federal report found that 60% of the mind-altering drugs, 71% of the antidepressants, and 80% of the amphetamines are prescribed for women. Women are prescribed more than twice the quantity of drugs as men for the same psychological syumptoms" (Mendelsohn, 1982:60). In 1980, Valium remained firmly atop *Pharmacy Times'* ranking of most prescribed drugs.[1] The drug industry's commitment to advertising clearly pays off in sales and profits. But what are the other consequences?

The widespread use of psychoactive substances as a legitimate, positively valued method for helping people to cope is part of a trend that some observers have called the "medicalization of Western societies" (Illich, 1976 or Conrad & Schneider, 1980). Increasingly, over the last century, more and more behavioral problems have been reconceptualized from misbehavior that should be subject to punishment to medical problems that should be subject to medical intervention— often with the use of drugs. Examples include stimulant medications (e.g., Ritalin) for hyperactive children, amphetamines for overeating, Antabuse for alcoholism, and methadone for heroin abuse. This is to say nothing of the use of even more potent (and toxic) psychotropic agents like Thorazine to control behavior among the more intractable populations of mental hospitals, prisons, or even the residents of nursing homes. The new medical technology, especially mood-altering drugs, places great power to control behavior in the hands of physicians. Moreover, this power is largely unchecked because it is exercised under the veil of a traditional ideology emphasizing the physician's unquestioned responsibility for the patient. We have all learned to do what the doctor orders.

Some more pessimistic visions of the future, in light of present trends, portend a therapeutic state in which people are gently and willingly drugged into pacification, unable to see or care that some of the sources of their anger or depression might be found in racist or sexist institutions, working conditions in their factories and offices, or the ways their children are taught in school. To paraphrase Marx: Valium would become the opiate of the people. For good or ill, the emerging medical technology provides the ultimate answer to problems of social control. Administered from outside, quietly controlling moods and behavior from within, drugs are the almost perfect alternative to the police state dominated by troops, secret police, and prison camps. Anger is replaced by illusion, fear by fantasy, moral outrage by sleepwalking compliance.

To be sure, the medicalized view of deviance has its brighter side: it can be more humanitarian than the criminal model; it can be helpful to the individual by minimizing selfblame and offering an optimistic likelihood for change (Conrad & Schneider, 1980, p. 250). However, the darker side of medicalization "includes (1) the dislocation of responsibility from the individual; (2) the assumption of the moral neutrality of medicine; (3) the problems engendered by the domination of expert control; (4) powerful medical techniques used for social control; (5) the individualization of complex social problems; (6) the depoliticization of deviant behavior; and (7) the exclusion of evil." (p. 259). Conrad and Schneider conclude that "It is this darker side that leaves us skeptical of the social benefits of medicalizing deviance." (p. 259)

Peter Schrag (1978) nicely captures the complex issues relating legal and illegal drug use when he says,

> Clearly, the drugs are often useful—useful to the client; useful to the institution, the doctor, and the community. The disturbing questions arise from the uncertain relationships between the two classes of beneficiaries and out of the collective didactic effects of the behavior the drugs induce. When is the client the real, long-term beneficiary of his medication, and when is the doctor or the institution or the community? When does it liberate and when does it create indefinite dependence or teach the individual that he is just the victim of his own chemistry? Here the numbers themselves become significant: some 30 or 40 million Americans can't all be crazy or "sick." The very pervasiveness of the drugs has thus helped blur, if not eradicate, the already tenuous distinction between mental illness and mental health, between therapy and control, and between treatment and manipulation. In that respect, the new drugs are altogether different from alcohol or tobacco which, while they may be as pharmacologically specific as many prescription drugs, are consumed in innocence—free, that is, from the ideology of specificity—and without the blessings of medical mediation. In the West, the consumer of alcohol assumes personal responsibility for his drinking; the consumer of Valium yields it to a doctor who, in prescribing, legitimizes its use and validates the ideology of specific action. At the same time, however, the politcal and social ideas associated with the newer drugs—including the legitimacy of mood and behavior control itself—have gradually become attached to all sorts of other things, including alcohol, street drugs, behavior modification, and almost every narcissistic movement from encounter therapy to the Reverend Sun Myung Moon's Unification Church. It's not surprising, therefore, that many of those phenomena have been represented either as corollaries or alternatives to drugs, or that they are constantly involved in controversies as to whether they are really liberation or brainwashing. (pp. 145–146)

SUMMARY

The meaning of the term "drug" varies widely; in this chapter drugs included physical substances ingested or injected into the body with the intention of altering moods or perceptions. Drugs alone do not have specific effects. Drug effects grow out of an interaction of factors including the substance's chemical properties, the physical and mental condition of the user, and the setting in which the drug is taken.

Alcohol is a drug, a central nervous system depressant that is potentially addictive. Frequent users acquire a tolerance for it and alcohol addicts suffer severe withdrawal symptoms. In addition to alcohol, we reviewed the other major drugs and their effects. Historically in the United States, the period from 1962 through 1967 marks the initiation of widespread marijuana use. After 1967, use rates of almost all recreational drugs climbed. Age overshadows all other demographic characteristics (race, rural–urban, social status) in differentiating drug users. Young adults have the highest rates in every recreational drug use category.

Our explanations of drug abuse began with alcoholism. According to a biogenetic explanation, some evidence supports the likely role of hereditary predispositions to alcoholism among some people. The best-known conceptualization of alcoholism is the Jellinek disease model that has been part of official Alcoholics Anonymous ideology for many years. Recent criticisms and challege to this traditional model were reviewed. At the sociological level of explanation we considered the importance of norms and cultural integration of drinking patterns. How people act when they are drunk varies greatly from culture to culture. Being drunk is not simply a matter of losing one's inhibitions. Moreover, there are cultural differences in rates of alcoholism. Usually, alcoholism rates are low in groups whose customs integrate drinking with social and religious practices that provide clear guidelines for when, how much, and in what situations one should drink. In American culture, drinking seems to perform the latent function of allowing a time out from normal expectations of proper behavior.

The history of changing laws regarding alcohol is an excellent example of the political side of the deviance defining process. Prohibition and its repeal were the outgrowth of intense political struggles among various interest groups. Not only laws governing alcohol use, but public images of alcoholism have changed over time and influenced public policy.

One of the principal explanations of marijuana use has been social learning theory. The evidence strongly points to the role of social learning in differential association with peers as a key to understanding marijuana use among young people. Likewise, cessation of marijuana use is heavily influenced by one's social situation. The issue of decriminalizing marijuana was shown to be intensely political. Marijuana's role as a youth culture symbol and the moral overtones of the argument are apt to drown out rational cost/benefit analyses in the public debate.

Our review of the history of opiates revealed that attempted legal restrictions on trafficking and use are rather recent. Indeed, throughout much of the period from the 16th to the 20th centuries, Western countries, especially Britain and the United States, actively promoted the lucrative opium trade. Today's international heroin industry is rooted in a prior political economy of exploitation.

Finally, we considered the use of legal drugs. Central to this concern are the links between the American drug industry, physicians, and their patients—especially women. The ever-increasing use of mind-altering substances, both legal and illegal, should provoke our concern about future techniques of social control.

NOTE

1. A study of hospital emergency room visits during 1980, recorded under the Drug Abuse Warning Network (DAWN), reports

> a total of 21,627 mentions of tranquilizer abuse. Forty-five percent of these mentions (9,864) were mentions of diazepam, commonly prescribed under the brand name Valium. In 88% of the cases where the patient's source of obtaining the tranquilizers was reported to DAWN (13,492), the patient had obtained the tranquilizers through his or her own legal prescription. Although, among the DAWN emergency rooms studied, mentions of tranquilizer abuse have declined substantially over the past few years, tranquilizers are still the most frequently mentioned drugs of abuse [excepting alcohol].... [T]here were more mentions of tranquilizer abuse in 1980 (21,627) than there were of narcotics (10,794 mentions), hallucinogens (4,379 mentions), cannabis (2,922 mentions) and cocaine (1,992 mentions) combined (20,086 mentions). (Porpora, 1982, pp. 4-5.)

REFERENCES

Akers, R. L.
    1973 *Deviant behavior: A social learning approach.* Belmont, Calif.: Wadsworth.
Akers, R. L., Krohn, M. D., Lanza-Kaduce, L., & Radosevich, M.
    1979 Social learning and deviant behavior: A specific test of a general theory. *American Sociological Review, 44,* 636-655.
Alcohol Health and Research World
    1974 The economic costs of alcohol misuse. *Alcohol Health and Research World* (Winter), pp. 19-26.
Alexander, R.
    1930 *Narcotics in India and South Asia.* London: Unwin Brothers.

Bales, R. F.
  1946 Cultural differences in rates of alcoholism. *Quarterly Journal of Studies on Alcohol, 6,* pp. 482–498.
Bates, W., & Crowther, B.
  1977 Drug abuse. In E. Sagarin & F. Montanino (Eds.), *Deviants: Voluntary actors in a hostile world.* Glenview, Ill.: Scott Foresman.
Becker, H. S.
  1963 *Outsiders: Studies in the sociology of deviance.* New York: The Free Press.
Berry, R. E., Jr., & Boland, J. P.
  1977 *The economic cost of alcohol abuse.* New York: The Free Press.
Brown, J. W., Glaser, D., Waxer, E., & Geis, G.
  1974 Turning off: Cessation of marijuana use after college. *Social Problems, 21,* 527–538.
Chafetz, M.
  1971 Introduction. In *First special report to the U.S. Congress on alcohol and health.* Washington, D.C.: National Institute on Alcohol Abuse and Alcoholism.
Chambliss, W. J.
  1978 The political economy of smack: Opiates, capitalism and the law. In R. J. Simon (Ed.), *Research in law and sociology,* vol. 6. Greenwich, Conn.: Jai Press.
Cisin, I., Miller, J. D., & Harrell, A. V.
  1977 *Highlights from the national survey on drug abuse: 1977.* Washington, D.C.: National Institute of Drug Abuse.
Clinard, M. B., & Meier, R. F.
  1979 *Sociology of deviant behavior.* New York: Holt, Rinehart and Winston.
Conrad, P., & Schneider, J. W.
  1980 *Deviance and medicalization.* St. Louis: Mosby.
DuPont, R. L., & Greene, M. H.
  1973 The dynamics of a heroin addiction epidemic. *Science, 181,* pp. 716–722.
Durkheim, E.
  1966 *The rules of sociological methods.* S. A. Solovay & J. H. Mueller (Trans.) & E. G. Catlin (Ed.). New York: The Free Press.
Fishburne, P. M., Abelson, H. I., & Cisin, I.
  1979 *National survey on drug abuse: 1979.* Rockville, Md: National Institute on Drug Abuse.
Glassner, B., & Berg, B.
  1980 How Jews avoid alcohol problems. *American Sociological Review, 45,* 647–664.
Goddard, J. L.
  1981 The medical business. In P. Conrad and R. Kern (Eds.). *The sociology of health and illness.* New York: St. Martin's Press.

Goode, E.
   1969   Marijuana and the politics of reality. *Journal of Health and Social Behavior, 10* (June), pp. 83–94.

Goode, E.
   1978   *Deviant behavior: An interactionist approach.* Englewood Cliffs, N.J.: Prentice-Hall.

Goodwin, D.
   1976   *Is alcoholism hereditary?* New York: Oxford.

Gusfield, J. R.
   1963   *Symbolic crusade.* Urbana, Ill.: University of Illinois Press.

Gusfield, J. R.
   1967   Moral passage: The symbolic process in public designations of deviance. *Social Problems, 15*, pp. 175–188.

Haberman, P. W., & Baden, M. M.
   1978   *Alcohol, other drugs and violent death.* New York: Oxford.

Henley, J. R., & Adams, L. D.
   1973   Marihuana use in post-collegiate cohorts: correlations of use, prevalence patterns, and factors associated with cessation. *Social Problems, 20,* pp. 514–520.

Hills, S. L.
   1980   *Demystifying social deviance.* New York: McGraw-Hill.

Illich, I.
   1976   *Medical nemesis.* New York: Bantam.

Inciardi, J. A.
   1981   Marijuana decriminalization research: A perspective and commentary. *Criminology, 19,* pp. 145–159.

Jellinek, E. M.
   1952   Phases of alcohol addiction. *Quarterly Journal of Studies of Alcohol, 13,* pp. 673–684.

Jellinek, E. M.
   1960   *The disease concept of alcoholism.* New Haven, Conn.: Hillhouse Press.

Johnson, B. D.
   1973   *Marihuana users and drug subcultures.* New York: Wiley.

Kandel, D. B., Truman, D., Faust, R., & Single, E.
   1976   Adolescent involvement in legal and illegal drug use: a multiple classification analysis. *Social Forces, 55,* pp. 438–458.

Koh, T. T. B.
   1974   Drug use in Singapore. *International Journal of Criminology and Penology, 2,* pp. 51–64.

Linsky, A. S.
   1971   Theories of behavior and the image of the alcoholic in popular magazines, 1900–1966. *Public Opinion Quarterly, 34,* pp. 573–581.

Lubbock, B.
   1933   *The opium clippers.* Glasgow: Brown, Son and Ferguson.

MacAndrew, C., & Edgerton, R. B.
   1969 *Drunken comportment: A social explanation.* Chicago: Aldine.

McCaghy, C. H.
   1968 Drinking and deviance disavowal: The case of child molesters. *Social Problems, 16,* pp. 43–49.

McCoy, A. W.
   1972 *The politics of heroin in Southeast Asia.* New York: Harper and Row.

Mendelsohn, R. S.
   1982 Male practice: How doctors manipulate women. Chicago: Contemporary Books.

Mizruchi, E. H., & Perrucci, R.
   1970 Prescription, proscription and permissiveness: Aspects of norms and drinking behavior. In George R. Maddox (Ed.), *The Domesticated Drug.* New Haven: College and University Press.

New York State Division of Substance Abuse.
   1981a *Drug use among college students in New York State.* Unpublished paper available from NYS Division of Substance Abuse, Albany, N.Y.

New York State Division of Substance Abuse.
   1981b *Drug use among New York State's household population.* Unpublished paper. Op. cit.

Orcutt, J. D.
   1975 Deviance as a situated phenomenon: Variations in the social interpretation of marijuana and alcohol use. *Social Problems, 22,* pp. 346–355.

Orcutt, J. D.
   1976 Ideological variations in the structure of deviant types: A multivariate comparison of alcoholism and heroin addiction. *Social Forces, 55,* pp. 419–437.

Owen, D.
   1934 *British opium policy in China and India.* New Haven: Yale University Press.

Pastor, Jr., P. A.
   1978 Mobilization in public drunkenness control: A comparison of legal and medical approaches. *Social Problems, 25,* pp. 373–384.

Pattison, E. M., Sobell, M. B., & Sobell, L. C.
   1977 *Emerging concepts of alcohol dependence.* New York: Springer Publishing.

Porpora, D.
   1982 Physicians' prescriptions of tranquilizers and tranquilizer abuse. Paper presented at the Annual Meeting of the Eastern Sociological Society, Philadelphia.

Rogers, J. M.
   1971 Drug abuse—by prescription. *Psychology Today, 5,* p. 16ff.

Rubin, V., & Comitas, L.
   1975 *Ganja in Jamaica: A medical anthropological study.* The Hague: Mouton.

Schrag, P.
  1978 *Mind control.* New York: Pantheon.
Schneider, J. W.
  1978 Deviant drinking as disease: Alcoholism as a social accomplishment. *Social Problems, 25,* pp. 361–372.
Scott, J. M.
  1969 *The white poppy: A history of opium.* London: Heineman.
Snyder, C.
  1958 *Alcohol and the Jews.* New Haven: Yale University Press.
Spradley, J. P.
  1970 *You owe yourself a drunk: An ethnography of urban nomads.* Boston: Little, Brown.
Trice, H. M., & Roman, P. M.
  1970 Delabelling, relabelling, and alcoholics anonymous. *Social Problems, 17,* pp. 538–546.
U.S. Senate Hearings
  1977 *Occupational alcoholism prevention and treatment act of 1977.* Subcommittee on Alcoholism and Drug Abuse.
Van Dyke, C., & Byck, R.
  1982 Cocaine. *Scientific American, 246,* pp. 128–141.
Wen, U. C.
  1961 Opium in the Straits Settlements, 1867–1910. *Journal of Southeast Asian History, 2,* pp. 52–75.

Chapter 6
ELITE DEVIANCE

THE AMERICAN CLASS STRUCTURE
  Who Are the Elites?
  Elites and the Exercise of Power
THE WHITE-COLLAR CRIME TRADITION
  Problems of Definition
ELITE OCCUPATIONAL DEVIANCE
  Illegal and Unethical Behavior in the Professions
  Official Deviance
CORPORATE DEVIANCE
  What Is a Corporation?
  Why Study Corporate Crime?
  The Costs of Corporate Crime
  Types of Corporate Deviance
  How Much Corporate Deviance Is There?
  Explanations of Corporate Deviance
  Control of Corporate Deviance
SUMMARY

This chapter deals with deviant behavior among those at the highest levels of American society. Our initial task, therefore, will be to identify who the elites are—to compare their wealth and power to the rest of the people in the American social structure. The elites whose deviance will concern us fall into two broad categories. First, there is the relatively small number of individuals who exercise great political power and who are accorded exceptionally high prestige in the society. Specifically, we will examine deviant behavior closely linked to the occupations of these high-status individuals. Second, there is the relatively small number of corporations which control an ever larger share of this nation's economy. We normally conceive of any social behavior, deviant or normal, as the product of individual motives, initiative, choices, or responsibilities. Increasingly in our society, however, corporations—very large, complex, bureaucratic organizations—have become actors that behave both for the good and the ill of many others. Therefore, a large portion of this chapter is devoted to corporate deviance and criminality.

For too long, say some critics (for example, Liazos, 1972 or Thio, 1973), students of deviance have concentrated on the poor, the powerless, or the pathological as the inspiration of their theories and subjects of their studies. Recently, with a burst of research on deviance committed by elites, this balance has begun to shift. And with it has come a more complete recognition that our study of deviance should never be excluded by class boundaries or alleged lack of individual psychopathology. As the evidence cited in this chapter amply demonstrates, deviance can become a way of life even for those at the top.

THE AMERICAN CLASS STRUCTURE

Who Are the Elites?

Individuals. At the very top of the American social hierarchy sits roughly 1% of the population that controls a disproportionate share of the country's wealth and exercises great economic and political power.

The power of this class derives from the weighty concentration of vast economic resources in their relatively few hands: 0.5% of American households own 22% of the individual wealth and control 60–70% of the corporate wealth. It is this very small class of superrich capitalists who

> make investment decisions that in turn open or close employment opportunities for millions of others; they contribute money to political parties, and they often own newspapers or television companies, thereby gaining impact on the shaping of the consciousness of all classes in the nation. The capitalist class tends to perpetuate itself: it passes on assets and styles of life (including networks of contact with other influentials) to its children. This creation of lineage is of sufficient importance to them that they are active in creating and supporting preparatory schools and universities for their children and for carefully selected newcomers who can be socialized into their world view. (Gilbert & Kahl, 1982, pp. 348–349)

Below the capitalist elite is the upper-middle class of university-trained managers, professionals, and bureaucratic administrators. Constituting about 14% of the population, this group distinguishes itself from the capitalist class by having its status grounded in educational credentials and relatively high income as opposed to the inherited wealth and lineage of the upper elite. The upper-middle class is less culturally unified than the capitalist class by common membership in elite social groups, elite prep schools and colleges, listing in social registers, and the like. However, the upper-middle-class life-style incorporates the symbols that many Americans identify as the epitome of success. Taken together, the upper 15% of the American population, made up of capitalists and the upper-middle class, can be usually considered the society's elite individuals. Characteristics of the remaining 85% of the population below them are summarized in Table 6.1.

Corporations. In the same way that a great deal of wealth and power are concentrated in the hands of a small proportion of individuals, relatively few very large corporations control a large segment of the American economy. As Clinard and Yeager put it: "The current size of U.S. corporations staggers the imagination." (p. 31). Some representative indicators are:

- In 1983 the total annual sales of the *Fortune* 500 largest industrial corporations was $1.6 trillion ($1,686,700,000,000).
- Annual revenues of Exxon, General Motors, and Mobil the world's largest industrial corporations, each exceed or approach $60 billion, greater than that of any government of the world except those of the United States and the Soviet Union.

TABLE 6.1. THE AMERICAN CLASS STRUCTURE*

Proportion of population	Class	Education	Occupation	Income, 1978	Budget level (Labor Department)
1%	Capitalist	Prestige university	Investors, heirs, executives	$300,000 or more, mostly from assets	—
14%	Upper middle	College, often with postgraduate study	Upper managers and professionals; medium businessmen	$30,000 or more	Above higher budget
65%	Middle	At least high school; often some college or apprenticeship	Lower managers; semi-professionals; sales, nonretail; craftspeople; foremen	About $20,000	Intermediate budget
	Working	High school	Operatives; low-paid craftspeople; clerical workers; retail sales workers	About $15,000	Between intermediate and lower budgets
20%	Working poor	Some high school	Service workers; laborers; low-paid operatives	Below $10,000	Under lower budget
	Underclass	Primary school	Unemployed or part-time; welfare recipients	Below $7,000	Under poverty line

Source: D. Gilbert and J. A. Kahl, 1982; p. 348.
*Model of the American class structure: Classes by typical situations

- Exxon has three times as many overseas employees as the U.S. State Department.
- Of the more than 200,000 corporations in the U.S., 2,000 (or 1%) account for one half of all U.S. business.
- The 500 largest industrial corporations account for two-thirds of all industrial sales and three-quarters of all manufacturing assets.

Many key industries in the United States are dominated by fewer than four corporations as indicated in Figure 6.1. Moreover, the tendency toward concentration has been growing. The 200 largest corporations controlled one half of all manufacturing assets in 1950; by 1975 they controlled two-thirds.

Elites and the Exercise of Power

The control of economic assets by elite individuals and corporations is most important, in reference to the study of deviance, to the extent that wealth can be effectively translated into political power—for with political power comes the ability to have the law enacted and enforced in one's favor. Two sorts of evidence serve to demonstrate how elites disproportionately influence the political process. The first is the direct link between capitalist and upper-middle classes to the political process, at the national level, in the Congress and Cabinet posts. Beginning with the House of Representatives, over three-quarters of the membership since 1948 have come from among lawyers, business owners, or professionals (Table 6.2). "The representation of blue-collar workers or white-collar employees has been scanty indeed. Evidence going back to the beginning of this century shows that this recruitment pattern has been utterly consistent" (Gilbert & Kahl, 1982, p. 242).

The Senate has a similar recruitment base with the vast majority having been professionals or business owners. As Gilbert and Kahl note, "The Senate is at the very least an upper-middle-class institution. But a significant minority of senators can be described as upper class. In the 92nd Congress, 20% qualified on the basis of social credentials, including *Social Register* listings, prep school attendance, or membership in exclusive clubs" (p. 242). In 1979, at least one-third of the 100 Senators were millionaires.

The Congress is important as the national law-making body. The enforcement of laws falls primarily on the executive branch of government whose administrative policy and procedure decisions are heavily influenced by the composition of the Cabinet. Here again, the domination of elites—especially the corporate elite—is remarkably evident.

ELITE DEVIANCE

(percentage share of market held by top four firms)

Industry	Leading Firms
Aluminum	Alcoa, Reynolds, Kaiser*
Automobiles	General Motors, Ford, Chrysler
Synthetic fibers	Dupont, Union Carbide, Celanese, Monsanto
Flat glass	Pittsburgh Plate, Owens-Illinois, Corning, Libbey
Electric bulbs	General Electric, Westinghouse, Sylvania
Telephone equip.	Western Electric
Copper	Anaconda, Kennecott, Phelps Dodge, American Smelt
Cereal foods	Kellogg, General Foods
Electric Tubes	RCA
Gypsum	Johns Manville, U.S. Gypsum, National
Cigarettes	Reynolds, American, Philip Morris, L&M
Typewriters	Litton, IBM
Salt	International, Morton
Rubber tires	Goodyear, Firestone, Uniroyal
Soap-detergents	Procter & Gamble, Colgate, Lever Bros.
Steel ingots & shapes	U.S. Steel, Bethlehem, Republic

FIGURE 6.1. THE GROWTH AND DEVELOPMENT OF THE CORPORATION

*Only the names of leading firms in each industry are identified. In some cases there is only a single dominant company, in others there may be two, three, or four.

Freitag (1975) found that over 76% of Cabinet members over the period 1897 to 1976 had interlocks with business as either corporate directors or officers (62%) or corporate lawyers (14%). The pattern is highly stable during the entire period.

To be sure, the strong tendency for Congress and Cabinet members to be recruited from the upper echelons of the society does not guarantee a uniform political viewpoint. However, people who share upper- or upper–middle–class origins are likely to be more sympathetic to views and interests common to those at the top of the class structure than those toward the bottom (Gilbert & Kahl, 1982, p. 243).

The second avenue through which elites influence the political process is more indirect. For example, upper–class members dominate numerous policy–forming organizations that heavily influence political candidates and often represent a major recruiting source for presidential appointees. Among such organizations are the Council on Foreign Relations; the Committee for Economic Development; the Business Council; the Ford, Rockefeller, or Carnegie foundations; or elite–sponsored research at major universities like Harvard, Yale, Princeton, or Columbia (Domhoff, 1978). One researcher (Dye, 1976) found that 42% of the directors of foundations, 25% of the directors of elite universities, and 40% of the directors of civic organizations could be classified as members of the upper–class (Kerbo & Fave, 1979, p. 17). More specifically, in relation to criminal justice policy, Quinney (1974, p. 67) notes that 63% of the members of the 1965 Presidential Crime Commission had business and corporate connections, and 95% had held high level domestic government positions.

In sum, we can say that the American class structure is characterized by a relatively small elite of capitalists (1%) and upper–middle–class individuals (14%). Paralleling the concentration of wealth in the hands of these individuals is a comparable concentration of corporate wealth

TABLE 6.2. OCCUPATIONS OF MEMBERS OF THE HOUSE OF REPRESENTATIVES (%)

Occupation	1948	1952	1956	1960	1964	1968	1970
Lawyer	58%	51%	49%	48%	52%	66%	52%
Business owner	13	22	21	23	20	12	16
Farm owner	5	7	9	3	6	2	4
Manager	—	2	4	—	4	6	8
Professional	16	13	13	26	10	10	14
White collar	2	2	2	—	4	2	2
Other	5	2	2	—	4	—	4
Total	100	100	100	100	100	100	100

Source: J. Nagle, *System and succession: The social bases of political elite recruitment* (Austin: University of Texas Press, 1977), p. 74.

held by relatively few large corporations. The evidence is very persuasive that these elite individuals and corporations are able to translate their economic power into political decisions largely in their interests both directly by political control of legislative and administrative positions and indirectly through organizations that influence public policy.

THE WHITE-COLLAR CRIME TRADITION

In his 1939 presidential address to the American Sociological Association, Edwin H. Sutherland (1883–1950) challenged traditional criminology. First, he questioned the assumption, based upon official statistics like the FBI's *Uniform Crime Index,* that crime is concentrated in the lower classes. Sutherland charged that such official measures of crime included only the sorts of offenses such as theft, burglary, and robbery that lower-class people are likely to commit while excluding illegal activities common to the well-to-do such as tax evasion, embezzlement, or price fixing. Subsequently, most students of deviance have agreed with this critique.

Sutherland also argued that students of crime must extend their view beyond the strict violation of the criminal law in their search for offenses and offenders. He said that criminologists should include in their subject matter administrative and civil law violations as well because it is under the jurisdiction of these bodies of law that most crimes of the rich and powerful are pursued. Indeed, he even went so far as to suggest that because the wealthy and powerful create the law and have the law enforced largely in their own interests, criminologists should be the ultimate, unbiased arbiters of what constitutes crime for purposes of determining the subjects of their inquiry. In other words, criminologists should not confine their investigations to activities prescribed by the criminal law. Instead they should invoke their own standard of those "wrongful and injurious practices" that should constitute crime, even if the behavior in question has not been officially labeled criminal by law.

Subsequently, Sutherland published his pioneering book *White Collar Crime* (1949) in which he reported on violations of the 70 largest corporations in the United States over the period from 1890 to 1945. He counted as crimes restraint of trade, misrepresentation in advertising, unfair labor practices, and financial fraud, among others. During the 45-year period, the 70 corporations had a total of 980 adverse decisions. "Every one of the 70 corporations has a decision against it, and the average number of decisions is 14. Of these 70 corporations, 98% are recidivists; that is, they have two or more adverse decisions" (Sutherland, 1956, p. 80). He concluded that "90% of the 70 largest corporations in the United States are habitual criminals."

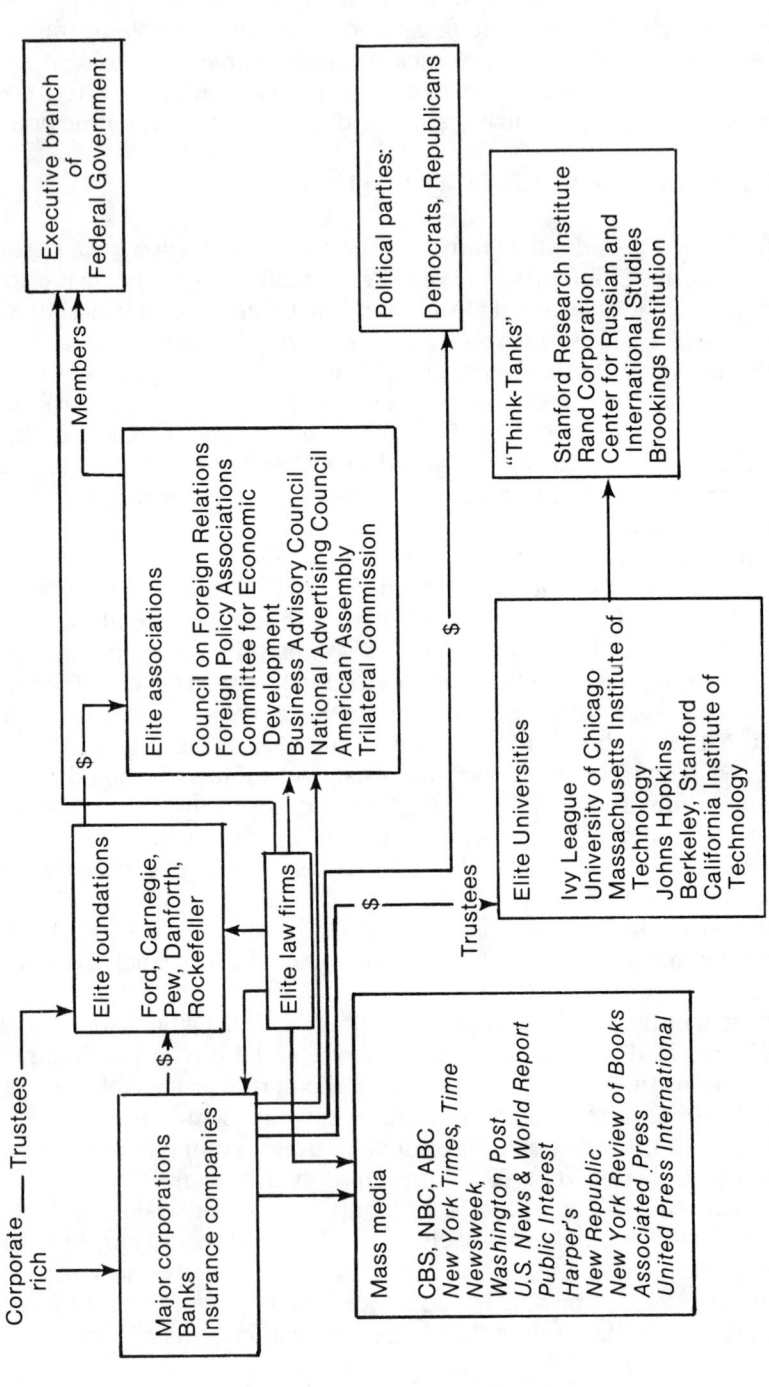

FIGURE 6.2. CAPITALIST ELITE—RULING ELITE LINKAGES
Source: Adapted from G. W. Domhoff, State and ruling class in corporate America, *The Insurgent Sociologist*, 3 (Spring, 1974), pp. 3–16. Used with permission.

Although Sutherland has been rightly criticized for overinterpreting his data and inflating his rhetoric (Klockars, 1977), the thrust of his argument remains viable: Crime is not necessarily caused by (or even correlated with) poverty and its alleged attendant pathologies. Crime is not confined to the lower class. Moreover, crime is not necessarily due to psychological pathology. As Sutherland mockingly put it:

> Business leaders are capable, emotionally balanced, and in no sense pathological. We have no reason to think that General Motors has an inferiority complex or that the Aluminum Company of America has a frustration–aggression complex or that U.S. Steel has an Oedipus complex, or that the Armour Company has a death wish or that the DuPonts desire to return to the womb. The assumption that an offender must have some such pathological distortion of the intellect or the emotions seems to me absurd, and if it is absurd regarding the crimes of businessmen, it is equally absurd regarding the crimes of persons in the lower economic class. (1956, p. 96)

Problems of Definition

Sutherland defined white-collar crime as crime committed by a person of respectability and high social status in the course of his occupation. In practice, Sutherland himself used the concept in reference to acts as varied as medical fee splitting by doctors, political corruption, embezzlement, tax fraud, antitrust violations, and labor law violations. Subsequently, others have applied the term to the production and sale of unsafe products or to environmental pollution. The main difficulty is that these applications of Sutherland's original definition exceed its conceptual boundaries. For example, the original definition states that the crime is "committed by a *person*...." To be sure, this may clearly be the case in a physician's medical fee splitting or an individual's tax evasion. However, the legal actor in the case of antitrust or labor law violation is more likely to be a corporation. This suggests that we should take care not to confuse deviant actions committed by individuals with those committed by corporations. Such a distinction forms the basis for the two major types of elite deviance we will consider in this chapter, elite occupational deviance and elite corporate deviance.

Elite occupational deviance is *an illegal or unethical act committed for personal gain by an individual of high social status and respectability in the course of that person's occupation or profession.* The examples we will examine briefly are certain practices in the professions among doctors, lawyers, and college professors, and political corruption among government officials. The central features that distinguish occupational deviance are the commission of the offense for direct personal gain and the relatively autonomous behavior of the offender.

Elite corporate deviance consists of *actions that violate criminal, civil, or administrative law (acts of omission or commission) that are intended to benefit the corporation itself. Such actions result from decisions by officers in a corporation (executives or managers) in accordance with corporate goals (primarily corporate profit), standard operating procedures, and cultural norms of the organization* (adapted from Kramer, 1981, pp. 7–8). Examples of corporate deviance include securities fraud, price fixing, labor law violations, violation of health and safety regulations, and pollution law violations. The key characteristics of corporate deviance are commission of the offense in the pursuit of corporate gain (profit, expanded market share, market stability), and the collective or organizational basis of the behavior. The decision to act illegally is made and implemented by numerous individuals through the bureaucratic procedures of the corporate organization. Many researchers in this field, following Sutherland's lead, use the term corporate crime to cover the same actions encompassed by our definition of corporate deviance. Subsequently in this chapter, therefore, the two terms will be taken to refer to the same general phenomena and will be used interchangeably.

ELITE OCCUPATIONAL DEVIANCE

Illegal and Unethical Behavior in the Professions

In an era when the word "professional" connotes proficiency in and dedication to one's work, there are few occupations from streetwalker to paid athlete to brain surgeon that do not claim to be a profession. As used by sociologists of work, however, the term is applied rather more narrowly to refer to occupations of relatively high status invested with a great deal of trust on the part of clients to manage their affairs honestly and in the public interest. Doctors, lawyers, and professors nearly meet the ideal characteristics of a profession including lengthy training to learn an abstract body of knowledge, autonomy and self-regulation on the job, the existence of their own associations, and a set of professional norms usually set down in a code of ethics. In fact, the professions and their clients rely heavily upon the long educational process necessary for certification to practice as the principal means of social control. The professions depend upon instilling each practitioner with a strong ethical conscience, in the absence of which the license to practice becomes a license to steal, or worse.

Physicians. Doctors are near the pinnacle of the society in both income and prestige. The old-time dedication of the western "Doc" and the contemporary wisdom of a television Marcus Welby symbolize part of the underlying image. At the same time, physicians are increasingly faced with public hostility often made manifest in malpractice suits and reaction to disclosure of scandals such as massive Medicaid fraud.

At least one of the offenses frequently committed by physicians is usually associated with street criminals. Drug addiction rates among doctors are extremely high; the rate for physicians is estimated to be 100 times that for the general population (Hessler, 1974). The reasons are thought mainly to be the stress and strain of professional obligations combined with easy access to drugs and a capacity to avoid detection. However, other deviant activities such as performing unnecessary surgery, ordering excessive laboratory tests, fee padding or fee splitting (referral of a patient to a high priced specialist who then pays off the referring physician) appear to be motivated primarily by greed. The extent of such illegalities is frightening.

> Dr. Jervey (a past president of the Federation of State Medical Boards) and others with long experience in this field estimate that at least one physician in twenty is a severe disciplinary problem, that between 15,000 and 20,000 private practitioners (as many as one in nine) are repeatedly guilty of practices unworthy of the profession. Most of these physicians commit offenses that are unethical rather than prosecutable: substandard care, abandonment, overcharging, and the like. But, Dr. Jervey concludes, between 2,500 and 7,500 are actually breaking the law through narcotics violations, frauds, and other felonies. (Lewis & Lewis, 1978, pp. 252–253.)

One sociological answer to why so many high-status professionals engage in deviant behavior lies in an analysis of the profession's autonomy. Professional autonomy is the characteristic of many occupations that lends them so much prestige. It is also thought by some to be a major contributor to deviance. As Lewis and Lewis put it:

> If you are like most laymen, you take comfort in the belief that doctors of medicine are kept in careful rein by stringent laws, rigorous government agencies, and exacting professional groups. Unfortunately, if you think this you are mistaken.
> Actually, the privately practicing physician is largely a free agent, scarcely subject to regulation. Once he secures a license he has virtually a lifetime franchise to practice at his own discretion. There are few statutory standards he must meet, for the laws are generally silent as to what constitutes acceptable performance by physicians. Even where restrictions are clear, enforcement is spotty; the state boards charged with overseeing the profession are seldom active on matters of discipline. Within the profession itself the disciplining of colleagues has little support; physicians do not like to police their fellows, and this reluctance is reflected at every level of organized medicine (p. 248).

Lawyers. Some lawyers regularly engage in outright illegal activities including various forms of criminal financial manipulation on behalf of clients such as tax fraud, securing perjured testimony from witnesses, and threatening or intimidating witnesses. More on the border between the outright illegal and the merely unethical are inflated fee setting and ambulance chasing. The latter activity often involves watching carefully for opportunities to offer accident victims legal services to sue for liability damages. The present rise in the frequency and size of awards in medical malpractice suits lies behind increasing tensions between the medical and legal professions. Doctors charge that aggressive, greedy lawyers push clients to file malpractice actions. The lawyers counter that they are merely protecting their clients' interests in the face of an inadequately self-regulated medical profession.

The problem of legal fee setting underscores how the autonomy, lack of regulation, and the abstract quality of the services rendered coalesce into a virtual invitation to take unethical or illegal advantage of clients. Blumberg, describing the "practice of law as a confidence game," says the following:

> In varying degrees, as a consequence, all law practice involves a manipulation of the client and a stage management of the lawyer-client relationship so that at least an *appearance* of help and service will be forthcoming. This is accomplished in a variety of ways, often exercised in combination with each other. At the outset, the lawyer-professional employs with suitable variation a measure of sales-puff which may range from an air of unbounding self-confidence, adequacy, and dominion over events to that of complete arrogance. This will be supplemented by the affectation of a studied, faultless mode of personal attire. In the larger firms, the furnishings and office trappings will serve as the backdrop to help in impression management and client intimidation. In all firms, solo or large-scale, an access to secret knowledge and to the seats of power and influence is inferred or presumed to a varying degree as the basic vendible commodity of the practitioners. (Blumberg, 1978, pp. 267-277)

Statistics do not exist on the amount of illegal or unethical behavior among lawyers. Certainly it would be unfair and incorrect to assume that every laywer is a shyster or that every physician cares only for money. Indeed, it is probably a wonder, given the heavy reliance upon self-regulation, that deviance in these professions is not far more prevalent than it is. Dansereau summarizes the situation well.

> Given present goals and means, current practices are likely to continue. Persistence of the competition between the business and the professional ethic will probably find mere mortals frequently succumbing to the temp-

tation to serve Mammon. As long as professional attention is poorly balanced between cure and prevention and oriented more toward the dollar than toward service, a favorable climate for professional deviance exists. The presence of interprofessional conflicts and competitions for client loyalty are other potential contributors to that climate. (Dansereau, 1974, p. 89).

Professors. While feeling rather free to debunk those in other professions, college professors have been loath to expose their own deviant ways to the scrutiny of the researcher or the public. Possibly, many people regard professors generally immune to temptation—after all, big money is not one of the inducements to enter the groves of academe. However, money is not the only medium of exchange in our society that is liable to corruption. Especially in hierarchical situations in which women are subordinate to men, as is the situation of female students to male faculty, sexual harassment becomes a possibility.

The phrase sexual harassment means "interactions between people of unequal status—an inequality that can be psychological as well as social or economic in nature—(that) may be perceived by the less powerful as aggressive attacks, hostile acts of persecution" (Franklin, et al., 1981, p. 1). Sexual harassment involves: (1) unwanted sexual attention from members of the same or a different sex; (2) the presence of intimidation or coercion when the aggressor is in a position of greater authority than the victim; and frequently, (3) the suggestion that institutionally inappropriate rewards or penalties will result from compliance or refusal to comply. More concretely, it includes examples like the following:

> A Yale undergraduate charged her political science professor with sexual harassment, alleging that he offered her an "A" in exchange for sexual favors. She refused, received a "C" in the course, and has since filed a lawsuit against the university.
>
> A senior communications major at a state university in California testified before the California state legislature in 1973 that she knew of "at least 15 professors who offered students " 'A's for sex."
>
> A female cadet at West Point resigned from the military academy in 1977 after charging her male squad leader with improper sexual advances. The Academy dismissed her charges when the squad leader denied any wrongdoing. (Sandler et al., 1981, p. 52.)

Only recently have data been available to allow estimates of the prevalence of sexual harassment on college and university campuses.

In a random survey of 269 senior women at a major university 30% reported receiving unwanted sexual attention from at least one instructor during their four years of college (Benson & Thomson, 1981). In a smaller study, 8% of the women reported unwanted and offensive touching and 2.6% reported that a male instructor had suggested or demanded sexual relations in exchange for an academic reward. (Wilson & Kraus, 1981)

The problem is complex, subtle, and can be emotionally traumatic. For example,

> A graduate student complained to her college counselor: "What was it that I did that led him to believe I was interested in him in anything but a professional sense? I am quite outgoing and talkative; could that be interpreted wrongly? I realized how utterly vulnerable I was in a situation like this. He is an immensely powerful person with many contacts and if I insult him, he can harm me and my career in a hundred different ways. Everything that happened would be interpreted in his favor, if it ever became public. It would be said that I got my signals wrong, that he was just truly interested in helping me in my career. I realized that should he try to hurt my professional advancement as a result of this kind of situation, there would be no person or formal mechanism to (whom I could) carry my grievances, no person I could complain to that would have any real power to help me. I was left feeling frustrated and defenseless . . ."
> . . . Sexual harassment takes an emotional toll as well. A wide range of symptoms has been reported by victims of harassment: insomnia, headaches, neck and backaches, stomach ailments, decreased concentration, diminished ambition, listlessness, and depression. Sexual coercion makes the educational atmosphere intolerable, forcing the student, in many cases, to withdraw from a course of study or change her career plans. But the overwhelming feeling is helplessness—knowing that if one complains, nothing will likely be done or, worse yet, she will be labeled a "troublemaker." (Sandler et al., 1981, pp. 53–54)

Certain qualities of higher education that impede an honest confrontation with the problem of sexual harassment have been identified (Dziech & Faaborg, 1982). First, the professional autonomy of faculty activity, sometimes couched in terms of academic freedom to teach and deal with students as they see fit, can serve as a smoke screen for the sexual harasser. "Collegiality" can become a remarkably cohesive bond in the face of harassment charges. Other features of higher education that are conducive to harassment or protection of the harasser are: lack of uniform teaching methods; the absence of uniform goals in education; a diffusion of power and authority at college campuses; "tolerance" of "eccentric" faculty; and a tendency among educators to examine problems at great length before taking steps to resolve them.

Of course, sexual harassment is hardly confined to the university. A 1976 national survey of 9,000 clerical and professional women revealed that 92% had experienced overt physical harassment, sexual remarks, and leering with a majority regarding this behavior as a serious problem at work (Sandler, 1981). A massive survey of federal workers found that 16% had experienced "severe" harassment (pressure for dates, touching, pressure for sexual favors, etc.) and 1% had been victims of actual or attempted rape or sexual assault in the workplace (Diamond et al., 1981). Indeed, as Gordon puts it, "sexual harassment is not a matter of manners or style. It is a fundamental form of oppression, and one of the most widespread in our society" (Gordon, 1981, p. 14). By reinforcing woman's image as being "fair game" when outside the confines of the home, sexual harassment serves as a subtle but effective tool of domination. Academia should be one of the primary arenas in which the problem is openly recognized, confronted, and effectively fought.

Official Deviance

With the growth of government in the 20th century, the opportunities for official corruption have expanded in kind. James Michael Curley, the colorful mayor of Boston in the early 20th century, is reputed to have looked into his shaving mirror each morning and said, "Well James Michael, what can I do for you today?" And apparently he managed to do very well, creating a political machine nearly as renowned as Boss Tweed's Tammany Hall of New York City almost 50 years earlier. However, even these legendary standards of political corruption among elected officials do not match today's possibilities if only because government is comprised of so many more people—including elected, appointed, and career civil officials.

Official deviance is, to be sure, *occupational* deviance; but there are, as Geis (1977) notes, several characteristics which justify treating it as a special category.

> Political white–collar crime differs from other forms of white–collar crime primarily in the occupational setting in which the offense takes place. A person who gains an elective or appointive office acquires with it considerable power to confer favors and to use public resources for personal gain. The officeholder also obtains control of persons and agencies which can be used to engage in illegal activities and to prevent their detection. Political white–collar crime, therefore, offers structural opportunities for violation that differ from those involved in other forms of white–collar crime.

> There are, as well, additional variations which would appear to justify delineation of political white-collar crime as a separable entity. Among the more notable of these are that political office is regarded as a public trust, and that the political incumbent has a specific duty to enforce the laws. Thus, one of the ugliest aspects of the Watergate affair was the contrast between the behavior of the participants and the public pronouncements of the leading members of the Nixon administration, with their demands for draconian measures against traditional offenders. (Geis, 1977, p. 207).

Thus, official deviance is unique because, being committed by those empowered to enforce the law, it is especially difficult to detect and prosecute. Moreover, since crime by those entrusted to uphold the law is especially morally repugnant, widespread disclosures of official deviance are apt to be the object of considerable public moral outrage and, in the long term, have a corrosive effect upon peoples' willingness to abide by the law throughout the society.

Among official elites, two broad types of deviance, oriented toward personal gain, prevail. The first is epitomized by the activities and events that led to Spiro Agnew's resignation as Vice President in 1972. Agnew, according to accounts of evidence in the hands of federal investigators, had accepted bribes from construction firms under contract in Maryland while he was Baltimore's county executive. He continued to receive them even while Vice President. Agnew was forced to resign the vice presidency as part of a plea bargaining arrangement in which he was allowed to plead *nolo contendere* ("I do not wish to contend") to tax evasion and resign in exchange for not going to jail. Agnew, who was not independently wealthy, once indicated that he continued to take bribe money as Vice President because he needed supplementary income to keep up with the high life-style of Washington's political luminaries.

The second type of elite official deviance, exemplified by the Watergate affair which led to the resignation of President Richard Nixon, is distinguished by the primary goal of maintaining power as opposed to enhancing personal wealth. The Watergate case began with a crude attempt at political espionage—a break-in and bugging of the Democratic national headquarters—and a subsequent failed attempt to cover up presidential knowledge of the scheme. Of course, embedded in the complex machinations revealed by the Watergate investigations are to be found the payoffs, the bribes and the "hush money" characteristic of political corruption at all levels of government. Taken together, the Agnew and Watergate episodes seem to reveal that in some cases of official deviance the primary goal is ill-gotten money while in other cases soiled money is more a means employed to advance the end of retaining or enhancing political power.

Corruption in American cities is frequently associated with the supply of illegal services or commodities such as gambling, prostitution, or drugs. Because the demand is high and the business of providing these prohibited items is so profitable, politicians are frequent targets of bribes aimed at clearing the way for these illegal enterprises with a minimum of interference from the police. As Robert K. Merton has put it:

> The distinctive function of the political machine for their criminal, vice and racket clientele is to enable them to operate in satisfying the economic demands of a large market without due interference from the government. Just as big business may contribute funds to the political party war-chest to ensure a minimum of governmental interference, so with big rackets and big crime. In both instances, the political machine can, in varying degrees, provide "protection." In both instances, many features of the structural context are identical: (1) market demands for goods and services; (2) the operators' concern with maximizing gains from their enterprises; (3) the need for partial control of government which might otherwise interfere with these activities of businessmen; (4) the need for an efficient, powerful and centralized agency to provide an effective liaison of "business" with government. (Merton, 1957, p. 80)

Theories of Official Deviance. There are four explanations of official deviance that variously emphasize: (1) individual morality; (2) the social functions of corruption; (3) the expansion of government; and (4) corruption as integral to capitalism. The first, which attributes official deviance to lapses of individual morality, is a "bad person" theory. Thus, to explain the actions of Agnew or Nixon we might search for the sources of character flaws that allowed them to fall to temptation. This is the most popular sort of theorizing among the general public; it is the least threatening to the status quo because it challenges only the integrity of the individuals involved and not that of the political-economic system; and it is the least satisfying sociologically.

The social functions approach is well summarized by the previous quote from Merton. Closely akin to this approach is the argument that organized crime and its attendant corruption were an inevitable part of American life as one route by which immigrants from whom legitimate opportunities were often blocked sought "social ascent and [a] place in American life" (Bell, 1953:142). The result was a massive growth of illegitimate business which generated more than sufficient revenues to finance the corruption of political elites.

Jack Douglas (1977) argues that official deviance will increase with the number of officials—that is, with the expansion of government. In the past 30 to 40 years, government has expanded greatly with the emergence of the welfare state. The inevitable result he sees is more official deviance and ever-increased public anger.

> There is a clear general principle in this. *The bigger the scale of government, and the more rules it seeks to enforce against its own agents, the more real official deviance there will be—inevitably.* So, it is not surprising to find that citizens see more acts of official usurpations of power. They are inevitably there, and they will continue to grow as government expands and its rules multiply. Since we have reason to believe that the sense of moral outrage about official deviance is greater by some multiplier factor than that of private deviance, we can expect that the sense of moral outrage over increased government deviance, and the resulting sense of alienation and revolt, will accelerate. (Douglas, 1977, p. 407)

Finally, official deviance has been explained as simply an endemic aspect of a capitalist system. Pearce suggests, for example, a "view which stresses the significance of 'grass roots' organization, of corruption and of ruling-class tolerance" (Pearce, 1976, p. 115). In this instance, political corruption is tied to organized crime. Organized crime, in turn, is seen as a servant of the capitalist elite by performing such dirty work as labor racketeering, union busting, supplying drugs to defuse potentially revolutionary, destitute ghetto dwellers, and even as international assassins as in alleged accounts of schemes to kill Fidel Castro. After an intensive case study of organized crime in an American city, William Chambliss concluded

> I have argued, and I think the data demonstrate quite convincingly, that the people who run the organizations which supply the vices in American cities are members of the business, political, and law enforcement communities—not simply members of a criminal society. Furthermore, it is also clear from this study that corruption of political-legal organizations is a critical part of the life-blood of the crime cabal. The study of organized crime is thus a misnomer; the study should consider corruption, bureaucracy, and power. (Chambliss, 1977, p. 328)

CORPORATE DEVIANCE

What Is a Corporation?

> As you sit sipping a can of Miller's Lite and munching on your "Whopper" from Burger King while watching a Paramount Picture on your Philco TV, you are probably not even aware that Philip Morris is receiving the proceeds from the beer you bought, that the Pillsbury family is the ultimate proprietor of your local Burger King, that the movie was brought to you by the same company that produces the sugar you put in your coffee, and that Henry Ford owns the company that made your TV.

> When you go out to choose between buying a Ford, Chrysler or Chevrolet, you probably do not think about the fact that if you had been buying a car at the beginning of the century you would have had 181 U.S. auto manufacturers competing to sell you their motorcars. When you decide between flying United or Eastern, it probably does not cross your mind that the Rockefeller family will be happy in either case since the Rockefellers' bank, Chase Manhattan, is a major stockholder in one and Laurance Rockefeller, in the other. Most of us know more about actors, actresses, football players and comic strip heroes than we do about corporate executives and stockholders. Yet, we are all aware that corporations play a central role in our lives. Two out of every five U.S. citizens work in them. They receive five out of every six dollars that we spend. And probably more than any other institution, what corporations do shapes our lives and our society.
>
> The market economy and bureaucratically administered organizations together dominate our society. And the large corporation is both a model of a bureaucratically administered organization and the most important actor in the market economy. As such it is the core institution of modern society. Trying to understand the contemporary world without having a clear analysis of the modern corporation would be like trying to understand medieval society without examining the church. (Evans & Schneider, 1981, pp. 216–217)

First, as stated in the quote above, a corporation is a large, bureaucratically administered organization. Indeed, this structural characteristic is one of three that help to distinguish the modern corporation. Second, the corporation is controlled from the top through its managers. This is, however, a very sticky point because some analysts argue that since the days of the great "robber barons" like Rockefeller or Carnegie, control of corporations has effectively passed from stockholders to professional managers—the corporate executives (Berle & Means, 1932). Others (Zeitlin, 1974) insist that control still remains vested in the hands of superrich capitalist class owners who hold and manipulate critical masses of stock. While sorting out whether large stockholders or managers (who themselves are frequently large stockholders) exercise dominant control is important, for our purposes we can say that corporate policy and operational decision making are in the hands of elite capitalists and managers.

Third, the primary goals of the corporation are growth and profitability. Even some corporate executives add that giant corporations should widen their sights beyond the single-minded pursuit of profit to include social obligations to the society. However, most corporate owners and executives would probably lean toward the position taken by economist Milton Friedman that profit making must be uppermost.

> The view has been gaining widespread acceptance that corporate officials ... have a "social responsibility" that goes beyond serving the interests of their stockholders. ... Few trends could so thoroughly undermine the very foundation of our free society as the acceptance of a social responsibility other than to make as much money for their stockholders as possible. (Friedman, 1962, pp. 133–134)

Because we are going to be considering questions of deviance and criminality, it is important also to understand how a large corporation is organized and how it is treated in law. Corporations come into existence when they are granted a charter by a state. The charter specifies the purpose of the corporation and may place limits on its activities. In large corporations, the stockholders usually elect a board of directors each year who oversee the corporate policies and management. Day-to-day operations are controlled by the executive officers who disperse their authority through the managerial chain of command. Legally, corporations are treated as an intangible person. As one observer has put it by analogy:

> Like natural (individual) persons, corporations are born (chartered), grow (enlarge assets, sales or profits), marry (merge), divorce (spin off), have children (organize subsidiaries), become healthy or ill (incur profits or losses), migrate (are licensed to conduct business in new jurisdictions), become parts of the hierarchical structures (become components in a holding company complex), and die (dissolve and surrender their charters). (Jacoby, 1973, p. 21)

Treatment of corporations legally as though they were individuals presents serious problems in controlling them. As Stone states "... the corporation *itself* (as lawyers are fond of reminding one another) is a *persona ficta,* a 'legal fiction' with 'no pants to kick or soul to damn' " (Stone, 1975, p. 3). In this legal situation, trying to decide who or what to blame for misdeeds and figuring out how to punish them, or it, is a difficult problem. Much of the discussion of corporate deviance that follows hinges on how the organizational complexity of the modern corporation and its curious status in law impinge on our capacity to understand and control it.

Why Study Corporate Crime?

Marshall B. Clinard and Peter C. Yeager (1980) have written the most comprehensive book presently available on corporate crime in the United States. Drawing heavily upon another leading authority in the field, Gilbert Geis (1974), they state elegantly the rationale for devoting attention to corporate crime.

The study of corporate crime disputes traditional explanations of crime and offers insights into the distribution and exercise of power. More specifically, the argument that poverty or individual pathology "causes" crime, for example, fails completely to account for lawbreaking by corporate executives, who are affluent and, presumably, well-adjusted persons.

Corporate crime is indicative of the distribution of power in our society. An examination of the statute books indicates the kinds of corporate acts that are now included within the criminal and other legal codes and those that go unproscribed. These laws show the influence of corporate power on legislation. On the other hand, shifts of power occur, and some corporate activities (for example, pollution and disregard for product and worker safety) have been successfully challenged by interest groups such as environmentalists, consumers, and labor unions, and the corporations subsequently subjected to government regulation.

Corporate crime provides an indication of the degree of hypocrisy in society. It is hypocritical to regard theft and fraud among the lower classes with distaste and to punish such acts while countenancing upper-class deception and calling it "shrewd business practice." A review of corporate violations and how they are prosecuted and punished shows who controls what in law enforcement in American society and the extent to which this control is effective. Even in the broad area of legal proceedings, corporate crime generally is surrounded by an aura of politeness and respectability rarely if ever present in cases of ordinary crime. Corporations are seldom referred to as lawbreakers and rarely as criminals in enforcement proceedings. Even if violations of the criminal law, as well as other laws are involved, enforcement attorneys and corporation counsels often refer to the corporation as "having a problem": one does not speak of the robber or the burglar as having a problem. (p. 21).

Corporate crime justifies our efforts to understand it because corporations influence our lives so extensively. To better comprehend their misdeeds is to better understand our own social condition.

The Costs of Corporate Crime

The House of Representatives' Subcommittee on Crime began hearings in 1978 on white-collar crime. Chairman John Conyers reports that "it had become exceedingly clear that white-collar crime is the most serious and all-pervasive crime problem in America today" (1980, p. 288). The costs of corporate crime can be divided into three broad categories: (1) economic costs; (2) physical costs; and (3) social and moral costs (Kramer, 1981).

Economic Costs. Just as with ordinary street crimes, the costs of corporate crime are difficult to measure. Nevertheless, estimates consistently reveal the economic costs to the public to be great. The Department of Justice places the total annual loss to taxpayers from reported and unreported violations of federal regulations by corporations at $10 to $20 billion (Clinard & Yeager, 1980, p. 8). A joint Congressional committee conservatively estimated that "the short-term dollar cost to the American public of certain white-collar crimes—not including product safety, environmental, chemical, and antitrust violations such as price fixing, and not including fraud against government programs—is roughly $44 billion per year, eleven times the $4 billion estimate for annual losses attributable to crimes against property" (Conyers, 1980, p. 288). The Senate Judiciary Committee estimates that faulty goods, monopolistic practices, and other violations cost consumers between $174 and $231 billion annually (Clinard & Yeager, 1980, p. 8). These estimates lead inescapably to a single conclusion: ". . . the economic costs associated with corporate crimes such as consumer fraud, antitrust and restraint of trade violations, commercial bribery, tax violations, and others, simply dwarf the financial costs of conventional property crimes like robbery, burglary and larceny" (Kramer, 1981, p. 9).

Physical Costs. The standard most Americans apply when gauging the seriousness of an activity is physical harm (Schrager & Short, 1980). Recognizing this, some corporation executives have claimed that many of the practices with which they have been charged are possibly "sharp or shady business techniques," maybe even "illegal," but hardly "criminal." Such a claim is patently false. Much corporate crime can more appropriately be termed corporate violence. The toll is staggering:

> Over 100,000 deaths per year are attributable to occupationally related diseases, the majority of which are caused by knowing and willful violation of occupational health and safety laws by corporations.
>
> Many of the industrial accidents that kill 14,200 workers and disable 2 million others per year would be prevented but for dangerous working conditions in violation of federal law.
>
> Air, water, and soil pollution in violation of federal standards contributes substantially to hundreds of thousands of deaths.
>
> The Consumer Product Safety Commission estimates that "approximately 20 million serious injuries are annually associated with unsafe and defective consumer products (unsafe food and drugs, defective autos, tires, appliances, contraceptive devices, and others). One hundred ten thousand of these injuries result in permanent disability and 30,000 result in death." (Kramer, 1981, p. 10–11)

To be sure, the public generally fears criminal activities like burglary, robbery, or homicide more than the disguised rip-offs of price fixing or the creeping death of occupational diseases or pollution. Nevertheless, when compared to the average of 20,000 murders reported to the police annually and officially classified as "criminal homicides," the physical, life-threatening costs of corporate violations amply earn the label criminal violence.

Social and Moral Costs. The economic losses and physical harms of corporate crime are severe, but some observers have found even greater damage to social relations. The President's Commission on Law Enforcement and Administration of Justice stated that corporate crimes "are the most threatening of all—not just because they are so expensive, but because of their corrosive effect on the moral standards by which American business is conducted" (President's Commission, 1967, p. 5). When the people at the top wantonly disobey the law a dangerous example is set for those below—an example that threatens the very legitimacy of the existing economic and legal systems. Conklin states correctly that

> Business crime also sets an example of disobedience for the general population. Crimes by the upper class, especially if they do not lead to conviction and imprisonment, serve as rationalizations for the lower classes to justify their own criminal behavior. Bitterness at class and racial discrimination in the criminal justice system also makes traditional offenders resistant to rehabilitation. Unpunished violations by white-collar offenders create disrespect for the law and engender a desire for revenge against those who protect their own but punish society's outcasts. For example, consumer fraud and exploitation was one underlying cause of the frustrations which led to the riots in black ghettoes during the 1960s. (1977, p. 8)

To summarize, we can return to Congressman Conyers.

> The full extent of America's white-collar crime is still unknown because so much goes undetected. The federal government simply lacks the statistic-gathering capability to monitor it. But we do know that such crime eats away at the national income and destroys the nation's physical and moral health.
> Such crime contributes heavily to productivity losses in the workplace, which in turn is a major source of inflation. White-collar crime cheats consumers of the real value of goods and services that they purchase. It maims and kills unwitting workers and consumers. The pervasive double standard under which street criminals typically receive stiff punishment while white-collar criminals frequently get by with mere slaps on the wrist creates cynicism toward the law and abets criminal behavior. (1980, p. 290)

Types of Corporate Deviance

Of the several schemes for categorizing corporate deviance that have been devised (Edelhertz, 1970 or Clinard & Yeager, 1980), the one best suited for our purposes applies the principle of who is victimized by the illegal activity. The most obvious recipients of potential harm are customers who may be victims of price–fixing, false advertising, or dangerous products; employees who may be subject to illegal and unsafe working conditions or have their economic power attenuated by unfair labor practices; and the public–at–large which suffers from pollution, public health and safety violations, or the corruption of government through mechanisms like illegal political contributions (Schrager & Short, 1978, pp. 413–415). A fourth group, owners or stockholders, can also be victims when an unscrupulous company management commits securities fraud or mismanages corporate resources in a way that the stockholders' equity becomes worthless (Ermann & Lundman, 1982, p. 24). Figure 6.3 summarizes the gains to perpetrators and the losses to victims of several illegal corporate actions. We will next turn to an example from each of these four categories.

Customers as Victims. Price fixing is an agreement among the sellers of a particular product that they will charge a uniform price for it. The goal of price fixing is to eliminate price competition, stabilize the market, and increase profits for the companies involved. Price fixing is in direct violation of the Sherman Antitrust Act, passed by Congress in 1890 and intended to insure the maintenance of competitive markets in the American economy. Despite its illegality, price fixing has been frequent. Sutherland (1949, p. 8), in his study of 70 large corporations in a 45–year period prior to 1945, found that legal decisions were made against 44 of the 70 in 125 suits. About 60% of the corporations were repeat offenders. The federal government continued to steadily process around 300 cases every ten years during the 1940s, 1950s, and 1960s (Posner, 1970) and there is no sign that either the amount of price fixing or legal actions against it are becoming less frequent (Clinard & Yeager, 1980, p. 141).

The most famous single price fixing case is the electrical equipment conspiracy of 1960. Certainly one of the largest on record, it involved General Electric, Westinghouse, and 27 other firms which agreed to fix prices on heavy electrical equipment such as generators or turbines. In secret meetings, using coded messages, and taking great care to destroy any incriminating evidence, the participants set prices in their industry in violation of the law (Geis, 1977). Despite elaborate precautions, evidence of the scheme slowly emerged from complaints by customers, employees who confessed to investigators, and numerous other sources.

Type of illegal corporate action	Gain for the perpetrator	Loss to the victim
AGAINST CUSTOMERS		
Antitrust violations	Reduction of competition; increased market share; increased economic power	Greater cost of consumer goods; reduced choice of products/manufacturers
False advertising	Increases market and consumption by creating an artificial demand for worthless or dangerous products	Waste of the consumers' income on worthless or dangerous products
Production and sale of hazardous goods	Reduced costs of production; lowered expenses for engineering, testing, development, etc.	Increased danger to the consumer that may lead to injury or death
AGAINST EMPLOYEES		
Occupational health and safety violations	Reduced costs of production; lowered expenses for safety equipment, medical tests, etc.	Increased danger to workers that may lead to injury or death
Labor law violations	Reduced labor costs through diminished collective bargaining power of the workers	Reduces the workers' income
AGAINST PUBLIC		
Pollution or public health and safety violations	Reduced costs of production; "solves" various "problems" like disposal of dangerous materials; lowers cost of pollution control	Increased danger to the public that may lead to sickness, injury, or death
Illegal political campaign contributions	Increased political power to influence the making and enforcement of laws in the violator's interest	Loss of legitimate capacity to influence the workings of government, particularly among people without great sums of money
AGAINST OWNERS		
Securities fraud	Creation of financial capital by sale of fraudulent or falsely inflated stock	The owner of the security finds him/herself holding worthless stock—similar to counterfeit money

FIGURE 6.3. GAINS TO PERPETRATORS AND LOSSES TO VICTIMS OF SELECTED TYPES OF ILLEGAL CORPORATE ACTIONS

The aspect that makes this case so noteworthy, aside from its magnitude, is the imposition of short jail sentences for four executives, two division managers, and one sales manager. In addition, the more common penalties, fines, were levied in amounts totaling almost $2 million. The companies also had to settle claims against them by customers who were harmed by the price fixing. The profitability of the conspiracy, while it lasted, is indicated by the results for one defendant. "(A) mid-1964 calculation showed that 90% of some 1,800 claims had been settled for a total of $160 million, but General Electric could derive some solace from the fact that most of these payments would be tax-deductible" (Geis, 1977, p. 120).

Although price fixing cases are regularly pursued by the authorities and some are successfully prosecuted, the ones that reach the courts undoubtedly represent only a small proportion of the total violations. As Clinard and Yeager state,

> From all indications, it is clear that violation of the nation's antitrust laws is anything but uncommon. In recent years, the *Wall Street Journal* has reported on criminal, civil, and administrative prosecutions in a wide variety of industries, including paper goods, electrical wiring, apparel, resins used to make paint, citrus fruit, computers, beer, plywood, armored car services, photography, and toilet seats....
>
> Corporate executives themselves indicate that price fixing is widespread. A survey of major corporation presidents conducted by the Nader study group found that nearly 60 percent of those responding (100) agreed that "many ... price fix" (Nader and Green, 1972, p. 17). (Clinard & Yeager, 1980, p. 141).

The massive costs to customers of these undetected violations can only be imagined.

Employees as Victims. In 1980 the House of Representatives' Subcommittee on Crime issued a report of hearings on corporate crime. Among the cases outlined was the role of several companies in the knowingly dangerous exposure of employees to asbestos. Asbestos is a heat resistant, strong, flexible, fibrous mineral that lends itself to a large number of commercial applications. The extent of risk from exposure of the general public to the material is unknown, but the risk to workers in the asbestos industry, where levels of contact with it are high, have been well documented.

> Asbestosis, a nonmalignant scarring of the lungs, has been associated with 10% of the deaths among asbestos workers surveyed in epidemiological studies. The disease often makes breathing so difficult that victims are unable to climb stairs. Mesothelioma, a rare cancer of the linings of

the chest or abdominal cavities, is associated exclusively with asbestos exposure and is usually fatal within a year after symptoms appear. Mesotheliomas have occurred in approximately 7% of worker exposures, and have even affected family members who reportedly contracted the disease by inhaling residue from a worker's clothing. The mineral also increases the risk of lung cancer, which accounts for the greatest number of asbestos-associated deaths. (Subcommittee on Crime, p. 22)

Evidence that asbestos represents a health hazard began accumulating in the early 1900s. "By 1935, the main elements of the problem are known. Chyrsotile asbestos, virtually the only fiber then in use, could cause widespread disease. This disease could be fatal and malignancy might also be a result of exposure" (p. 23). Nevertheless, until 1960 the problem did not attract major attention and regulations were few. Then several studies were published that provided clear evidence of the hazardous results from exposure to asbestos fibers.

Historically, the response of industry executives to evidence of danger to workers has been close to an outright cover-up. As the Subcommittee report states:

> During pretrial discovery proceedings in recent product liability suits against the asbestos industry, documents dating from 1933-1945 were obtained which included correspondence among senior executives, lawyers, physicians, consultants, and insurance representatives for Johns-Manville Corporation, Raybestos-Manhattan Incorporated and other asbestos companies.
>
> South Carolina Circuit Court Judge James Price (who reviewed the material), is quoted as saying "it shows a pattern of denial and disease and attempts at suppression of information" so persuasive that he ordered a new trial for the family of a dead insulation worker whose earlier claim had been dismissed. Judge Price noted that correspondence further reflects a conscious effort by the industry in the 1930s to downplay, or arguably suppress the dissemination of information to employees and the public for fear of promotion of lawsuits. Judge Price also noted compensation disease claims filed by asbestos insulation workers against several companies—which quietly settled them—including eleven asbestosis cases settled out of court by Johns-Manville in 1933, "all predating the time (1964) when these companies claim they first recognized the hazard to insulators." Judge Price concluded that settlement of these claims "constitute compelling proof of actual notice to certain manufacturers that asbestos-containing thermal insulation products indeed caused disease in workers."

The future

With an estimated 8 to 11 million workers having been exposed since World War II, the potential for asbestos-related occupational disease and cancer appears to be significant. Because of the latency period associated with this disease, it is reported that deaths from asbestosis and asbestos-related cancer in the year 2000, and later, will occur even if we ban the use of the substance today. (Subcommittee on Crime, 1980, p. 24).

Moreover, the asbestos industry has fought strenuously against proposals to tighten the minimal standards for exposure to the substance in the workplace. Similar accounts could be gathered for other industries—including mining (black lung), textiles (brown lung), and chemicals (numerous carcinogens). The cost in employee health and lives is dreadful.

The Public–at–Large as Victims. Sometimes the harm of corporate violations can be somewhat indirect and diffuse. Such is the case of campaign contribution violations in which companies seek unfair influence over legislation or governmental regulation. Likewise, violation of pollution laws may have only a slow, cumulative effect upon public health and mortality. However, there are cases in which corporate law violations have an immediate, devastating impact. The Buffalo Creek–Pittston Coal Company disaster that "resulted from the company's knowing maintenance of an illegal dam" (Schrager & Short, 1978, p. 415) is such an example.

Background
Buffalo Creek, West Virginia, is a mountain hollow, some 17 miles in length. Three small forks come together at the top of the hollow, to form the creek itself. In early 1972, approximately 5,000 people lived in this area, in what amounted to a continuous string of 16 villages.

Middle Fork served for several years as the site of an enormous pile of mine waste, known as a "dam" to local residents and an "impoundment" to the Buffalo Mining Company. The impoundment was there because it solved two important disposal problems for the company:

1. Each time four tons of coal are removed from the ground, one ton of slag—a wide assortment of waste materials—is also removed, and must be disposed of.

2. Additionally, more than 500,000 gallons of water are required to prepare four tons of coal for shipment, and this, too, must be disposed of.

The Buffalo Mining Company began to deposit its slag in Middle Fork as early as 1957, and by 1972 was dumping approximately 1,000 tons per day. Traditionally, the company had deposited its solid waste into Middle Fork, and its liquid effluent into nearby streams. However, by the 1960s, coal operators were under a great deal of pressure to retain this water until some of the impurities had settled out of it. The companies were also beginning to see the utility in having a regular supply of processing water on hand. Buffalo Mining Company responded to this by dumping new slag on top of old, in such a way as to form barriers behind which waste water could be stored and reused.

Middle Fork was described as an immense black trough of slag, silt and water, a waste sink arranged in such a way as to create small reservoirs behind the first two impoundments, and a large lake behind the third.

The Episode

According to subsequent accounts, during the night of February 25, 1972, Buffalo Mining Company officials continually monitored the Middle Fork waste site. They were reportedly uneasy because the lake water seemed to be rising dangerously close to the dam crest. The past few days had been wet ones, but such seasonal precipitation was not considered unusual. Toward dawn, company officials were concerned enough to have a spillway cut across the surface of the barrier in an effort to relieve pressure. The level continued to rise, but the company issued no public warnings. Testimony disclosed that the senior officials on the site met with two deputy sheriffs who arrived on the scene to aid in an evacuation in the event of trouble. The officials contended at the time that everything was under control, and the deputies left.

Just before 8:00 a.m., February 26, a heavy-equipment operator inspected the surface of the dam and found that not only was the water within inches of the crest—which he already knew—but that the structure had softened dramatically since the last inspection.

Within minutes the dam had collapsed. The 132 million gallons of waste water and solids roared through the breach. The wave reportedly set off a series of explosions, raising mushroom-shaped clouds in the air, and picking up "everything in its path." One million tons of solid waste were said to be caught in the flow.

Impact

A 20 to 30 foot tidal wave traveling up to 30 miles per hour devastated Buffalo Creek's 16 small communities. More than 125 people perished and hundreds of others were injured. Over 4,000 survived but their 1,000 homes as well as most of their possessions were destroyed.

A few hundred of the 4,000 survivors decided not to accept the settlement for real property damage offered by the coal company as reimbursement. Instead, they brought suit against the Pittston Corporation.

On Wednesday, June 26, 1974, two and one half years after the incident, the 600 or so Buffalo Creek plaintiffs were awarded 13.5 million dollars by the Pittston Corporation in an out-of-court settlement. (Subcommittee on Crime, 1980, pp. 1–3)

Owners as Victims. Legally, the people who own a corporation are its stockholders. And, of course, many of the stockholders who invest in a company are not superrich capitalists or huge institutional investors like banks or insurance companies, but average individuals who buy shares totaling no more than a few hundred or a few thousand dollars. These investors basically entrust their money to the management of the company with the understanding that the company will be run to yield them a fair return on their investment. The Equity Funding securities fraud case exemplifies a dramatic instance in which stockholders became the victims of fraudulent management practices.

The Equity Funding Corporation of America (EFCA) was a combination insurance–investment company. The scandal involved inflating the value of Equity stock by creating fake insurance policies on the company's record books. "Phony customers were large in number. When the fraud was discovered, there were 56,000 bogus policies as compared to 41,000 real ones. There were also accounting irregularities that claimed $200 million in nonexistent assets" (Ermann & Lundman, 1982, p. 43). Beginning in 1960, but not uncovered until 1973, the financial manipulation

> ... was a crime which involved an estimated loss of $2 billion. The apparent motive behind this complex fraud was to create a good earnings record (which) would increase the value of the stock and thereby enrich the conspirators, who held large amounts of stock and who received more through the years as bonuses. Furthermore, inflated reported earnings and assets made it possible for EFCA to acquire other companies in exchange for its stock and to borrow money with which to make other acquisitions and finance the company's operations which were losing huge amounts each year (Parker, 1976, pp. 120–121). (Conklin, 1977, p. 46)

When the scheme began to unravel, the company's stockholders were left with little or nothing for their investment. In this case, many of the investors could hardly afford the loss.

> By the time this huge financial empire crumbled, millions of investors lost billions of dollars. As William Blundell (1976) points out, the victims tended to be "the little people who bleed and suffer for months and years and perhaps the rest of their lives. In this sense the toll taken by Equity Funding was one of the most horrible of any modern crime." As with most business and securities crimes, the Equity Funding conspirators, if convicted, received relatively light fines and sentences when compared to their "street crime" counterparts. (Johnson & Douglas, 1978, p. 151)

How Much Corporate Deviance Is There?

A recent study of legal actions against 582 of the largest U.S. corporations during 1975–1976 provides a base line for estimating the volume of corporate violations. Marshall B. Clinard (1979) analyzed information from a variety of sources to understand the legal actions initiated and completed against corporate violators. At the outset, we are cautioned that because many violations are not reported and others do not result in a formal charge, ". . . official actions taken against corporations are probably only the tip of the iceberg of total violations, but they do constitute an index of illegal behavior by the large corporations" (Clinard & Yeager, 1980, p. 111). Therefore, the data reported represent minimal figures of government actions against major corporations. Even the undercount of these detected violations may run as high as one-fourth to one-third.

With these qualifications, Clinard presents in its most positive light the fact that a majority of the corporations studied were the object of at least one enforcement action.

> *The world of the giant corporations does not necessarily require illegal behavior in order to compete successfully. The fact that [nearly] 40% of the corporations in this study did not have a legal action instituted against them during a two-year period by 24 federal agencies attests to this conclusion.* On the other hand, more than 60% had at least one enforcement action initiated against them in the period. An average of 4.8 actions were taken against the 300 parent *manufacturing* corporations that violated the law at least once. Moreover, a single instance of illegal corporate behavior, unlike "garden variety" crime, often involves millions of dollars and can affect the lives of thousands of citizens. This study found that almost one-half of the parent manufacturing corporations had one or more serious or moderate violations and these firms had an average of 3.1 such violations. (Clinard, 1979, pp. xix–xx)

Generally, large corporations had a disproportionately greater number of violations. The automobile, drug, and oil industries were the most frequent violators accounting for almost one-half of all violations. Eighty percent of them had one or more serious or moderately serious violations. Corporations are not usually subjected to the full force of the law. Eighty percent of the fines imposed were $5,000 or less; less than 1% of the fines exceeded one million dollars. Indeed, the most frequently imposed sanction of the 1,446 levied was a warning (44%) followed by monetary penalties (23%) and a variety of injunctions or consent orders. The type of violation also influenced the severity of the sanction. "Corporate actions that directly harm the economy were more likely to receive the greater penalties, while those affecting consumer product quality were responded to with the least severe sanctions" (Clinard, 1979, pp. xx).

Finally, a certain number of violators are chronic repeat offenders. Clinard and Yeager put the problem this way:

> The rates of recidivism (relapse into prior criminal habits after punishment) vary from about 25 to as high as 60% for ordinary crime. It is

> interesting to compare these rates with those in the field of corporate sanctions. In Sutherland's (1949) study of 70 of the 200 largest nonfinancial corporations a high rate of recidivism was found. He studied sanctions imposed during the life of each corporation, an average of 45 years; he found that the average corporation had had a decision rendered against it—that is, had an enforcement action taken against it—14 times and that 97.1% were recidivists in the sense of having two or more adverse decisions against them. (pp. 26-27)

The data from the 1975-1976 Clinard study reveal a similar pattern of repeated offenses.

> Of the 477 manufacturing corporations, 210, or approximately one-half, had two or more legal actions completed against them during 1975 and 1976; 18.2% had five or more. For serious and moderately serious violations, 124 firms, or one-fourth, had two or more actions, and 7.8% five or more. If one could extrapolate the number of sanctions over the average equivalent time period used by Sutherland (1949), the result would far exceed his average of fourteen sanctions. (p. 27)

Overall, then, available data reveal corporate violations and their repetition to be frequent; offenders tend to be concentrated in certain large industries; and the sanctions applied to violators are generally very light.

Explanations of Corporate Deviance

The range of theories to explain corporate deviance parallels theories that explain the types of deviance we have previously considered. The categories of explanation used to organize the following discussion are: social-psychological factors; the culture of the corporation; the structure of the corporation; the structure of the economy; and societal reaction and social control.

Social-Psychological Factors. The earliest coherent theory of corporate deviance is Sutherland's learning theory explanation of white-collar crime. We can see from Sutherland's application of this learning theory that it is intended to encompass corporate deviance.

> The data which are at hand suggest that white-collar crime has its genesis in the same general process as other criminal behavior, namely, differential association. The hypothesis of differential association is that criminal behavior is learned in association with those who define such behavior favorably and in isolation from those who define it unfavorably, and that a person in an appropriate situation engages in such criminal behavior

if, and only if, the weight of the favorable definitions exceeds the weight of the unfavorable definitions. This hypothesis is certainly not a complete or universal explanation of white-collar crime or of other crime, but it perhaps fits the data of both types of crimes better than any other general hypothesis. (Sutherland, 1949, p. 234)

Sutherland goes on to describe how the initiate is introduced to the ways of corporate deviance and how he or she learns both the techniques for violating the law and the rationalizations for engaging in illegal practices.

As a part of the process of learning practical business, a young man with idealism and thoughtfulness for others is inducted into white-collar crime. In many cases he is ordered by the manager to do things which he regards as unethical or illegal, while in other cases he learns from those who have the same rank as his own how they make a success. He learns specific techniques of violating the law, together with definitions of situations in which those techniques may be used. Also, he develops a general ideology. This ideology grows in part out of the specific practices and is in the nature of generalization from concrete experiences, but in part it is transmitted as a generalization by phrases such as "we are not in business for our health," "business is business," or "no business was ever built on the beatitudes." These generalizations, whether transmitted as such or abstracted from concrete experiences, assist the neophyte in business to accept the illegal practices and provide rationalizations for them. (p. 240)

The importance of rationalizations for high-status business executives who participate in corporate illegality cannot be overemphasized. Rationalizations like "everybody does it," "the law only holds back free enterprise," or "it isn't really 'criminal' " are common. As Conklin (1977) states, rationalizations of this sort "may be even more important in explaining business crime than in explaining juvenile deliquency, because businessmen probably have a stronger need to deny criminal intent" (pp. 86–87).

A supplement to Sutherland's learning approach emphasizes the personal characteristics of those who climb to the top management of large companies. First we must understand that only a small proportion of people persistently strive for such top posts and that those who do are apt to be different from those who fail to make it to the top or do not try. Summarizing his analysis, Gross (1978) says:

... The men at the top of organizations will tend to be ambitious, shrewd and possessed of a nondemanding moral code. Their ambition will not be merely personal, for they will have discovered that their own goals are best pursued through assisting the organization to attain its goals. While this is less true, or even untrue at the bottom of the organization, those at the top share directly in the benefits of organizational goal achievement, such as seeing their stock values go up, deferred compensation, and fringe benefits.

Further, being at or near the top, these persons are those most strongly identified with the goals of the organization. . . .

Finally, if the organization must engage in illegal activities to attain its goals, men with a nondemanding moral code will have the least compunctions about engaging in such behavior. Not only that, as men of power, pillars of the community, they are most likely to believe that they can get away with it without getting caught. Besides, they are shrewd. (p. 71)

Culture of the Corporation. While the evidence indicates that corporate deviance is widespread, it is by no means true that every large corporation is equally likely to commit crime. Recall that in the Clinard study, 40% of the corporations did not have legal action brought against them during a two-year period. To explain why some corporations tend to deviate from the law more than others, some theorists have identified attitudes or forces that when overemphasized in the organization contribute to illegal behavior. Stone (1975, p. 237) cites a desire for profits, expansion, and power; a desire for security; fear or failure; and group loyalty and identification with corporate goals. Clinard and Yeager (1980) suggest that a significant contributor is the moral tone established by the corporation's elite.

> Lawbreaking can become a normative pattern within a corporation, with or without pressure for profits or from the economic environment. In confidential interviews with a number of board chairmen and chief executive officers of very large corporations, a consensus emerged that the top management, particularly the chief executive officer, sets ethical tone. The president and chief executive officer of a large manufacturing corporation noted that "by example and holding a tight rein a chief executive . . . can set the level of ethical or unethical practices in his organization. This influence can spread throughout the organization." As another high executive pointed out, price fixing or kickbacks must be "congenial to the climate of the corporation." Still another board chairman said, "Some corporations, like those in politics, tolerate corruption." (p. 60)

Possibly some industries are more inclined than others to engender a callous attitude toward obedience of the law. Concluding a study of illegal activity in the American liquor industry, Denzin (1977) quotes a high-ranking official in one distilling firm:

"We break the laws every day. If you think I go to bed at night worrying about it, you're crazy. Everybody breaks the law. The liquor laws are insane anyway." (p. 919)

Structure of the Corporation. The most fundamental structural characteristic of large, modern corporations is that they are bureaucracies. The term bureaucracy refers to a mode of social organization that tends toward rationality in decision making, impersonality in social relations, routinization of tasks, and centralization of authority. Those who work in corporate bureaucracies are, because of the nature of their organizational environment, prone to view problems in a very narrow, technical sense. As a result, "... the rational/technical ethos of bureaucracy transforms even those issues with grave moral import into practical concerns" (Jackall, 1980, pp. 355-356). For example, when the drug company Richardson-Merrill, manufacturer of an anticholesterol agent MER/29, discovered that the drug might cause side effects such as hair loss, reduced libido, cataracts or partial blindness, the "company's executives considered the adverse reports as obstacles to be undercut, in this case with fabricated data, and concentrated on developing more aggressive marketing strategies to overcome the drug's tarnished image." (pp. 355-356)

Large, complex, bureaucratic organizations also tend to fragment work—to make people responsible only for a very tiny portion of the final product. Thus, "... bureaucracy separates men and women from the consequences of their actions; such depersonalization reinforces the avoidance of responsibility endemic to hierarchical, segmented structures" (Jackall, 1980, p. 356). In modern bureaucracies, the expectations of obedience to higher authority coupled with a complex division of labor provide the ideal setting to legitimize the excuse for almost any behavior. With a clean conscience, most people in the organization can say, "I was only doing what I was told to do."

Referring to the large-scale organizations that increasingly dominate modern life, Gross (1978) states flatly that "all organizations are inherently criminogenic." (p. 56). The seeds for criminality are sown into bureaucratic structures because "organizations find themselves under heavy pressure to meet their goals, with a structure which means that responsibility for tasks is delegated, enabling some units to pass off onto other units the risky consequences of questionable behavior, but in which trouble with the law is one of many environmental contingencies which must be handled" (p. 61) Thus, modern bureaucratic organizations which provide a highly efficient, effective mechanism for the solution of complex technical problems do not provide a good setting for moral reflection or a sense of individual responsibility. An environment which facilitates crime is the result.

Structure of the Economy. The underlying precepts of American business ideology include the primacy of profit as a goal in free enterprise. "The bottom line"—the final figure on an accounting statement that indicates a company's level of profitability—is the ultimate criterion upon which most corporate executives are judged. This situation implies an anomic condition analogous to Merton's (1957) imbalance of cultural goals and institutionalized means that creates structural pressures to deviate. Merton argues that an overemphasis on cultural success goals (e.g., a great deal of money and comfortable surroundings) coupled with blocked legitimate means to achieve those goals (e.g., racial or ethnic discrimination in education or employment) will lead those whose opportunities are blocked to "innovate" by committing crime to reach the success goals. The theory predicts that those most likely to be discriminated against—people at the bottom of the social hierarchy—will be most likely to commit crime primarily in response to blocked opportunities. Obviously, the high-level corporate manager does not face the same sort of blocked opportunity structure as a typical ghetto resident. Instead, the pressure to deviate in his or her case comes from the intense pressure to attain the corporate cultural goal—maximum profits. This powerful stress on goal attainment is frequently coupled with minimal concern for the legality or ethics of the means to succeed. Thus, the structural imbalance for those in the large corporation may be due mainly to an excessive emphasis on goals as compared to means. The disjunction between the concern for goals and means that Merton used to explain lower-class deviance may also be the structural foundation for deviance at the top. This is especially true in an economy in which the motivating dynamic is alleged to be competition.

Of course success in a capitalistic economy, whether gained by legal or illegal means, frequently leads to the elimination of competition. Thus, for example, America's early domestic automobile industry which had well over 150 manufacturers is now dominated by three. Markets dominated by only a few suppliers are called oligopolies and oligopolistic conditions are ripe for certain kinds of corporate crime, especially price fixing. (For other oligopolistic industries, see Figure 6.2.) When only a few firms supply most of the goods in a particular industry, there are powerful pressures to stabilize the market and maximize profits by price fixing.

The introduction of sophisticated technology into the business and financial world is another factor in the economy that has opened up new opportunities for crime. The use of computers, "electronic money," and modern telecommunications to conduct banking and business have created entirely new ways to steal, replete with a jargon to describe the techniques including "Trojan horse, salami, superzapping, logic bombs, data leakage, data diddling, piggybacking and scavenging" (Parker, 1980, p. 203). Research to date indicates that the rapid introduction of modern business technology, for all its obvious benefits, carries with it the potential for crimes that are hard to detect, amount to huge losses per incident, and require radical departures from traditional images of criminals, crime, and crime control.

A more general approach to economic theorizing about the causes of corporate deviance is rooted in a critique of modern capitalism itself. In broad outline, the analysis might begin with the period of rapid industrial growth and concentration of capital during the last half of the 19th century. During this period, the likes of Carnegie and Rockefeller amassed huge personal fortunes and created vast industrial empires. Business was almost totally unregulated. However, the success of these capitalists posed two obvious dilemmas that paved the way for the growth of government. First, the concentration of wealth, if allowed to continue unabated, would destroy the competitive capitalist system itself as the most successful entrepreneurs eliminated their competition and acquired control over more industries. In part, to save the system from itself, regulatory laws like the Sherman Antitrust Act (1890) were intended to limit monopolies and preserve competition. Second, the increasingly unequal distribution of wealth—the distinction between the superrich and the rest—became a source of mass discontent with potentially revolutionary consequences. Thus, in fits and starts, over the first three-quarters of the 20th century, government became an agency for redistributing wealth in the form of progressive income taxation, social security, health benefits, and poverty programs. (It can be argued that this redistribution mostly amounted to the transfer of wealth from the middle class to the lower class leaving the upper-class elites relatively untouched.) Thus, the federal government grew both as regulator of business and redistributor of wealth into what is now frequently called welfare state capitalism.

Critics of welfare state capitalism focus on how the relationship between large corporations and the state (the government) which is assigned the task of regulating corporate actions actually encourages ineffective legal constraints and promotes corporate crime (Barnett, 1981). Ultimately, the reasons are grounded in the power of elites to influence government that were outlined at the outset of this chapter. Recall that business elites have in the past and still continue to dominate the legislative (Congress) and executive (Cabinet) branches of government. To be sure, the state is under pressure from both corporate offenders and their victims (consumers, employees, and the public-at-large) to frame the law and have it enforced to their advantage. However, in the end, "the real economic impact and the control over information and financial resources which characterized large corporations grant to them an economic and political power that is great relative to that generally possessed by the victims of corporate crime" (Barnett, 1981, p. 4). As a result, on balance the law more often favors corporate interests as do the funding and priorities of regulatory or enforcement agencies. This ineffective legal constraint creates a situation in which the relative risks and probable costs of corporate illegal activity are low compared to the likely gains. In this state of affairs, the commission of corporate crime is a perfectly rational action. Summarized briefly then, this theory postulates that overall the state is controlled by and operates in the interests of corporate capitalists in opposition to the interests of consumers, workers, and the general social welfare.

Societal Reaction and Social Control. Labeling, or societal reaction theory, proposes that attempts to control deviance often have the unintended consequences of increasing the likelihood of the undesired behavior rather than deterring it. For example, by subjecting a young delinquent to the stigmatizing process of a public trial, the theory suggests, we push him or her further into a criminal self-concept while closing off avenues to succeed in nondelinquent ways. Thus, the efforts to control or deter the behavior actually end up encouraging or amplifying it. (See the discussion of Scheff's theory of *Being Mentally Ill* in Chapter 3 for a detailed account of the theory's dynamics.) The policy implications of the theory are that we should *avoid* officially labeling people deviant as much as possible to minimize the negative effects of stigmatizing them. Generally, experts on corporate deviance take a very different view of labeling as a deterrent against corporate illegality. Indeed they allege that a major reason for the failure effectively to control corporate crime is a lack of publicly imposed penalties. Braithwaite and Geis (1982) argue this way:

> Such an observation has important implications. Although the labeling hypothesis makes it unwise to use publicity as a tool to punish juvenile delinquents, it is sound deterrence to broadcast widely the names of corporate offenders. Corporations and their officers are genuinely afraid of bad publicity arising from their illegitimate activities. They respond to it with moral indignation and denials, not with assertions that "if you think I'm bad, I'll really show you how bad I can be," as juvenile delinquents sometimes do.
>
> Chambliss argues that white-collar criminals are among the most deterrable types of offenders because they satisfy two conditions: They do not have a commitment to crime as a way of life, and their offenses are instrumental rather than expressive. Corporate crimes are almost never crimes of passion; they are not spontaneous or emotional, but calculated

risks taken by rational actors. As such, they should be more amenable to control by policies based on the utilitarian assumptions of the deterrence doctrine. (pp. 301–302)

Whereas labeling theory may apply to many other types of deviance, most analysts contend that it does not apply to white-collar or corporate criminality. Such a position leads inevitably to the conclusion that "corporate crime is a conceptually different phenomenon from traditional crime" (Braithwaite and Geis, 1982, p. 294) primarily due to the high status and power of its perpetrators relative to its victims. Moreover, failure to enforce vigorously the laws against corporate violations can erode or neutralize moral indignation about these crimes thereby, in a certain sense, legitimating them (McCormick, 1977). Both the failure to define many harmful corporate actions as criminal and the failure to enforce the laws that do exist has been long recognized. Sutherland (1949) enumerates some of the reasons for this:

> The less critical attitude of government toward businessmen than toward persons of lower socio-economic status is the result of several relationships. (a) Persons in government are, by and large, culturally homogeneous with persons in business, both being in the upper strata of American society. (b) Many persons in government are members of families which have other members in business. (c) Many persons in business are intimate personal friends of persons in government. Almost every important person in government has many close personal friends in business, and almost every important person in business has many close personal friends in government. (d) Many persons in government were previously connected with business firms as executives, attorneys, directors, or in other capacities. In times of war, especially, many persons in government retain their business connections. (e) Many persons in government hope to secure employment in business firms when their government work is terminated. Government work is often a step toward a career in private business. Relations established while in government, as well as inside information acquired at that time, carry over after the person joins a business firm. (f) Business is very powerful in American society and can damage or promote the governmental programs in which the governmental personnel are interested. (g) The program of the government is closely related to the political parties, and for their success in campaigns these political parties depend on contributions of large sums from important businessmen. Thus, the initial cultural homogeneity, the close personal relationships, and the power relationships protect businessmen against critical definitions by government. (pp. 248–249)

Sutherland goes on to say that because business is tightly organized and closely linked to government, corporate harms are less likely to be defined as criminal or when they are so defined, to receive law enforcement attention. In contrast, consumers, employees, and the general public are less well organized and less influential with government. This *differential social organization* must be redressed, says Sutherland, if harmful, illegal corporate actions are to be effectively curbed.

While differential social organization persists, "the public today regards white-collar and corporate crime as serious offenses—in fact, as equal to, and even more serious than, many 'ordinary' crimes, such as burglary and robbery" (Clinard and Yeager, 1980, p. 5). The lack of strict laws and stringent enforcement cannot be correctly justified by claims that the public does not perceive corporate crime as worthy of legal attention. Rather, the evidence indicates that the public regards corporate criminality as serious; that the public generally supports existing laws aimed against it; and that the public would like to see the laws more vigorously enforced. (Conklin, 1977, p. 24)

Control of Corporate Deviance

Approaches to controlling corporate crime can be organized for discussion into three broad categories: legal and penal reform; consumer, employee, and public action; and changes in corporate attitudes and structure.

Legal and Penal Reform. The first step in initiating any criminal legal action is to uncover evidence that a crime has been committed. Usually, in the case of ordinary crimes such as theft or assault, the individual or organization that is harmed will report that a crime has occurred to the authorities. Corporate crimes, in comparison, frequently involve many victims, each of whom is harmed so imperceptibly that none of them is motivated to report their victimization if they even know it has happened. Employees being harmed by illegally handled toxic substances at work or residents of a city exposed to health-endangering violations of pollution standards probably would not know of their victimization until it was too late unless there was monitoring of the situation. Thus, ordinary "street crime" control can rely heavily on *reactive* enforcement—enforcement that is activated when a victim makes a complaint, while corporate crime control requires *proactive* enforcement—enforcement that requires monitoring and seeking out violators.

The proactive nature of corporate crime control suggests two strategies for pursuing it more effectively. First, more could be done to protect "whistle blowers"—people in an organization who go to the authorities or to journalists to expose illegal or unethical corporate conduct. In some cases, whistle blowers have been subject to harsh discipline, harassment, job loss, or even physical harm. Although some protections already exist for informants, additional ones such as relieving them of the burden of legal fees if they win in court might encourage more to come forward (Ermann and Lundman, 1982, p. 165). Second, larger and more effective enforcement staffs are needed to pursue corporate crime. Clinard and Yeager (1980) state flatly that "the regulatory agencies, both federal and state, lack resources to deal effectively with white–collar and corporate crime. Since corporate crime is organizational crime, its detection, investigation, and prosecution are time consuming" (p. 316). In addition, successful prosecution of corporate crime requires an investment in highly specialized personnel like accountants, engineers, and laboratory technicians.

Even in cases reaching the courts and resulting in conviction, the penalties are generally very light. During 1975 to 1976, 80% of the corporations fined received penalties under $5,000 (Clinard and Yeager, 1980, p. 125). In cases where fines are somewhat larger, as compared to the gross revenues of the corporate violators, they amount relatively to less than the average parking ticket for an individual earning $15,000 a year. Thus, in Table 6.3, the $50,000 criminal fines handed out to the nine 1976 defendants of a major price fixing case averaged well under the equivalent of $1 for an individual. Summarizing the implications of a court sentencing study, Seymour (1973) underlines the disparities in the treatment of common criminals and white–collar criminals. "To the family whose son has been sentenced to prison for four years for stealing a check from the mails, a suspended sentence for the man who has defrauded investors out of $150,000 represents rank unjustice. To the inmates of Attica prison, newspaper accounts of a corporate executive who received a $1,000 fine for evading $60,000 in income taxes provide a reason for hatred. These disparities generate a practical threat to society in the form of unrest and bitterness" (Seymour, 1973, p. 821).

In addition to satisfying at least minimal standards of justice, stiffer penalties for corporate wrongdoing can be encouraged as a deterrent. Braithwaite and Geis (1982) show how individual corporate criminals are likely to be deterred by severe penalties because "they have more of those valued possessions that can be lost through a criminal conviction, such as social status, respectability, money, a job, and a comfortable home and family life" (p. 302). They go on to say:

> In general, the arguments about the deterrability of individuals convicted of corporate crimes are equally applicable to the corporations themselves. Corporations are future–oriented, concerned about their reputation, and quintessentially rational. Although most individuals do not possess the information necessary to calculate rationally the probability

TABLE 6.3. LARGE, NONSUBSIDIARY CORPORATIONS INVOLVED IN 1961 AND 1976 PRICE-FIXING CASES

Corporation	Gross revenues[b]	Criminal fine[c]	Equivalent for individual earning $15,000[d]
1961 Defendants[a]			
Allis–Chalmers	$ 502,200,000	$127,500	$ 3.75
Carrier	266,300,000	7,500	0.42
Cutler–Hammer	118,300,000	45,000	5.70
Federal Pacific	88,200,000	65,000	10.95
Foster Wheeler	197,900,000	20,000	1.50
General Electric	4,456,800,000	437,500	1.47
I–T–E	111,500,000	92,500	12.30
Ingersoll Rand	181,400,000	20,000	1.65
McGraw–Edison	329,200,000	70,000	3.15
Square D	115,300,000	75,000	9.75
Wagner Electric	65,900,000	10,000	2.25
Westinghouse	1,913,800,000	372,500	2.85
Worthington	189,000,000	20,000	1.50
1976 Defendants[e]			
American Can	3,142,500,000	50,000	0.24
Champion International	2,910,500,000	50,000	0.26
Diamond International	887,100,000	50,000	0.84
Federal Paper	393,600,000	50,000	1.80
International Paper	3,540,000,000	50,000	0.21
Mead	1,599,300,000	50,000	0.47
Potlatch	624,100,000	50,000	1.20
St. Regis	1,642,100,000	50,000	0.45
Weyerhauser	2,868,400,000	50,000	0.26

Source: M. D. Ermann & R. J. Lundman, 1982, p. 148.

[a]1961 nonsubsidiary defendants are those defendants listed separately in *Moody's Handbook of Common Stocks, Fourth Quarter* (New York: Moody's Investors, 1966).

[b]As listed in *Moody's Handbook.*

[c]1961 data reported in *The New York Times,* 7 February 1961, p. 26 and 2 February 1961; 1976 data reported in Notice of Hearing on Proposed Class Action Settlements and Proposed Plan of Distribution In Re Folding Carton Antitrust Litigation, U.S. District Court, Northern District of Illinois, Eastern Division, MDL 250, July 26, 1979.

[d]To determine equivalent for individual earning $15,000, we first divided the criminal fine by 1961 gross revenues. The resulting figure was then multiplied by $15,000. For example, Allis–Chalmers was fined $127,500 and had gross revenues of $502,200,000; $127,500 divided by $502,200,000 equals .00025, and .00025 times $15,000 equals $3.75, the equivalent for an individual earning $15,000.

[e]1976 nonsubsidiary defendants are those defendants listed separately in *Moody's Handbook of Common Stocks: Winter 1979–80 Edition* (New York: Moody's Investors Services, 1980).

of detection and punishment, corporations have information-gathering systems designed precisely for this purpose....

Although the fine itself may be an ineffective deterrent when used against the corporate criminal, other sanctions associated with the prosecution—unfavorable publicity, the harrowing experience for the senior executive of days under cross-examination, the dislocation of top management from their normal duties so that they can defend the corporation against public attacks—can be important specific deterrents. (pp. 302–303)

Other effective sanctions might be to forbid repeat violators from acting in such formal roles as company directors, lawyers, accountants, and the like. And at the most extreme level, "capital punishment for the corporation is one possibility: The charter of a corporation can be revoked, the corporation can be put in the hands of a receiver, or it can be nationalized" (Braithwaite & Geis, 1982, p. 307).

In respect to sanctions, it is important to emphasize the role of publicity. Clinard and Yeager (1980) found from conversations with federal and state enforcement officials, as well as with corporate executives "that mass media publicity about law violations probably represents the most feared consequence of sanctions imposed on a corporation." (p. 318) Likewise, Hopkins (1980) concludes that "for most companies, the real mechanism of deterrence was concern about loss of reputation, both that of the company and, more particularly, that of individual managers" (Hopkins, 1980, p. 212). Thus, the present evidence suggests that stiff sanctions accompanied by widespread publicity can add to deterrence of corporate deviance.

Consumer, Employee, and Public Action. The consumer movement, in both its private and public aspects, has grown slowly over the past twenty years. Perhaps a watershed was Ralph Nader's (1965) carefully documented attack on General Motor's design and sale of the Corvair in *Unsafe at Any Speed.* Likewise, private organizations, such as the Consumers Union which publishes *Consumer Reports,* have had an influence in sharpening public awareness and increasing corporate responsibility. On the public front, the Consumer Product Safety Commission, the Federal Trade Commission, and the Food and Drug Administration are among the federal agencies that regularly review complaints about products and order suspension of sale or recall of those deemed unsafe.

Employee pressure for healthful, safe working conditions has been applied mainly through union efforts. The Occupational Health and Safety Administration is the federal agency that has been created to oversee such standards in the workplace. Both consumer- and employee-oriented federal agencies have their counterparts in many state and local governments.

Two points regarding government regulation bear mention. First, not all regulation is necessarily to the benefit of consumers, employees, or the public. Pfeffer (1974) argues convincingly that "There is evidence that administrative regulation and licensing has actually operated against the public interest; and that rather than protecting the public from the industry, regulation has frequently operated to protect and economically enhance the industry or occupation" (p. 478). Thus, certain trade, pricing, or advertising regulations have actually increased consumer costs in the airline or trucking industries and professions such as undertaking or law. Second, isolated examples of bad regulations or poor judgment in enforcement should not be used to sustain a more general attack on efforts to control corporations. "Although it is true that some rules may be overzealous, as also happens within a corporation itself, it is unreasonable to include in this category the vast majority of laws that regulate trusts, advertising, environmental pollution, taxes, and other important areas of corporate behavior" (Clinard and Yeager, 1980, p. 71). Government action in the public interest requires both sensible regulation and deregulation with an eye not merely to the number but the intent and effect of the rules in question.

Finally, the effectiveness of public action depends significantly upon improved information about corporate deviance. In order to improve our knowledge there must be centralized collection of data on corporate violations along with federal and state enforcement actions. At present, there is no standard system for the accumulation and publication of information on corporate crimes comparable to the FBI's *Uniform Crime Reports* issued annually for street crimes. Conklin (1977) has suggested that development and regular issuance of such a business crimes report would help to increase public awareness.

Changes in Corporate Attitudes and Structure. The most effective social control for individuals, it has been said, is effective socialization to abide by the norms of the society. Likewise, underlying any strategy to control corporations is a viable set of ethical principles to guide the conduct of business. The strengthening of business ethics starts with the tone set by the boards of directors and managements of individual corporations. Beyond this, influential business organizations like the U.S. Chamber of Commerce, the National Association of Manufacturers, or the Business Roundtable could direct attention to ethical standards. Business schools should continue to pay more attention to ethics and social responsibility as part of the curriculum for the future corporate elite.

Changes in corporate organization have been identified by some as the potentially most fruitful ways of controlling corporate crime. First, stockholders should be provided with more information on how "their" corporation is being run by the management and a more realistic opportunity to effect corporate decision making through the board of directors. As presently constituted and run, most large corporations operate with little or no concern for the interests of small shareholders even though collectively these people may own a majority of stock in the company. Stone (1975) has suggested that large corporations should not be permitted to have their managers sit on the board; that steps should be taken to insure that directors get critical information regarding company operations; and that the general public have representation on boards of directors.

At the management level, McVisk (1978) has argued that the liability of corporate executives for the behavior of their companies must be clarified. After all, in a giant organization employing thousands of people producing hundreds of products, how can the corporate executive legitimately be responsible for criminal actions? The approach he proposes calls for a clear definition of the duties of all corporate personnel. The chief executive officer would be charged with the responsibility "of instituting the necessary systems within the company to insure compliance" and "other officers and employees of the corporation would share liability to the extent that their function within the system was not carried out" (p. 90). Thus, corporate executives would be made criminally liable for failure to institute adequate organizational safeguards against corporate crime.

Even more sweeping reforms have been proposed. For example, Nader et al. (1976) call for federal, as opposed to state, chartering of corporations. At present, states compete for corporate chartering fees by trying to outdo one another in loosening restrictions on corporate behavior. Tiny Delaware has been the most successful. "The state is 'home' for half of the nation's 500 largest industrial firms. In 1979 it realized $64,000,000 in revenues from corporate chartering" (Ermann & Lundman, 1982, p. 161). Of course, Delaware does not begin to have the resources necessary to cope with violations by these giants. A federal chartering system could, for example,

> require full disclosure of corporate operations, give stockholders the right to amend corporate bylaws and to recall any director, provide more opportunities for stockholders or stockholder groups to nominate some board members, provide a full-time staff to the board of directors to monitor independently corporate operations, establish safeguards to respect the privacy of all employees, and require a community impact statement when a corporation plant is to be relocated. Federal chartering would also make possible more effective regulation of corporations by various federal agencies, both in preventing illegal activities and in enforcement actions against violators. (Clinard & Yeager, 1980, p. 212)

Finally, control might be more effectively exercised if such vast economic power was not allowed to concentrate in so few hands. A policy of deconcentration and divestiture might restrict large corporations' sizes, their acquisition, mergers, and general capacity to dominate totally a particular industry. In many countries, including the United States, federal ownership or nationalization of key monopolies or oligopolies such as utilities and transportation systems is successful. Public ownership, the most fundamental of all proposed reforms, is also the most controversial. Thus, there are those who see the control of corporate deviance as an organizational problem as opposed to one of economic control that would be ameliorated by nationalization. Two experts argue that:

> Nationalized corporations still would be organizations with essentially the same goals they currently have. Security, growth, and autonomy are important goals for *all* organizations. Corporate deviance is the product of organizational patterns that serve these goals. Deviance does not result from avarice by or for powerless shareholders. In fact, government and other nonprofit organizations also routinely are deviant. (Ermann & Lundman, 1982, p. 175)

Whatever the approach, whether through legal and penal reform, public action, changes in corporate organization, or altering the place of giant corporations in the economy, the options for controlling corporate deviance are varied and largely untried. As huge business organizations continue to dominate our lives, policies designed to encourage the best and restrain the worst that they have to offer should become a part of our public discourse.

SUMMARY

America's elites can be usefully defined as the upper strata of individuals who form the superrich capitalist class and the upper–middle class, together comprising about 15% of the population; in addition, there are elite corporations whose staggering size and wealth permit them to dominate the American economy. These elite individuals and corporations are able effectively to transform their economic wealth into political power by a variety of direct and indirect means. As a result, a major factor in the evolving conceptions of crime and the administration of justice in the United States has been the ability of elites to have the law made and enforced in their interests.

The study of elite deviance is rooted in Sutherland's development of the concept *white-collar crime*. The thrust of his argument was that crime is not merely a lower-class activity and need not be explained in terms of psychopathology. Extending Sutherland's pioneering work, others have distinguished deviant actions committed by high-status individuals and corporations. We defined *elite occupational deviance* as an illegal or unethical act committed for personal gain by an individual of high social status and respectability in the course of that person's occupation or profession. In contrast, *corporate deviance* consists of actions that violate criminal, civil, or administrative law that are intended to benefit the corporation itself. Such actions result from decisions by officers in a corporation (executives or managers) in accordance with corporate goals (primarily corporate profits), standard operating procedures, and cultural norms of the organization.

Two major areas of elite occupational deviance were considered with examples. First, illegal and unethical behavior among professio '˙ included problems like physicians' fee splitting, lawyers' fee-setti.. practices, and sexual harassment by academic professors. Second, deviance by politicians and government officials received our attention. Four explanations of official deviance variously emphasize individual morality, the social functions of corruption, the expansion of government, and corruption as integral to the capitalist system.

Our review of corporate deviance began with a description of what a corporation is and how it operates. Although they are large, bureaucratic, hierarchically controlled organizations in pursuit of profits, corporations have a curious status in law as intangible persons. Both their organizational complexity and legal status are important for our understanding of corporate deviance.

The costs of corporate crime are immense. The economic toll certainly exceeds many times the annual losses from conventional property crimes like burglary, larceny, and robbery. The physical costs in damaged health and lost lives from violation of occupational health and safety and pollution laws are staggering. Possibly even more damaging are the social and moral costs from the disrespect for the law that wanton violation by the society's elites conveys to the rest of the population. All of these harms were demonstrated in examples from four types of corporate deviance characterized by customers as victims, employees as victims, the public-at-large as victims, and owners as victims. A recent study by Clinard helps us to estimate the amount of corporate crime. He found that over a two-year period (1975 to 1976) among 582 of America's largest corporations, 60% had at least one enforcement action initiated against them. Corporate offenders are concentrated in certain large industries; and penalties for violations generally are very light.

Explanations of corporate crime range from the social psychological to the sociological. Explicitly rejecting psychopathological explanations, Sutherland emphasized social psychological learning in his theory of differential association to account for corporate deviance. As part of their socialization in the corporation, people learn both the techniques for violating the law and how to rationalize having done so. The personal traits (ambition, shrewdness, and a nondemanding moral code) that often characterize people who rise to the top of large organizations also contribute to an atmosphere favoring corporate deviance. In fact, it appears that in some companies and industries, law violation has become a part of the corporate culture.

Sociological explanations focus on the structure of the corporation, the structure of the economy, and the failure of social controls. As large, bureaucratic organizations, corporations tend to fragment authority and responsibility for their actions. Deviance is more easily committed in an atmosphere not conducive to moral reflection or individual responsibility. Excessive emphasis on competing for maximum profits is central to one economic theory of corporate crime. And a general critique of welfare state capitalism emphasizes how corporate economic power is translated into political power. Thus, the government passes weak laws to control corporate deviance that have inadequate enforcement provisions making the commission of corporate crime a low–risk, rational action for the perpetrator. Put simply, efforts to control corporate crime have been feeble.

Finally, we presented several public policy reforms aimed at controlling corporate deviance more effectively. These included legal and penal reform; consumer, employee, and public action; and changes in corporate attitudes and structure.

REFERENCES

Barnett, H. C.
   1981   Corporate capitalism, corporate crime. *Crime and Delinquency, 27,* pp. 4–23.

Bell, D.
   1953   Crime as an American way of life. *Antioch Review, 13,* pp. 131–153.

Benson, D. J., & Thomson, G. E.
   1981   Sexual harassment on a university campus: The confluence of authority relations, sexual interest and gender stratification. Paper delivered at the Annual Meeting of the American Sociological Association, Toronto.

Berle, A. A., & Means, G. C.
   1932   The modern corporation and private property. New York: MacMillan.

Blumberg, A. S.
   1978   Practice of law as a confidence game. In John M. Johnson and Jack D. Douglas (Eds.), *Crime at the top.* New York: Lippincott.

Blundell, W. E.
   1976   Swindled. New York: Dow Jones Books.

Braithwaite, J., & Geis, G.
   1982   On theory and action for corporate crime control. *Crime and Deliquency, 28,* pp. 292–314.

Chambliss, W. J.
   1977   Vice, corruption, bureaucracy, and power. In J. D. Douglas & J. M. Johnson (Eds.), *Official deviance.* Philadelphia: Lippincott.

Clinard, M. B.
   1979   *Illegal corporate behavior.* Washington, D.C.: U.S. Government Printing Office.

Clinard, M. B., & Yeager, G. C.
   1980   *Corporate Crime.* New York: The Free Press.

Conklin, J. E.
   1977   "Illegal but not criminal." *Business crime in America.* Englewood Cliffs, N.J.: Prentice-Hall.

Conyers, J., Jr.
   1980   Corporate and white-collar crime: A view by the chairman of the house subcommittee on crime. *American Criminal Law Review, 17,* pp. 287–300.

Dansereau, H. K.
   1974   Unethical behavior: Professional deviance. In C. D. Bryant (Ed.), *Deviant Behavior: Occupational and organized bases.* Chicago: Rand McNally.

Denzin, N. K.
   1977   Notes on the criminogenic hypothesis: A case study of the American liquor industry. *American Sociological Review, 42,* pp. 905–920.

Diamond, R., Feller, L., & Russo, N. F.
   1981   *Sexual harassment action kit.* Washington, D.C.: The Federation of Organizations for Professional Women.

Domhoff, G. W.
   1978   *The powers that be: Processes of ruling-class domination in America.* New York: Random House.

Douglas, J. D.
   1977   A sociological theory of official deviance and public concerns with official deviance. In J. D. Douglas & J. M. Johnson (Eds.), *Official deviance.* Philadelphia: Lippincott.

Dye, T. R.
   1976   *Who's running America?* Englewood Cliffs, N.J.: Prentice-Hall.

Dziech, B., & Faaborg, L.
   1983   *The lecherous professor.* Boston: Beacon Press.

Edelhertz, H.
   1970   *The nature, impact and prosecution of white-collar crime.* Washington, D.C.: U.S. Department of Justice, Law Enforcement Assistance Administration.

Ermann, M. D., & Lundman, R. J.
  1982 *Corporate deviance.* New York: Holt, Rinehart and Winston.
Evans, P. B., & Schneider, S. A.
  1981 The political economy of the corporation. In S. G. McNall (Ed.), *Political Economy: A critique of American society.* Glenview, Ill.: Scott, Foresman.
Franklin, P., Moglen, H., Zatlin-Boring, P., & Angress, R.
  1981 *Sexual and gender harassment in the academy.* New York: The Modern Language Association of America.
Freitag, P.
  1975 The cabinet and big business: A study of interlocks. *Social Problems, 23,* pp. 137-152.
Friedman, M.
  1962 *Capitalism and freedom.* Chicago: University of Chicago Press.
Geis, G.
  1974 *Upperworld crime.* In A. Blumberg (Ed.), *Current perspectives on criminal behavior: Original essays in criminology.* New York: Knopf.
Geis, G.
  1977 The heavy electrical equipment antitrust cases of 1961. In G. Geis & R. F. Meier (Eds.), *White-collar crime.* New York: The Free Press.
Geis, G., & Meier, R. F.
  1977 *White collar crime.* New York: The Free Press.
Gilbert, D., & Kahl, J. A.
  1982 *The American class structure.* Homewood, Ill.: Dorsey.
Gordon, L.
  1981 The politics of sexual harassment. *Radical America* (summer), pp. 7-14.
Gross, E.
  1978 Organizational crime: A theoretical perspective. In N. K. Denzin (Ed.), *Studies in symbolic interaction,* vol. 1. Greenwich, Conn.: JAI Press.
Hessler, R. M.
  1974 Junkies in white: Drug addiction among physicians. In C. D. Bryant (Ed.), *Deviant behavior: Occupational and organized bases.* Chicago: Rand McNally.
Hopkins, A.
  1980 Controlling corporate deviance. *Criminology, 18,* pp. 198-214.
Jackall, R.
  1980 Crime in the suites. *Contemporary Sociology, 9,* pp. 354-371.
Jacoby, N.
  1973 *Corporate power and social responsibility.* New York: Macmillan.
Johnson, J. M., & Douglas, J. D.
  1978 *Crime at the top.* New York: Lippincott.

Kerbo, H., & Fave, R. D.
1979 The empirical side of the power elite debate. *The Sociological Quarterly, 20,* pp. 5–22.

Klockars, C. B.
1977 White collar crime. In E. Sagarin & F. Montanino (Eds.), *Deviants: Voluntary actors in a hostile world.* Morristown, N.J.: General Learning Press.

Kramer, R. C.
1981 Toward the study and control of corporate crime: Some preliminary issues and questions. Paper presented at the Annual Meeting of the Society for the Study of Social Problems, Toronto.

Lewis, H. R., & Lewis, M. E.
1978 A crisis for patients. In J. M. Johnson & J. D. Douglas (Eds.), *Crime at the top.* New York: J. B. Lippincott.

Liazos, A.
1972 The poverty of the sociology of deviance: Nuts, sluts and 'preverts.' *Social Problems, 20,* pp. 103–120.

McCormick, A. E., Jr.
1977 Rule enforcement and moral indignation: Some observations on the effects of criminal antitrust convictions upon societal reaction processes. *Social Problems, 25,* pp. 30–39.

McVisk, W.
1978 Toward a rational theory of criminal liability for the corporate executive. *The Journal of Criminal Law and Criminology, 69,* pp. 75–91.

Merton, R. K.
1957 *Social theory and social structure.* New York: The Free Press.

Nader, R.
1965 *Unsafe at any speed: The designed-in dangers of the American automobile.* New York: Grossman.

Nader, R., & Green, M. J.
1972 Crime in the suites: Coddling the corporation. *New Republic* (April 29), pp. 27–31.

Nader, R., Green, M., & Seligman, J.
1976 *Taming the giant corporation.* New York: Norton.

Parker, D. B.
1976 *Crime by computer.* Totowa, N.J.: Charles Scribner's Sons.

Parker, D. B.
1980 Computer-related white-collar crime. In G. Geis & E. Stotland (Eds.), *White-collar crime: Theory and research.* Beverly Hills, Calif.: Sage.

Pearce, F.
1976 *Crimes of the powerful: Marxism, crime and deviance.* London: Pluto Press.

Pfeffer, J.
1974 Administrative regulation and licensing: Social problem or solution? *Social Problems, 21,* pp. 468–479.

Posner, R.
   1970   A statistical study of antitrust enforcement. *Journal of Law and Economics, 13,* pp. 365–419.

President's Commission on Law Enforcement and Administration of Justice.
   1967   *The challenge of crime in a free society.* Washington, D.C.: U.S. Government Printing Office.

Quinney, R.
   1974   *Critique of legal order.* Boston: Little, Brown & Company.

Sandler, B. R., & Associates
   1981   Sexual harassment: A hidden problem. *Educational Record, 62,* pp. 52–57.

Schrager, L. S., & Short, J. F., Jr.
   1978   Toward a sociology of organizational crime. *Social Problems, 25,* pp. 407–419.

Schrager, L. S., & Short, J. F., Jr.
   1980   How serious a crime? Perceptions of organizational and common crimes. In G. Geis and E. Stotland (Eds.), *White–collar crime: Theory and research.* Beverly Hills, Calif.: Sage.

Seymour, W. N., Jr.
   1973   Social and ethical considerations in assessing white–collar crime. *The American Criminal Law Review, 11,* pp. 833–34.

Stone, C. D.
   1975   *Where the law ends: The social control of corporate behavior.* New York: Harper and Row.

Subcommittee on Crime of the Committee on the Judiciary, U.S. House of Representatives.
   1980   *Corporate crime.* Washington, D.C.: U.S. Government Printing Office.

Sutherland, E. H.
   1949   *White–collar crime.* New York: Holt, Rinehart and Winston.

Sutherland, E. H.
   1956   Crimes of corporations. In A. Cohen, A. Lindesmith, & K. Schuessler (Eds.), *The Sutherland papers.* Bloomington, Ind.: Indiana University Press.

Thio, A.
   1973   Class bias in the sociology of deviance. *The American Sociologist, 8,* pp. 1–12.

Wilson, K. R., & Kraus, L. A.
   1981   Sexual harassment in the university. Paper delivered at the Annual Meeting of the American Sociological Association, Toronto.

Zeitlin, M.
   1974   Corporate ownership and control: The large corporation and the capitalist class. *American Journal of Sociology, 79,* pp. 1073–1119.

Chapter 7
DEVIANCE, CONTROL AND SOCIAL POLICY

IMAGES OF DEVIANCE IN WESTERN HISTORY
  Sin, Crime, and Sickness
  The Medicalization of Deviance
THE POLITICS OF DEVIANCE
  The Social Construction of Deviance
  The Emergence of Social Policy
  The Responsibility of the Human Sciences
THE PRACTICE OF CONTROL
  Overreach and Underreach of the Criminal Law
  Deviance as Control

Several tasks are proposed for this concluding chapter. First, we will place in very broad historical perspective an overview of approaches to deviance and control in Western culture. Second, there is a discussion of the process by which social policy in regard to deviance emerges in contemporary American society. Third, based on the theory and evidence from the previous chapters, we will recommend more effective alternatives to present social control practices. The parting remarks constitute a critical assessment of how the production, maintenance, and control of deviance are frequently tied to those interested in maintaining the status quo. The underlying theme is that deviance and its control are inseparable from the broader social structures in which they occur.

IMAGES OF DEVIANCE IN WESTERN HISTORY

Sin, Crime, and Sickness

Three approaches to explaining deviance have competed for ascendancy throughout Western history. Sometimes two or all three of them—deviance as sin, as crime, or as sickness—have existed side by side with approximately equal acceptance. In virtually every period there have been some adherents to each of the three. However, within very broad time frames, one image of deviance has tended to dominate others. Not surprisingly, moreover, the reigning image of deviance in a particular period is linked to that period's dominant groups and social institutions. For example, in a medieval, feudal society dominated by theological reasoning and ecclesiastical authority, theories of deviance emphasized sin, evil, and fall from grace. The clergy, whose authority was anchored in theological doctrine and tradition, were the primary social control practitioners. The social control practices, reflecting the apparent need to atone for sin or expunge evil, often involved penance or corporal punishment. In contrast, our present capitalistic welfare state is a society dominated by giant corporations, large, bureaucratic government, and technocrats (highly trained scientists, engineers, and other skilled professionals). In this technologically oriented society, the management of deviance is increasingly placed in the hands of specialists. The ascendant image of deviance conceptualizes wrongdoing as evidence of sickness. Medical, psychiatric, and social scientists, along with various helping professionals (social workers, probation officers, counselors) increasingly preempt or share in social control decisions with the courts. Techniques of social control include drugs and surgery intended to "cure" the behavior in question.

Figure 7.1 summarizes these broad historical trends in Western images of deviance and the practice of social control. Notice that each historical period tends to have its own characteristic images of deviance and approaches to social control.[1] Thinking in such a grand historical frame of reference is useful for uncovering large-scale patterns. However, the cautionary words with which we began require reemphasis. Specific exceptions and reversals of the general tendency to move from images of deviance as sin, to crime, to sickness exist. Indeed, within the last hundred years or so in American society there has been a cyclical pattern in deviance designations between images of crime and sickness (Conrad & Schneider, 1980, p. 274). For example, through the 19th century to the present, opiate addiction has been alternately defined as no problem, to a medical problem, to a crime, and to a current hybrid medical–legal designation. Throughout the same period, alcoholism has carried a mixed designation of immorality, illegality, and sickness with the medical model presently dominating. The prevailing definition of homosexual behavior has moved from sin to crime to sickness and, most recently, demedicalization. The effectiveness and the durability of the political struggle that was described in Chapter 2 to redefine the official American Psychiatric Association designation of homosexual behavior as a "nonillness" remains to be seen.

The deeper implications of changing images of deviance must remain beyond the scope of this book. However, a few words may suggest at least one direction in which further thought on the subject may lead. From the viewpoint of "images of deviance," the essential importance of a theory is not its truth or falseness, for virtually all theories become discredited and outmoded in time.[2] Rather, a theory is important because it makes manifest underlying assumptions about the nature of humans and their interactions. And, in so doing, theories of deviance serve as important guides for how people treat one another and the kind of society they construct. Put differently, theories and images of deviance, modes of social control, everyday interaction, and the social structure of the society in which they exist are all of the same cloth.

Historical period	Pre-industrial Feudal (pre-1500)	Mercantile/Early industrial capitalism (1500-1900)	Advanced welfare state capitalism (1900-present)
Dominant groups/institutions	Church, clergy monarchy, and nobility	Landed gentry, merchants, and industrial capitalists	Industrial capitalists and state technocrats
Image of deviance			
Identification	Sin/evil	Crime/illegal	Sickness/madness/crime
Responsibility	Individual in relation to God and Sovereign	Individual in relation to the Law and the State	Individual denied responsibility
Social control			
Practitioners	Clergy, monarchy, and nobility	Judges and courts	Medical, psychiatric, and social scientists, helping professionals and courts
Legitimation of authority	Tradition/Divine right/moral	Legal/rational/moral	Technical/rational/moral
Mode of response	Retributive/corporal/capital/penance	Restitutive/incarceration/capital/banishment	Rehabilitative/drugs or surgery/repressive/incarceration or capital
Image of the limits on human action	Supernaturalistic determinism/original sin	Free will/Utilitarian, rational choice	Naturalistic determinism/Bio-Psycho-social causes

FIGURE 7.1. BROAD HISTORICAL TRENDS IN WESTERN IMAGES OF DEVIANCE AND THE PRACTICE OF SOCIAL CONTROL

The Medicalization of Deviance

Over the past one hundred years, American society has been a particularly receptive environment for medicalized conceptions of deviance. Two careful observers of the medicalization trend summarize the reasons why.

> In a general sense, the American values of experimentation, newness, humanitarianism, pragmatism, and individualism have all contributed to a nurturing crucible for medicalization, for the medical perspective on deviance contains elements of all these values . . .
> . . . In recent years health itself has become a predominant value. American society, with its democratic system, is open to challenges of new definitions of deviance. Medical practice is independent and expansive. In a capitalist society, medicalization can create new markets and be highly profitable. In short, in American society medical conceptions of deviance have a cultural resonance both with dominant values and the organizational apparatus to promote and sustain them, creating a fertile environment for medicalization. (Conrad & Schneider, 1980, pp. 263, 265)

The most common alternative to medicalization in the past century has been to treat deviance as crime. Therefore, it would be appropriate to consider briefly the underlying distinctions between deviance conceived as crime versus deviance viewed as sickness. Probably most significant is the attribution of responsibility in each case. Crime is assumed to be an act motivated by some gain—money, power, revenge, or pleasure. A criminal is also presumed to be responsible for his or her conduct. Crime involves a moral choice to break or abide by the law. In contrast, in sickness the patient is deemed not responsible for his or her condition. There is no moral decision to get sick or stay well. Sickness merely involves a turn for the worse (Aubert & Messinger, 1958). Thus, when we treat someone as a criminal, we assume that the behavior in question involved a morally conscious choice for which the person can be held responsible. To say that behavior is a result of sickness implies that it occurred beyond the person's control, that the person is not responsible.

Beyond the attribution of responsibility, there are great differences in how crime and sickness are handled once they are suspected. Generally, as an ideal, the determination of guilt or innocence in crime is made by citizen peers of the accused who make up a trial jury. In the case of sickness, decisions about whether one is ill or well are made by professional experts, primarily doctors.

The trend toward medicalization of deviance has not usually happened by sharp transformations in the definition of a particular activity like homosexual behavior, drunkenness, or drug taking. Rather, in subtle stages, the practice of law and the practice of medicine have become more entwined. We can see it in the increasing use of expert psychiatric testimony in respect to "competency to stand trial" hearings and the successful use of the insanity defense in the celebrated cases such as that of attempted presidential assassin John Hinckley, Jr.[3] Michel Foucault (1975) sees the emergence of a new form of law presided over by judges who have an "immense 'appetite for medicine' " made manifest in their regular appeal to psychiatric experts. The mixing of law and medicine has "had a whole series of effects: the internal dislocation of the judicial power or at least of its functioning; an increasing difficulty in judging, as if one were ashamed to pass sentence; a furious desire on the part of judges to judge, assess, diagnose, recognize the normal and abnormal and claim the honour of curing and rehabilitation" (p. 304).

In the day-to-day practice of decision making, images of deviance as crime have become increasingly influenced by images of deviance as sickness. Moral judgments of right or wrong have coalesced with technical judgments of well or sick. The result is a subtle shift from a view of people personally responsible for their own behavior and who are judged guilty or innocent by citizen peers to a view of people who are irresponsible and whose behavior calls for evaluation by elite experts to determine pathology. The consequences extend well beyond the lives of deviants alone. First, with the blurring of the distinction between crime and sickness, the very capacity to view almost any misbehavior on a moral plane fades as moral-legal and medical-technical decision making meld. The moral frame required for a public understanding of popular protest breaks when virtually any sort of rule-breaking, including civil disobedience, is regarded as "sick" and is, therefore, to be dismissed as such. Medicalized deviant behavior loses all potential for political meaning.[4]

From a still wider perspective, looking beyond those labeled incorrigible, a medicalized, therapeutic ethos directs the efforts of people searching to relieve their malaise, not in the social arrangements into which they are bound, but only within themselves. They seek individualized "diagnoses" and "cures" as opposed to examining critically their society. And, whenever more decisions leave the moral-legal domain for the medical-therapeutic one, people yield the power to control their own lives to medical, behavioral, and social "experts." Democracy is thereby diminished. The society is moved still closer to Huxley's *Brave New World* of genetic engineering, behavior modification, and total elite social control.

THE POLITICS OF DEVIANCE

The Social Construction of Deviance

Late in the 19th century the French sociologist Emile Durkheim made his most enduring observation about deviant behavior. He said that it is *not* the intrinsic quality of a given act that makes it deviant; rather it is the definition of the act applied by the "collective conscience" of people in a society that confers on an act its deviant character (Durkheim, 1938, p. 70). Becker (1963) subsequently expanded on Durkheim's insight saying that

> *social groups create deviance by making the rules whose infraction constitutes deviance,* and by applying those rules to particular people and labelling them as outsiders. From this point of view, deviance is *not* a quality of the act the person commits, but rather a consequence of the application by others of rules and sanctions to an "offender." The deviant is one to whom that label has successfully been applied; deviant behavior is behavior that people so label. (p. 9)

Deviance is a product of enterprise and conflict. "Differences in the ability to make rules and apply them to other people are essentially power differentials (either legal or extralegal). Those groups whose special position gives them weapons and power are best able to enforce their rules" (Becker, 1963, p. 18). Deviance designations are the objects of conflict and disagreement; they are part of the political process of society. Likewise, of course, social policies aimed at controlling what has been identified as deviant are the products of political struggles. The two, deviance and the social policies adopted to control it, arise from a complex set of interactions between interest groups; the government; media image makers; medical, behavioral and social scientists; helping professionals; law enforcement personnel; the general public; and those who have been labeled deviant.

The Emergence of Social Policy

Neither images of deviance nor social policy are static. Rather than conceptualizing them as *things,* it is far better to see them as a *process* —a process that, like time, is forever changing, forever in motion. Moreover, the process that creates images of deviance and social policies to control it is very complicated, not entirely understood, and difficult to convey in only a few sentences. As a start, Figure 7.2 is a simplified, general model. There are several things about it that bear special emphasis.

First, the model represents social action in motion. In the process of deviance definition and social policy formation concerning any particular behavior, almost all of the influences indicated by the model's arrows are happening simultaneously. For the sake of illustration, let us run through a brief example of how the model applies to the specific case of alcohol use. Beginning at the far left of Figure 7.2, politically powerful interest groups would include the liquor industry, organizations like Alcoholics Anonymous, the Women's Christian Temperance Union, university research organizations, and the professional associations of social workers, counselors, and law enforcement personnel. Taken together, these groups influence media images of alcoholism by the written material they produce (papers, reports, brochures, and posters) and the public statements made by spokespeople on radio, television, and in the press. They also influence the types and amounts of government funding for research and the levels of support for programs to rehabilitate and control alcoholics.[5] The types and levels of government funding directly affect the work of scientists doing research on alcoholism, those who run programs for intervention and rehabilitation, and law enforcement personnel. Note how scientists, helping professionals, and law enforcement personnel are both recipients of government support for their work and politically powerful interest groups that influence what types and how much government support there will be. This kind of circular feedback of influence occurs at numerous other points throughout the model.[6]

Not only are influences in the social policy process often circular, sometimes there is even more direct feedback. For instance, the work of medical, behavioral, and social scientists is reflected in media images of alcoholism. Newspaper, news magazine, and radio and television reporters rely on researchers' reports and public statements during interviews for various news stories. At the same time, however, media and public images of what constitute "hot topics" for research influence, to some extent, researchers' choices of particular problems to study. For example, increased media and public attention directed at women as problem drinkers is likely to stimulate greater study of that specific problem by social scientists both directly in the scientists' selection of research problems and indirectly through the availability of funding.

Second, the social policy that emerges is embodied in the laws, administrative procedures and judicial rulings made by public officials. For example, in the case of public drunkenness, social policy in some states has recently undergone a transformation from criminalization to decriminalization. Such a change usually involves eliminating some

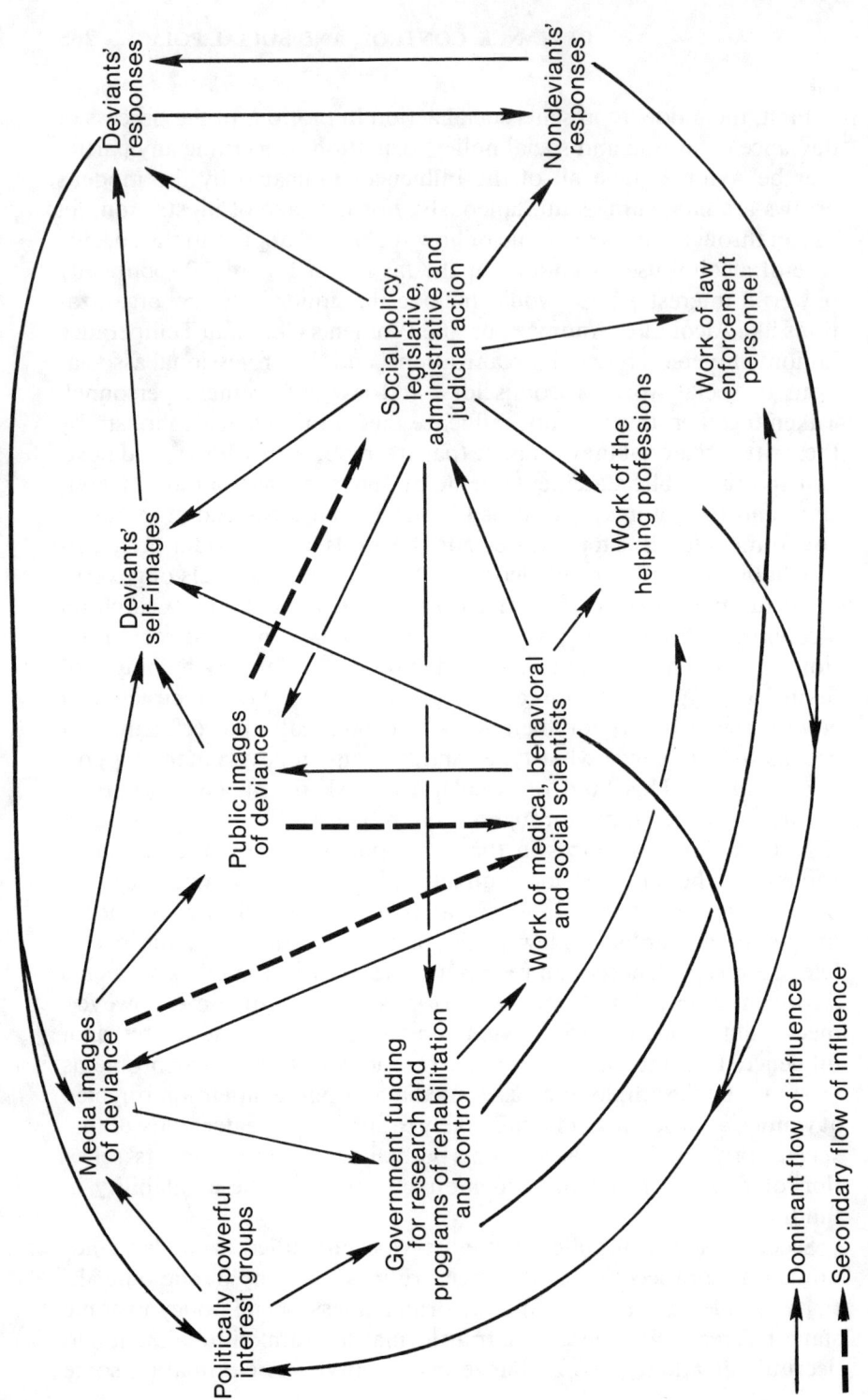

FIGURE 7.2. THE PROCESS OF DEFINING DEVIANCE AND CREATING SOCIAL POLICY

statutes concerning public drunkenness as a crime from the criminal law, addition of regulations to the public health code, and administrative edicts on how people who are identified as public drunks are now to be treated. In addition to influencing the work of law enforcement agents and helping professionals like social workers or detoxification specialists, the new social policy also will alter the public drunk's self-image as he or she sees the condition redefined from a problem handled primarily by the criminal justice system to one managed by welfare and medical personnel.

Third and finally, social policies produce responses from both non-deviants and those tagged with a deviant label. From the ranks of both may come politically powerful interest groups, like the Women's Christian Temperance Union or Alcoholics Anonymous, that either support or attempt to change whatever social policy is currently in force. In this sense, deviants themselves must be seen both as objects and participants in the social policy creation process. To repeat, definitions of deviance and social policies intended to control it emerge from a never-ending, dynamic set of interactions that influence one another in highly complex ways. Continuing to unravel the details of specific cases through sociohistorical analysis of the sort already done on topics such as drinking (Gusfield, 1963; Schneider, 1978), mental disorders (Szasz, 1961) and marijuana use (Musto, 1973; Galliher and Walker, 1977) remains an important item on the research agenda for students of deviance.

The Responsibility of the Human Sciences

Medical, behavioral, and social scientists should not underestimate the degree to which what they study and how they study it is influenced by government funding decisions and public, media images of what constitute worthy research targets. Nor should they minimize the impact of their work on (1) media images of deviance; (2) public images of deviance; (3) deviants' self-images; (4) the work of those in the helping professions; and (5) legal, administrative and judicial social policy. Theories widely accepted in the human sciences are part of the stuff of which deviance images are constructed and social policy decisions implemented. The responsibility of the human sciences in this realm is significant.

Theories of deviance have an even more far-reaching, if diffuse, importance. For example, some would argue (for example Matza, 1964 or Taylor et al., 1973) that social scientists' explanations of deviance have too often been excessively deterministic. In other words, the explanations seem to presume that the deviant is rather mindlessly propelled along an inevitable path by virtue of his or her genetic endowment, early childhood socialization, or pathology-producing social environment. The overriding image is a "billiard ball" conception of human behavior whereby people appear to be propelled into their actions by prior causes over which they have little or no choice or control. Such overly deterministic explanations are misleading in at least three ways. First, they ignore the role of human volition as a determinant of social action. To be sure, social conditions do limit or alter peoples' behavior. But humans who have the capacity to think, anticipate, and reflect—and this includes people labeled deviant as well, of course—can and do make choices about how they will behave. Thus, excessively deterministic images of deviance can dehumanize our images of those who are designated wayward and, ultimately, even dehumanize images of all others as well.

Second, a "billiard ball" conception of behavior removes the role of individual responsibility and accountability for a person's actions. How can one be blamed, made ashamed, or found guilty if the underlying explanation for his or her action is presumed to be beyond personal control? Third, and related to the second, an overdeterministic model of human behavior erases or masks the moral and political meaning of deviant actions. By removing the element of free choice and conscious decision from explanations of deviance, the answer to the question "Why did he do it?" need not go beyond a narrow technical explanation of the person's physical or psychological condition. A more adequate framing of the question, "Why did she *choose* to do it?" forces us to explore the conscious, human motivations—including the political and moral commitment—behind social action.

The main point is that theories of deviance inevitably embody fundamental assumptions about social action and human nature. Certainly far more attention is directed to the study of deviant than conforming behavior—especially the deviant behavior of the relatively powerless. After all, they are the ones who usually end up being defined as the problems. However, in a certain sense, it is through our extensive observation of deviants and theorizing about them that the human sciences produce what we think we know about human behavior more generally. Not too much unlike the lowly white rat, powerless deviants have usually been docile research subjects. Thus, the study of deviance and the underlying behavioral images that are part of deviance theories become part of general public discourse and explanations of human action. If we but listen carefully, we will hear them being applied to us all.

THE PRACTICE OF CONTROL

Overreach and Underreach of the Criminal Law

Beginning in the 1960s and into the present many social policy makers and their advisors in academe have called for decriminalization of certain illegal activities including prostitution, pornography, homosexual behavior, drunkenness, and drug use as long as the behavior in question only involves consenting adults. The argument goes that because these activities amount to willing exchanges between a supplier of some good or service and a customer, no victim's complaint accompanies the "crime." With no complaint, the law is extremely difficult to enforce (Schur, 1965). Indeed, the attempt to enforce laws that, due to the nature of the activities they proscribe are largely unenforceable, contributes to crime by enhancing disrespect for the law. As Morris and Hawkins (1970) put it:

> ... in many cases the attempt to use the criminal law to prohibit the supply of goods and services which are constantly demanded by millions of Americans is one of the most powerful criminogenic forces in our society. By enabling criminals to make vast profits from such sources as gambling and narcotics; by maximizing opportunities for bribery and corruption; by attempting to enforce standards which do not command either the respect or compliance of citizens in general; by these and in a variety of other ways, we both encourage disrespect for the law and stimulate the expansion of both individual and organized crime to an extent unparalleled in any other country in the world. (p. 27)

The leading humane alternative to criminalization of these activities is to treat them as medical problems, and we have already seen that the medicalization of deviance has its own dubious consequences. In addition to the reservations about medicalized conceptions of deviance already expressed, some commentators believe that substitution of medical personnel for law enforcement officers amounts only to dressing up in different clothing a fundamentally punitive approach.

> There is now considerable recognition that, however progressive they may seem at first glance, these efforts to define problematic situations in medical terms are far from being universally successful. As the trend toward politicization proceeds, the individuals involved become increasingly unwilling to accept medical definitions of their behavior; to gay liberation movement's repudiation of the concept that homosexuality is a disease or even "abnormal" is a striking case in point. Similarly, large-scale service programs that leave the individual subject to substantial

medical control (such as enforced "civil commitment" of addicts for treatment, or the granting of "therapeutic abortions" on approval by hospital medical boards) have been found to be inadequate modifications of what has remained a basically punitive policy. (Schur, 1974, pp. 43–44.)

Are there alternatives to criminalization or medicalization? Yes. One, called a social welfare approach, would proceed in two stages. First, decriminalize for consenting adults those exchange activities that generally yield no complaint. Second, offer and provide genuine help to people involved in such activities. They should not be coerced into accepting alternatives. Of course, the details would require lengthy description, but briefly, in practical terms, a social welfare model would ensure a respectable job and the realistic opportunity of an alternative livelihood for the street prostitute as opposed to the revolving door (jail-to-street-to-jail) system of criminal justice in which she is now trapped. The social welfare alternative would protect against job discrimination and provide the minimum of freedom from legal stigma for consenting adults engaging in homosexual behavior. Not unlike the present program of the Salvation Army, for the drunk there would be a place to sleep and a meal in a receptive environment as opposed to court appearances and "three hots and a cot" in a drunk tank, serving a life sentence in 30 day increments "on the installment plan." Maintenance facilities would be readily available for drug addicts along with medical and other social services.[7]

Inevitably, such a program must raise questions about its cost. Certainly the price should be no higher than the vast expenditures on criminal justice resources directed at these activities today. In 1983, prostitution and commercialized vice, other sex offenses (except rape), drunkenness, and drug abuse violations accounted for nearly 1,206,000 arrests or 17% of the total in the United States.[8] Each arrest represents valuable time spent by the police to say nothing of legal fees, court costs, and prison expenses. And, given the low socioeconomic status of these offenders, fines hardly represent a cost–effective alternative. Processing through the criminal justice system is probably the *most* expensive means imaginable for dealing with these activities. And this is to say nothing of the likely reduction in street crime if, for example, drug addicts did not have to engage in dangerous, often violent, activities to support a habit made more expensive by virtue of the supply being provided by the criminal underworld.

The proposal, then, is this. Decriminalize and treat as social welfare problems prostitution, pornography, homosexual behavior, drunkenness, and drug use. There are two main reasons. First, these activities and the people involved have been proven virtually undeterrable by a criminal justice system that is expensive and is actually undermined by attempting to enforce unenforceable laws against those activities. Second, whatever harm there is in these activities (and undoubtedly there is some to the deviant him- or herself and others in the society) can be minimized by treating them predominantly as social welfare problems rather than criminal or medical ones. Thus, in respect to several of the deviant activities taken up in previous chapters of this book, present social policy represents an *overreach* of the criminal law that would most beneficially be retracted.

Continuing the same line of reasoning, social policy in respect to elite deviance has been characterized by a distinct *underreach* of the criminal law. To repeat in brief the argument in Chapter 6, elite deviants—both individuals and corporations—are particularly sensitive to negative publicity arising from brushes with the criminal justice system. They have a great deal to lose if convicted—economic resources, status, and prestige. Moreover, the deviant acts they commit are unlikely to be crimes of passion or desperate need. Rather, they are more apt to involve very rational calculation of the relative gains and losses attached to law breaking. Thus, the criminalization, strict law enforcement, and severe sanctioning of elite deviance should be a favored social policy for two principal reasons. First, the activities and people involved in elite deviance are very likely to be deterred by the application of criminal sanctions. Moreover, public respect for the criminal justice system would be enhanced by the realization that elite "crimes in the suites" were being handled with severity comparable to "crimes in the streets." Second, the considerable harm done to clients, customers, employees, and the general public can be minimized, through deterrence, by treating elite deviance as serious criminal behavior rather than the benign neglect that is so often its fate under present social policy.

Deviance as Control

Deviants have long been recognized as harbingers of social change (Durkheim, 1938, p. 71). From Socrates in Athens to Bohemians in Greenwich Village or "flower children" in Haight–Ashbury, nonconformists have played a role in the evolution of beliefs, life-styles, and moral codes. A balanced picture requires taking note of how the production, maintenance, and control of deviance contributes to the status quo. Several ways are discussed below.

The first is found in the symbolic value of the deviance-defining process for those who succeed in discrediting others' custom or preference by having it officially declared illegal while their own remains legitimate. Status enhancement at the expense of others is the prize for the winners of deviance–defining "stigma contests" (Schur, 1980, p. 8). Recall in Chapter 5 Gusfield's (1963) interpretation of the mid–19th century American temperance movement as a symbolic struggle of status politics between nativist, Protestant, middle–class, rural people and immigrant, Catholic, lower–class city dwellers. The passage of the Prohibition Amendment was, for a time, one way of declaring where the power in the society resided. Particularly when a group in power feels threatened, launching a stigma contest against the threatening party (and, of course, winning) is often the surest way to demonstrate relative status and dominance. Today, some antipornography campaigns (Zurcher & Kirkpatrick, 1976) or the attacks on the Gay Rights movement (Bryant, 1977) can be viewed as efforts to keep the deviants, and those in sympathy with them, clearly in their place.[9]

Next, by successfully shaping popular images of deviance, public attention can be directed away from the transgressions of one social entity (usually the most powerful) at the expense of others (usually the powerless). The process of deviance designation can be thought of as the identification and ordering of a particular set of social problems on the public agenda for social action. For example, if the vast majority can be convinced that *the genuine*, high–priority social problems in the country are street crime and the allegedly related lower–class "pathological" activities such as street prostitution, pornography, homosexual behavior and alcoholism and other drug–taking, they will be less receptive to searching for and finding deviance among those at the top of the social hierarchy. Beyond merely deflecting attention, labeled deviants can become ready scapegoats to be blamed by those in power and provide targets for an aggressive populace when things are going badly. In a society with a faltering economy, the next best thing to war with another country to relieve the internal political pressure may be a "war on crime," an ideological witch–hunt like the McCarthyism of the 1950s, or a morality crusade against avowed deviants and misfits.

Deviance is profitable for those who study, prescribe, manufacture, and exercise social control techniques. Deviance supports an "enormous enterprise" (Palmer, 1973, p. 76) that includes at all levels of government police, judges, prison guards, probation officers, sociologists, psychologists, and doctors; in addition to private security firms, manufacturers of weapons, drugs, uniforms, vehicles, and so on. Deviance control is a sufficiently large industry with adequate political clout to ensure that its business will never decline substantially for want of offenders—real or imagined. If, as Erikson (1966) states, the amount of deviance found in a society is closely tied to "the size and complexity of its social control apparatus" (Erikson, 1966, p. 24), American society should not want for deviants in the foreseeable future.

Finally, popularly accepted images of deviance are central to legitimating modes of domination. Returning to the theme with which this chapter began, explanations and social policy in respect to deviance are generally consonant with the interests and ideas of a society's dominant groups. In medieval society the Church was the dominant institution; deviance was most commonly portrayed in terms of sin or evil; and social policy was predicated on reasoning that involved concepts like "original sin" or demonic possession. Today, in a world dominated by giant corporations, a massive government presence, and high technology, one contemporary trend is for deviance to be portrayed as sickness. Social control consistent with this image of deviance becomes a less public enterprise exercised by technical experts hidden behind a veil of professional–client confidentiality, by a haze of drugged psychotropic mind control, or behind the walls of large bureaucratic institutions. At the same time, economic troubles in our society mount. Elites in power frequently search desperately for others to blame and issues that deflect the great mass of peoples' attentions from the declining quality of their lives. And, too often, the strategy is to play upon fears and prejudices by calling for a repressive crackdown on the activities, many admittedly illegal, of the poor and powerless. Today, both the velvet–gloved manipulations of medicalized social control and iron–fisted, punitive retribution pluck responsive chords in the body politic. Possibly, contending alternatives will emerge. In any case, understanding the social construction of deviance and the social policies intended to control it provides one way to knowing better the society we have and anticipating the one likely in the future.

NOTES

1. This point is somewhat related to Erikson's (1966) observation that "Every human community has its own special set of boundaries (norms), its own unique identity, and so we may presume that every community also has its own characteristic styles of deviant behavior. Societies which place a high premium on ownership of property, for example, are likely to experience a greater volume of theft than those which do not, while societies which emphasize political orthodoxy are apt to discover and punish more sedition than their less touchy neighbors." (Erikson, 1966, pp. 19–20.)

2. This statement is no less true for the natural sciences like physics than it is for the behavioral and social sciences. See Kuhn, 1970.

3. Note in trials involving psychiatric testimony how prestigious expert witnesses for both the prosecution and the defense frequently arrive at contradictory conclusions despite vigorous claims of "scientific" precision and objectivity.

4. There have been conscious American government attempts to discredit people who have engaged in civil disobedience by implying their behavior was motivated by mental illness. FBI activities against Daniel Ellsberg and Dr. Martin Luther King come to mind. Likewise, President Lyndon Johnson applied Eric Hoffer's (1952) thesis to anti-Vietnam War demonstrators claiming that they merely represented the unfortunate attraction of society's "unstables and frustrated," normally dispersed and disorganized, to a single issue. In this way, the demonstrators' behavior could be explained away as "lunatic fringe" rather than moral. Indeed, during the 1960s in America when the level of social unrest prompted a rush for explanations, the most common metaphor was a "sick" society. The terminology was medical rather than moral (for example, an "unjust" society). The United States is certainly not alone in this regard. Witness the Soviet Union's practice of treating ideological dissidents as psychiatric cases for institutionalization.

5. Of course, various nongovernmental organizations support alcoholism research and rehabilitation programs also. Their omission from the model is one example of how it is simplified. Generally in respect to most types of deviance, government sponsored research and programs are the largest and most influential.

6. For a discussion of the theoretical rationale behind the type of feedback model proposed here, see Buckley's (1967) chapter on "Social Control: Deviance, Power, and Feedback Processes."

7. The approach suggested here does not imply that other criminal offenses like assault, theft, or robbery be dealt with in any way substantially different than presently. Thus, if a drug addict on maintenance doses can stay out of trouble (as numerous physician addicts do now, for example), then he or she should be left alone by the criminal law. If, on the other hand, an addict commits a serious crime like robbery, he or she should be subject to the full force of the criminal law for that criminal act regardless of the addiction.

8. This figure *excludes* arrests for driving under the influence of alcohol and other liquor law violations that together account for another 18% of the total annual arrests for the country.

9. Of course, in respect to pornography, there are crusaders from the political "right" who see the ready availability of sexually explicit materials as one sign of a degenerate "liberal" politics and life-style. At the same time, antipornography campaigns are being initiated from the feminist "left" by women who object to the demeaning images of women these materials so often portray.

REFERENCES

Aubert, V., & Messinger, S. L.
   1958   The criminal and the sick. *Inquiry, 1,* pp. 137–160.
Becker, H. S.
   1963   *Outsiders.* New York: Free Press.

Bryant, A.
  1977 *The Anita Bryant story: The survival of our nation's families and the threat of militant homosexuality.* Old Tappan, N.J.: Revell.
Buckley, W.
  1967 *Sociology and modern systems theory.* Englewood Cliffs, N.J.: Prentice-Hall.
Conrad, P., & Schneider, J. W.
  1980 *Deviance and medicalization: From badness to sickness.* St. Louis: Mosby.
Durkheim, E.
  1938 *The rules of sociological method.* S. A. Solovay & J. H. Mueller (Trans.) G. E. G. Catlin (Ed.). New York: Free Press.
Erikson, K. T.
  1966 *Wayward Puritans.* New York: John Wiley and Sons.
Foucault, M.
  1975 *Discipline and punish.* A. Sheridan (Trans.). Middlesex, England: Penguin.
Galliher, J. F., & Walker, A.
  1977 The puzzle of the social origins of the Marijuana Tax Act of 1937. *Social Problems, 24,* pp. 367–376.
Gusfield, J.
  1963 *Symbolic crusade.* Urbana, Ill.: University of Illinois Press.
Hoffer, E.
  1952 *The true believer.* New York: Harper and Row.
Kuhn, T. S.
  1970 *The structure of scientific revolutions,* 2nd ed. Chicago: University of Chicago Press.
Matza, D.
  1964 *Delinquency and drift.* New York: Wiley.
Morris, N., & Hawkins, G.
  1970 *The honest politician's guide to crime control.* Chicago: University of Chicago Press.
Musto, D. F.
  1973 *The American disease: Origins of narcotic control.* New Haven: Yale University Press.
Palmer, S.
  1973 *The prevention of crime.* New York: Behavioral Publications.
Schneider, J. W.
  1978 Deviant drinking as disease: Alcoholism as a social accomplishment. *Social Problems, 25,* pp. 361–372.
Schur, E. M.
  1965 *Crimes without victims: Deviant behavior and public policy.* Englewood Cliffs, N.J.: Prentice-Hall.
Schur, E. M.
  1974 A sociologist's view: The case for abolition. In E. M. Schur & H. A. Bedeau, *Victimless crimes: Two sides of a controversy.* Englewood Cliffs, N.J.: Prentice-Hall.

Schur, E. M.
   1980   *The politics of deviance.* Englewood Cliffs, N.J.: Prentice–Hall.
Szasz, T. S.
   1961   *The myth of mental illness.* New York: Harper & Row.
Taylor, I., Walton, P., & Young, J.
   1973   *The new criminology: For a social theory of deviance.* New York: Harper and Row.
Zurcher, L. A., Jr., & Kirkpatrick, R. G.
   1976   *Citizens for decency: Antipornography crusades as status defense.* Austin: University of Texas Press.

AUTHOR INDEX

Achilles, N., 63
Adams, L. D., 186
Agrest, S., 120
Akers, R., 73, 186
Alpern, D. M., 120
Ardrey, R., 14, 20
Atkinson, M., 39

Bachrach, L. L., 114, 116
Baden, M. M., 173, 174
Bales, R. F., 167, 179
Bandura, A., 14
Barnett, H. C., 241, 242
Barrett, D., 78
Bartell, G. D., 75
Beach, F. A., 54, 55
Becker, H. S., 4, 7, 10, 184, 185, 264
Bedeau, H. A., 20
Bell, A. P., 57, 59, 60, 61
Bell, D., 221
Benedict, R., 87
Benson, D. J., 218
Berg, B., 179
Berle, A. A., 223
Berry, R. E., Jr., 169, 174
Bieber, I., 71
Bingham, J., 111
Blumberg, A. S., 216
Boland, J. P., 169, 174
Boles, J., 39
Book, J. A., 98
Braithwaite, J., 18, 242, 243, 245, 247
Breed, W., 138, 140, 142, 152, 153
Brenner, M. H., 10, 102
Brown, J. W., 186, 187
Brownmiller, S., 53
Bryant, A., 272
Buckley, W., 274
Buffurm, P. C., 67
Bullough, B., 31
Bullough, V., 31
Byck, R., 168

Camus, A., 55
Catanzaro, R. J., 12
Cavan, R., 15, 144, 145, 146
Chafetz, M., 179
Chambliss, W. J., 18, 20, 144, 189, 190, 191, 192, 222
Cisin, I., 172
Clinard, M. B., 167, 206, 226, 228, 230, 234, 235, 236, 244, 245, 247, 248, 249, 251
Cloward, R., 17
Cohen, A. K., 17
Conklin, J. E., 227, 234, 237, 244, 248
Conover, D., 92
Conrad, P., 195, 196, 260, 262
Conyers, J. Jr., 225, 226, 227
Cory, D. W., 4
Coser, L. A., 14
Cressey, D. R., 12, 14
Crowther, B., 167
Cumming, E., 111
Cumming, J., 111

Dank, B. M., 61, 62
Dansereau, H. K., 217
Darrow, W. W., 78
Davis, K., 35, 36, 49
Davis, N., 37, 38, 39
Deisher, R., 30
Delph, E. W., 64, 65
Denfeld, D., 75
Denzin, N. K., 238, 239
Diamond, R., 219
Dohrenwend, B. P., 93, 94, 95, 97, 101
Dohrenwend, B. S., 93, 94, 95
Douglas, J. D., 144, 150, 221, 222, 234
Domhoff, G. W., 210, 212
Dunham, H. W., 15, 99, 100, 101, 122
Dupont, R. L., 192
Durkheim, E., 15, 16, 20, 138, 141, 142, 143, 144, 183, 264, 271
Dye, T. R., 210

277

Dziech, B., 218

Eaton, J. W., 95, 101
Eaton, W. W., 95
Edelhertz, H., 228
Edgerton, R. B., 178, 180
Ellis, L., 12
Erikson, K. T., 20, 272, 273
Ermann, M. D., 228, 234, 245, 246, 250
Essen-Moller, 98
Evans, P. B., 223

Faaborg, L., 218
Fang, B., 74, 75
Farberow, W. L., 130, 136, 138, 149, 151
Faris, R. E. L., 15, 99, 100, 101, 122
Farnsworth, D. L., 141
Fave, R. D., 210
Ferracuti, F., 17
Fishburne, P. M., 173
Flexner, A., 40
Ford, C. S., 54, 55
Fort, J., 170
Foucault, M., 263
Fox, R. G., 12
Franklin, P., 217
Friedman, M., 224
Freitag, P., 210
Freund, S., 4, 14

Gagnon, J. H., 28, 51, 78
Galliher, J. F., 267
Gandy, P., 30
Gebhard, P. H., 37
Geis, G., 18, 38, 219, 220, 224, 225, 228, 230, 242, 243, 245, 247
Gibbs, J. P., 144
Giddens, A., 130
Gilbert, D., 206, 207, 208, 210
Glassner, B., 179
Glueck, E., 12, 14
Glueck, S., 12, 14
Goddard, J. C., 193, 194
Goffman, E., 67, 112, 115
Goldstein, A., 120

Goode, E., 63, 162, 167, 188
Goodwin, D., 174
Gordon, L., 219
Gottesman, J. J., 98
Gove, W., 110, 111, 112
Gray, D., 37, 38
Green, M. J., 230
Greene, M. H., 192
Greenwald, H., 36
Gross, E., 237, 238, 239
Gusfield, J. R., 52, 181, 182, 267, 272
Gussen, J., 136

Haberman, P. W., 173, 174
Hall, S., 34
Hawkins, G., 269
Hendin, H., 138, 140, 141, 153, 154
Henley, J. R., 186
Henry, A. F., 14, 133, 146, 147, 148
Henshel, A., 74
Hessler, R. M., 214
Heston, L. L., 70, 98
Heyl, B. S., 30, 37
Hills, S. L., 176
Hirschi, T., 18
Hoffer, E., 274
Hollingshead, A. B., 96, 105
Hook, E. B., 12
Hooker, E., 72
Hopkins, A., 247
Hughes, C. C., 130
Humphreys, L., 64, 66
Hunt, M., 27, 28
Hyde, H. M., 43

Illich, I., 193, 195
Inciardi, J. A., 187
Ismach, J. M., 78

Jackall, R., 239
Jacobs, J., 151
Jacobs, P. A., 12
Jacoby, N., 224
James, J., 30, 35, 37
Jay, K., 78
Jellinek, E. M., 175
Johnson, B. D., 186

Johnson, J. M., 234
Johnson, V., 57, 58, 70, 71

Kahl, J. A., 206, 207, 208, 210
Kalish, R. A., 138
Kallmann, F. G., 4, 70, 98
Kandel, D. B., 186
Kerbo, H., 210
Kinsey, A. C., 56, 57, 58
Kinsie, P. M., 36
Kirkpatrick, R. G., 52, 53, 272
Kleiner, R. J., 103, 104
Klockars, C. B., 213
Kobler, A. L., 149
Kramer, R. C., 214, 225, 226
Kraus, L. A., 218
Kuhn, T. S., 273

LaFontaine, J., 129, 130
Laing, R. D., 104
Leighton, A., 130
Lemert, E. M., 41
Lester, D., 137, 138, 148, 158
Lewis, H. R., 214
Lewis, M. E., 214
Liazos, A., 9, 205
Licht, H., 55
Linsky, A. S., 104, 183
Lombroso, C., 12
Lorenz, K., 20
Lundman, R. J., 228, 234, 245, 246, 250

MacAndrew, C., 178, 180
McCaghy, C. H., 181
McCord, J., 14
McCord, W., 14
McCormack, T., 51, 52, 53
McCoy, A. W., 191
McIntosh, M., 55, 61
McKay, H. D., 15
McVisk, W., 249
Mannheim, H., 12
Maris, R. W., 138
Martin, W. T., 144
Masters, W. H., 57, 58, 60, 70, 71
Matza, D., 15, 17, 267

Means, G. C., 223
Mechanic, D., 118, 119, 120
Meier, R. F., 167
Mendelsohn, R. S., 195
Merton, R. K., 16, 17, 103, 122, 221, 240
Milazzo-Sayre, L. J., 97
Mitchell, W. J., 112
Mizruchi, E. H., 178
Morris, N., 269
Mott, F. D., 95
Muedeking, G. D., 44
Munter, P. K., 140
Musto, D. F., 267
Myers, J. K., 104

Nader, R., 230, 247, 249
Nagle, J., 210
Nunnally, J. C., 111

Ohlin, L. E., 17
Orcutt, J. D., 176, 186

Palmer, S., 272
Palson, C., 75
Parker, D. B., 103, 104, 234, 241
Pastor, P. A., Jr., 184
Pattison, E. M., 176, 177
Pearce, F., 222
Perrucci, R., 113, 178
Pfeffer, J., 248
Phillips, D. P., 148
Pokorny, A. D., 136
Polsky, N., 30, 49, 50
Porpora, D., 198
Powell, E. H., 138
Propper, A. M., 69

Quinney, R., 18, 210

Redlich, R. C., 96
Roberts, B. H., 104
Robins, E., 70
Roby, P. A., 40
Roemer, M. I., 95
Rogers, J. M., 169
Rogler, L. H., 105

Roman, P. M., 176
Rosen, G., 131
Rosenblum, K. E., 37
Rosenhan, D. L., 92, 112, 113
Rosenstein, M. J., 97
Roth, L. H., 14
Rothman, D. J., 86
Rowse, A. L., 55

Sagarin, E., 68, 69, 76, 77
Saghir, M. T., 70
Sampson, H., 106
Sandler, B. R., 217
Scheff, T. J., 8, 10, 106, 107, 108, 109, 111, 115, 118
Schields, J., 98
Schneider, S. A., 223
Schneider, J. W., 176, 195, 196, 260, 262, 267
Schrag, P., 169, 196
Schrager, L. S., 226, 228, 232
Schur, E. M., 7, 20, 269, 270, 272
Schwartz, R. D., 8
Scull, A. T., 11, 115
Seiden, R. H., 140
Seymour, W. N., Jr., 245
Shah, S., 14
Shaw, C. R., 15
Sheehy, G., 33, 34, 35
Sheldon, W. H., 12
Shields, J., 70
Shneidman, E. S., 136, 138, 149, 150, 151, 152
Short, J. F., Jr., 14, 133, 146, 147, 148, 226, 228, 232
Simon, W., 28, 51, 78
Skolnick, J. H., 8
Skultans, V., 86
Smith, J. R., 75
Smith, L. G., 75
Synder, C., 179
Sobell, L. C., 177
Sobell, M. B., 177
Spector, M., 74
Spitzer, S., 18
Spradley, J. P., 184
Srole, L., 93

Star, S., 111
Steele, M. F., 144
Stengel, E., 138
Stewart, P., 42
Stone, C. D., 224, 238, 248
Stotland, E., 149
Straus, J. H., 156
Straus, M. A., 156
Sutherland, E. H., 12, 14, 211, 213, 228, 236, 237, 243
Sykes, G. M., 15, 17
Szasz, T., 267

Tabachnick, N., 136
Taylor, I., 267
Thio, A., 9, 205
Thomson, G. E., 218
Toby, J., 18
Trice, H. M., 176
Tuckman, J., 151

Van Dyke, C., 168

Walker, A., 267
Wallace, A. F. C., 88
Walshok, M. L., 76
Walters, R. H., 14
Warren, C. A. B., 61
Weil, R. J., 95, 101
Weinberg, M. S., 57, 59, 60, 61, 64, 70, 73
Weinberg, S. K., 104
Williams, C. J., 64, 70, 73
Wilson, K. R., 218
Wilson, J. Q., 51
Winick, C., 36
Witken, H. A., 12
Wolfgang, M. E., 17
Worden, J. W., 140

Yarrow, M. R., 105
Yeager, P. C., 206, 224, 226, 228, 230, 235, 236, 244, 245, 247, 248, 249
Young, A., 78

Zeitlin, M., 223
Zurcher, L. A., Jr., 52, 53, 272

SUBJECT INDEX

Alcohol: and physical dependence, 164; and psychological dependence, 164; and loss of inhibitions, 176–178; American ambivalence toward, 179–180; cultural patterns of use, 178–180
Alcohol abuse: economic costs of, 173–174; and violent deaths, 173–174; arrest rates related to, 174
Alcoholics Anonymous, 175–176
Alcoholism: and heredity, 174–175; types of, 175; stages of, 175–176; rates of in different groups, 178–179; changing images of, 183
American Psychiatric Association: definition of homosexuality, 73–74
American Temperance Movement, 181
Amphetamines, 166
Anomie: theory, 16; and mental disorders, 103–104
Antipornography campaigns, 52–53
Asbestos industry: and corporate crime, 230–232
Atavism, 12
Auto accidents: and suicide, 136

Barbiturates, 169
Blue laws, 20
Buffalo Creek flood: and corporate crime, 232–233
Bureaucracy: and crime, 239

Call girls, 34–35
Cannabis, 170–171
Capitalism: rise of and opiates, 190–192; and political corruption, 222; and corporate crime, 241–242
Child-rearing practices: and suicide, 147–148
Chromosome composition: and antisocial behavior, 12
Cocaine, 166
College students: and suicide, 140

Conformity: as the norm, 6
Control theory, 17–18
Corporate chartering: control of, 249–250
Corporate consolidation: and crime, 240
Corporate crime: rationale for studying, 224–225; economic losses from, 225–226; as a cause of illlness and death, 226–227; detrimental effects on public morality, 227; price fixing, 228–230; as a cause of illness and death, 230–232; and the asbestos industry, 230–232; and the Buffalo Creek flood, 232–233; extent of, 234–236; and recidivism, 235–236; and social learning, 236–237; rationalizations for, 237; and new technology, 240–241; and capitalism, 241–242; and labeling, 242–244; deterrence of, 242; and government, 243–244; and differential social organization, 244; reactive versus proactive law enforcement, 244–45; penalties for, 245–247; publicity as a sanction against, 247; regulation and deregulation in respect to, 248; publicity as a sanction, 248; and the liability of executives, 249. *See also* Corporate deviance; White-collar crime
Corporate deviance. *See also* Corporate crime; White-collar crime
Corporate executives: personal characteristics conducive to crime, 237–238
Corporation: definition of, 223
Corporations: legal treatment of, 224; bureaucratic aspects and crime, 239; and diffusion of moral responsibility, 239; primacy of profit, 240
Crime: FBI Index of, 6, 211; "victimless," 7, 20; committed by corpora-

281

tions, 211–213; as compared to sickness, 262
Criminalization of deviance: effects of, 269; and medicalization of deviance, 269–270
Cultural relativity, 87
Cultural transmission, 17

Decarceration: and government policy, 115
Decriminalization: of marijuana, 188–189; of deviance, 270–271
Deinstitutionalization of mental patients, 115–117
Deterrence: punishment, 18; of corporate crime, 242
Deviance: approaches to definition of, 4–6; as a field of inquiry, 8–9; and body type, 12; genetic predisposition to, 12; and instincts, 14; and socialization, 14; and imitation, 14; and professional autonomy, 215–216; effects of criminalization, 269; and normative boundaries, 273; and domination, 273
Deviants: influence on social policy, 267; as scapegoats, 272
Differential association: theory of, 14–15; and white-collar crime, 236–237
Differential social organization: and corporate crime, 244
Domination: and deviance, 273
Drift hypothesis: and suicide, 145
Drinking: cultural patterns of, 178–180; functions of, 180–181; and individual responsibility, 180–181; dysfunctions of, 181; as a symbol, 182
Drug: definition of, 161
Drug addiction: among physicians, 215
Drugs: influences on effects of, 162–163; legal states of, 164–165; psychoactive properties of, 165–171; legal misuse of, 193; advertising of, 193–194; treatment of women with, 194–195; legal misuse of, 198
Drug-taking: as related to age, 172

Durkheim, Emile: types of suicide, 141–144

Elite corporate deviance: definition of, 214
Elite occupational deviance: definition of, 213
Elites: influence on government, 208–211; and political power, 241–242
Equity Funding case: and stock fraud, 233–234
Ethology, 20

False accusation, 8
Family socialization: and mental disorders, 105–106
Female sex role: and prostitution, 41
Firearms: and suicide, 137
Functionalism: theory of, 15; as applied to prostitution, 35–36; as applied to pornography, 49–50; as applied to deinstitutionalization of mental patients, 116–117; as applied to drinking, 180–181; as applied to political corruption, 221

Gay self-concept: and homosexual identity, 63
Gay subcultural: 61–67; bars, 63–64; baths, 64–65; medical risks of, 78
Government: and corporate crime, 243–244
Government funding: and social policy, 266

Hashish, 171
Heredity: and mental disorders, 98–99; alcoholism, 174–175
Heroin: 168; size of the industry, 192
Heterosexual behavior: compared to homosexual behavior, 57–58
Heterosexuals: compared to homosexuals, 60–61
Homicide: and age, 133; and suicide, 133; and suicide, 146–148; and suicide, 156

Homosexual identity: and gay self-concept, 61–63
Homosexual behavior: physical aspects of, 57; compared to heterosexual behavior, 57–58
Homosexuality: in different cultures, 54–56; acceptance of, 55; definition of, 56; in total institutions, 67–70; in male prisons, 67–69; as a learned role, 68–69; in female prisons, 69; in the military, 69–70; genetic aspects, 70–71; and psychopathology, 71–72; critique of psychoanalytic theories of, 72; as learned behavior, 72–73; and masturbation, 72–73; and labeling, 73; American Psychiatric Association definition of, 73–74
Homosexual role: emergence of, 55, 61
Homosexuals: and sexual problems, 58; different life-styles, 58–61; compared to heterosexuals, 60–61; effects of prejudice on, 60–61; effects of stigma on, 67
Human sexuality: as a continuum, 56–57
Human sciences: influence on social policy, 267–268

Imitation: and suicide, 148–149

Karposi's sarcoma: among homosexuals, 78

Labeling: theory of, 15; and homosexuality, 73; and mental disorders, 106–111; critique of theory, 110–111; and marijuana use, 184–186; as applied to corporate crime, 242–244
LSD, 170

Manic-depression, 92
Marijuana: and the law, 187–189; decriminalization of, 188–89; as a symbol, 188
Marijuana use: and learning, 184–186; and peer influences, 186; cessation of, 186–187
Masturbation: and pornography, 49, 50; and homosexuality, 72–73
McNaughten rule, 119–120
Medicalization: of deviance, 195–196; in American society, 262; consequences of, 263; and criminalization of deviance, 269–270; consequences of, 274
Mental disorder: definition of, 89; and criminal behavior, 89
Mental disorders: in different historical periods, 85–86; in different cultures, 86–88; classification of, 89–92; organic, 89–91; functional, 89–92; schizophrenia, 91–92; manic-depression, 92; difficulties of diagnosis, 92–93; "true" prevalence of, 93; and age, 94; and sex, 94–95; and race, 95; and rural-urban settings, 95; and social class, hospitals, 97; and heredity, 98–99; and social disorganization, 99–102; distribution and the chance hypothesis, 99; distribution and the selection hypothesis, 99–102; distribution and the drift hypothesis, 101–102; distribution and the stress hypothesis, 101–102; and the economy, 102–103; and anomie, 103–104; and family socialization, 104–106; and labeling, 106–111; and stigma, 111–112; legal aspects, 117–121
Mental patients: deinstitutionalization of 115–117
Mental hospitals: involuntary commitments, 112; as total institutions, 112–114; and depersonalization, 113; reduction in use, 114; See also Psychiatric hospitals
Mental hospital staff: stigma on, 113–114
Military: homosexuality in, 69–70

Nationalization of corporations: as a crime control measure, 250

Normative boundaries: and deviance, 273
Normlessness, 16

Official statistics: and suicide, 133–136
Opiates, 168; as a commodity, 189–193; in China, 190–192; and the rise of capitalism, 190–192
Opium, 168
Opium trade: American involvement in, 191–193
Opportunity structure, 17

Phrenologists, 12
Pimps: and prostitutes, 33–34
Political corruption: 219–222; as individual immorality, 221; social functions of, 221; and the expansion of government, 221–222; and capitalism, 222
Political power: and elites, 241–242
Pornography: definition of, 42–43; in different cultures, 43–44; and the invention of printing, 43; and the law, 43–45; *Roth v. United States,* 44; *Miller v. California,* 44–45; variety of, 45; effects of exposure to, 45–49; functions of, 49–50; consumers of, 50–51; as a functional alternative, 49–50; dominant themes of, 50–52; and masturbatory fantasies, 50–51; and violence, 51–52; feminist critique of, 53; as "victimless" crime, 53–54
Poverty: and suicide, 131–132. *See also* Social class
Price fixing, 228–230
Prisons: homosexuality in, 67–69
Professional autonomy: and deviance, 215–216
Prohibition Amendment, 3, 182
Prostitutes: streetwalkers, 32–34; and pimps, 33–34; call girls, 34–35
Prostitution: difficulties of defining, 29–30; in different cultures, 30–32; risks of, 33; functions of, 35–36; psychoanalytical motivations of, 36–37; predisposing factors, 37; attractions of, 37–38; precipitating factors, 38; process of career movement, 38–39; professionalization, 39; legal treatment of clients, 39–40; and social status, 40; and the sexual double-standard, 40–41; and the female sex role, 41; and the status of women, 39–42; and profit, 41
Psychiatric hospitals: public and private compared, 97. *See also* Mental hospitals
Psychodelics, 170
Public drunkenness: and the law, 183–184
Publicity: as a sanction against corporate crime, 247–248
Punishment: deterrence, 18

Recidivism: and corporate crime, 235–236
Research: definition of, 9–10
Residual rule-breaking, 8, 106–107

Schizophrenia, 91–92
Secret deviance, 7–8
Sexual double-standard: causes and effects of, 32; and prostitution, 40–41; and swinging, 75–76
Sexual harassment: definition of, 217; by professors, 217–219; effects of, 218; extent of, 217–218; impediments to eliminating, 218–219
Sickness: as compared to crime, 262
Social class, 18; and mental disorders, 97; in America, 205–211. *See also* Poverty; Social status
Social control of deviance: profits in, 272
Social learning: and homosexuality, 72–73; and corporate crime, 236–237
Social disorganization, 15–16; and mental disorders, 99–102
Social policy: formulation of, 10–11; creation of, 264; and government funding, 266; influence on deviants, 267; as influenced by the human sciences, 267–268; social welfare ap-

proach, 270–271; in respect to elite deviance, 271
Social status: and suicide, 138, 146–148. *See also* Social class
Social welfare: approach to social policy, 270–271
Stigma: and mental disorders, 111–112
Stock fraud: and the Equity Funding Case, 233–234
Subculture of violence, 17
Suicidal persons: common characteristics of, 152–153
Suicide: in primitive societies, 129–130; in Western history, 130–131; and poverty, 131–132; and homicide, 133, 146–148, 156; and age, 133; in the United States, 133; and official statistics, 133–136; and auto accidents, 136; completed versus attempted, 137; and firearms, 137; and social status, 138; among college students, 140; egoistic, 142; altruistic, 142; anomie, 142; fatalistic, 142; and stability of social relationships, 144; and the drift hypothesis, 145; and social status, 146–148; and child-rearing practices, 147–148; and imitation, 148–149; intentions of the victim, 150; intervention, 153–154
Suicide notes: genuine versus simulated, 151; repetitive themes, 151–152
Suicide prevention centers: effectiveness of, 153–154

Swingers: personality characteristics, 74–75; social backgrounds, 74–75
Swinging: introduction to, 75; motives of, 75; alleged virtues of, 75; and the sexual double-standard, 75–76; theoretical importance of, 76–77

Tearooms: and impersonal sex, 65–67; types of participants, 65–66; trade, 65, ambisexuals, 65–66; gays, 66; closet queens, 66
Theories of deviance: overview of, 11–19; and conceptions of human behavior, 267–268
Theory: definition of, 9; utility of, 11
Total institutions: homosexuality in, 67–70; mental hospitals, 112–114

Valium, 169, 195
Violence: and pornography, 51–52
Violent deaths: and alcohol abuse, 173–174
"Victimless" crime, 7, 20; pornography as, 53–54

Wealth: distribution of in America, 206–208
White-collar crime: and differential association, 236–237. *See also* Corporate crime; Corporate deviance
Women: status of and prostitution, 39–42

Book Manufacture
UNDERSTANDING DEVIANCE AND CONTROL: Theory, Research and Social Policy was typeset at Compositors, Inc., Cedar Rapids, Iowa. Printing and binding was at Edwards Brothers, Ann Arbor Michigan. Internal design was by F.E. Peacock art department. Cover design was by Mead Design, San Diego. The type face is Times Roman.